£20
B14881
C48.N
383764
AF864560

Central Bank, Peripheral Industry

Central Bank, Peripheral Industry
The Bank of England in the provinces, 1826-1913

Dieter Ziegler

Translated by Eileen Martin

Leicester University Press
(a division of Pinter Publishers Ltd)
Leicester, London

© Dieter Ziegler, 1990

First published in Great Britain in 1990 by Leicester University Press
(a division of Pinter Publishers Ltd)

All rights reserved. No part of this publication may be reproduced, stored in a retrieval system, or transmitted, in any form or by any means, electronic, mechanical, photocopying, recording or otherwise, without the prior permission of the Leicester University Press.

Editorial offices
Fielding Johnson Building, University of Leicester
University Road, Leicester, LE1 7RH

Trade and other enquiries
25 Floral Street, London, WC2E 9DS

British Library Cataloguing in Publication Data

A CIP cataloguing record for this book is available from the British Library

ISBN 0 7185 1338 X

Filmset by Mayhew Typesetting, Bristol, Great Britain
Printed and bound in Great Britain by Biddles, Kings Lynn and Guildford

'When the newspapers tell me that there is yet another financial crisis and that gold is being rushed from one country to another and I see photographs of excited City men jostling and scambling and of bank porters carrying boxes of bullion, I always feel that some idiotic game is going on and that it is as preposterous that the welfare of millions of real people should depend on the fortunes of this game as it would be if our happiness hung upon the results of the Stock Exchange golfing tournament . . . . I thought then how this City which is always referred to with such tremendous respect, which is treated as if it were the very beating red heart of England, must have got its money from somewhere, that it could not have conjured gold out of Threadneedle Street, and that a great deal of this money must have poured into it at one time — and a good long time ago — from that part of England which is much dearer to me than the City, namely, the industrial North.'

J.B. Priestley, *English Journey*

Contents

List of figures viii
List of tables ix
Preface x

1. Introduction 1

2. The Bank of England provincial branches 4
   2.1 Setting up the branches 1826/9 4
   2.2 Branches of the Central Bank 9
   Establishing the Bank of England note, 1826/9–1844 9
   The Bank and the 1844 Regulation Act 31
   2.3 Branches of a commercial bank 38
   The commercial decline begins 38
   The crisis in bill discounting 50
   The new upswing in lending 1889–1913

3. The limits to central bank policy 75
   3.1 From the 'Palmer Rule' to Peel's Act 76
   3.2 The Bank of England and the mid-nineteenth century crises 82
   3.3 Tenderness for domestic trade and industry? 88

4. The Bank and industry: the example of Birmingham 1880–1905 96
   4.1 The crisis in bill discounting 98
   4.2 The rise of the 'industrial branch' 1880–93 100
   4.3 A London scandal and the reverberations in Birmingham 1893–4 110
   4.4 The old policy under new management 1894–7 116
   4.5 The end of the industrial branch 121

5. The development of central bank policy and the English provinces — a reassessment 129

Notes 138

Bibliography 151

Index of People and Places 158

Subject Index 161

List of figures

2.1	Bank of England branch banknote circulation, 1829–66	27
4.1	Bank of England branches' lending and deposits, 1870–1913	97
4.2	Birmingham branch lending and deposits, 1870–1913	97

List of tables

2.1 Joint stock banks in England and Wales, 1826–56 10
2.2 Number of banks having a 'circulation account' with the Bank of England 14
2.3 Bank of England branch banknote circulation, 1829–44 17
2.4 Bills discounted at Bank of England branches, 1831–44 18
2.5 Lapsed country bank issues, 1844–74 36
2.6 Merger activity in British banking, 1870–1913 37
2.7 Bills discounted at Bank of England provincial branches, 1835–74 39
2.8 Average amount of deposits at the Bank of England provincial branches, 1853–75 48
2.9 Average amount held in bills at Bank of England provincial branches, 1853–70 51
2.10 Bills discounted at Bank of England provincial branches, 1870–89 52
2.11 Average amount held in bills at Bank of England provincial branches, 1870–89 53
2.12 Share of gross profits provided by interest on bills at the provincial branches, 1870–89 56
2.13 Profits and losses of Bank of England provincial branches, 1875/6–1889/90 57
2.14 Average amount of deposits at Bank of England provincial branches, 1875–1913 58
2.15 Profits and losses of Bank of England provincial branches, 1889/90–1912/13 60
2.16 Share of gross profits provided by interest on bills and advances at the provincial branches, 1889–1911 61
2.17 Average amount held in bills at the Bank of England provincial branches, 1890–1913 63
2.18 Average amount of advances granted at Bank of England provincial branches, 1887–1913 64
2.19 Credit/deposit ratio at Bank of England provincial branches, 1870–1913 68

Preface

This book is based upon my contribution to a research project called 'British Economic Policy and Manufacturing Industry, 1870–1913', directed by Sidney Pollard. While concentrating on monetary policy, I had to learn that contrary to my German experiences, British government was only scarcely involved in this branch of economic policy and that there were only two or three people in service 'who were thoroughly familiar with monetary problems' (Cairncross 1988, p. 46). Consequently, the government had to leave almost everything to a privately-owned institution, to the Bank of England. Once research was under way, I became increasingly sceptical about the 'conventional wisdom' that claims that the Bank of England became a fairly modern central bank before the First World War. These doubts were confirmed as I began to scrutinize the largely neglected history of the Bank's policy in the provinces — as Sidney Pollard had predicted.

To Sidney Pollard, who was largely responsible for my research strategy and with whom I discussed my ideas over a period of more than five years, I owe the greatest debt. For advice and encouragement I am also indebted to many colleagues, particularly to Phil Cottrell, Peter Hertner, Edwin Green, Alan Milward and Richard Tilly. Norman McCord was kind enough to let me have his notes on the Newcastle branch during the 1847 and 1857 financial crises. Without this unusually generous support the chapter about the Bank during the mid-nineteenth century could not have been written.

I have been given free access to the immensely rich Bank of England Archive and Record Office, where the most helpful staff ensured that research was made as problem-free as possible. In particular Henry Gillett and John Pullinger were of invaluable assistance in facilitating access to the Bank's records, catalogued and uncatalogued.

My research in London was financed by the Deutsche Forschungsgemeinschaft (DFG) during my research assistantship in Bielefeld 1983–6, and by the European University Institute (EUI) in Florence, for which I had a Deutscher Akademischer Austauschdienst (DAAD) grant 1986–8. The translation, which was carried out by Eileen Martin, was subsidized by the Bank of England and the EUI.

Finally, I should like to thank Wilma Diekmann and Michael Goerke who came to my aid with typing and processing at different stages of the project.

Bielefeld, February 1990.

1

Introduction

The development of central bank policy in England until the First World War can with some justification be regarded as well researched. Thanks to the archives of the Bank of England, which have been relatively freely accessible for some time, a very different picture has emerged in recent decades. Briefly, the state of research is as follows. After a period of intense theoretical monetary discussion, which reached its peak in the experimental phase of monetary policy after the end of the Napoleonic Wars, Peel's Bank Charter Act of 1844 laid down the basic lines of monetary policy which were not fundamentally changed by further legislation before the First World War. One of the main objectives of Peel's Act was to give a central bank the monopoly of the issue of banknotes, but apart from that Peel's Act was rather an 'anti central bank act'. The Bank of England was actually formally released from the central bank functions which were being discussed by contemporaries, that is, responsibility for the micro and macro-economic stability of the monetary system. Macro-economic stability, seen as the free convertibility of sterling into gold, was to be quasi-automatic through 100 per cent gold cover, as well as a fixed fiduciary issue, while micro-economic stability, that is the stability of and the confidence in the finance markets, was to be left solely to market forces. The financial intermediaries were to learn to keep their portfolios sufficiently liquid and the existence of a 'lender of last resort' was seen as only a hindrance to that lesson. Therefore the Bank of England was both a central bank of issue and a commercial bank and, owing to the rigid rules on cover, its function as central bank of issue was outside the decision-making powers of its directors. The dual nature of the Bank was evident in its division from 1844 into two departments, the Issue Department and the Banking Department.

The majority of the Bank of England directors welcomed the reform. Even before it was passed, they had taken the path of 'retreat' in central bank policy, which Peel's Act was to prescribe, and had concentrated on commercial bank functions which were transferred to the Banking Department when the Act was passed. The most visible expression of this change in outlook was that the Bank returned to the London money market to compete with the bill brokers, discount houses and commercial banks and, at the same time, began building up an investment portfolio to absorb its surplus funds.

However, crises in the mid-nineteenth century quickly taught the Bank that there were limits to its business policy. It could not fix its discount rate like a normal commercial bank; rather it had to relate Bank Rate to a liquid reserve which *de facto* was also the liquidity reserve of the money market. Hesitantly, but ultimately recognizably, the Bank took up its old function as lender of last resort to the London money market again towards the end of the nineteenth century and cooperation replaced competition.

> The Baring crisis of 1890 had been the turning point in the development of co-operation between the Bank and the joint stock banks — traces of mutual jealousy and suspicion were now few. Such co-operation was crucial to the effective application of Bank control. (Nevin and Davis 1970, p. 108)

In the international context the Bank played the part of 'principal violinist' (Foreman-Peck and Michie 1986, p. 405)[1] in the orchestra of the international capital flows and, in this way, it helped to ensure that the international gold standard would work smoothly.

It is evident from this admittedly very simple account that the policy of the Bank has been largely considered by previous scholars in the international context (the gold standard) and the London context (its function as lender of last resort). A more detailed review of the current state of research would not alter that impression. It is astonishing how little attention has been paid to the whole range of business objectives which the Bank of England itself postulated. In 1911 Governor Cole described these business aims as follows: 'While the Bank naturally keeps in view the interests of its shareholders, still, the first consideration of the Bank, in its decision as to the Bank rate, is the welfare of the trade of the country' (Mansion House Speech, 1 July 1911, quoted in Powell 1915, p. 662). The Bank of England still had commercial banking interests in 1911, even if Cole saw these as secondary, and this area of activity should at least be investigated. There was also a very broad, but unfortunately not very precisely formulated, central bank responsibility. It may be concluded from the formulation that the need for regulation — or at least the sphere of influence — of the Bank or its policy extended beyond the City of London. Nevertheless, relations between the Bank of England and British industry, most of which before the First World War was located in the provinces, have only been considered by Sayers. In his analysis he concentrated — quite as Cole would have expected — exclusively on the effects of the Bank Rate on the supply of credit in the provinces. Virtually nothing is known of the provincial branches of the Bank and of the 'institutionalization of relations between the Bank of England and industry', as one might say. Only the position of individual provincial branches before 1844 and, especially, their relation to the provincial banks of issue has been systematically studied.

The reason for this concentration of research on the pre-1844 period is certainly due to the branches having been allotted a central bank function before Peel's Act was passed, namely to establish Bank of England notes in the provinces. When Peel's Act seemed to offer a legal solution to the problem of the provincial banknote, the provincial branches lost their central bank function and became a part of the activity of the Banking Department, operated purely as commercial branches. The past lack of interest shown by historians in the post-1844 history of the Bank of England in the provinces can only seemingly be justified by this. For, if it is correct that the Bank also had to take the interests of its shareholders into account, conflicts must have arisen between the requirements of the emerging central bank and the dividend interests of the bank's proprietary. What influence these profit interests had on the decisions of the Bank, both in London and the provinces, is of major importance in an assessment of the state of development of central bank policy before 1914. If it is also correct that 'the welfare of the trade of the country' meant not only a strict observance of the rules of the game of the international gold standard, but also a certain 'tenderness for domestic industry and trade' (Sayers 1976, Vol. 1, p. 43) within the constraints that Peel's Act and the role as 'principal violinist' in the international concert permitted, then it is mainly in the provinces that we must look for proof of the correctness of Cole's statement.

This study draws mainly on hitherto neglected sources of the Bank of England branch banks office and the correspondence between individual branch agents and the head office. As far as the correspondents are concerned, in view of the huge range of material available, strict time and geographical limits had to be set. The following account based on these sources is therefore limited to the branches in Leicester and Birmingham. However, by using sources in the branch banks' office that affected all the branches, it is possible to distinguish general developments from the particular features of these two branches and so obtain a relatively full picture of the Bank of England in the provinces. Leicester is representative of the branches that were not commercial successes and were closed after a time. Birmingham was for a short time a kind of industrial branch of the Bank of England and its eventful history reflected more than any other changes in outlook at the head office.

2

The Bank of England provincial branches

2.1 Setting up the branches 1826/9

The first branches were set up as a direct consequence of the crisis of 1825/6. The collapse of two London banks in December 1825 caused the failure of a number of provincial banks. The government was quick to draw conclusions, namely that the banking system was not in a position to guarantee stable conditions for currency and credit and needed thorough reform (Clapham 1944, Vol. 2, pp. 102–7; Clapham 1930, Vol. 1, pp. 273–5; Morgan 1943, Ch. 4, pp. 75–99).

In the government's view the capital of many private banks of issue was quite inadequate. One of the main reasons for this was the privilege held by the Bank of England, whereby it was the only bank in England permitted to have more than six partners. However, only a minority of the banks seem to have been strictly affected by this limitation as, of the 552 licensed private issue banks in England and Wales in 1822, more than two-thirds had three or fewer partners. Only twenty-six banks had the legal maximum of six partners. Since limited liability was not available under general company law, each partner was liable, should the company fail, to settle its debts with his entire assets. Consequently very few persons would be strictly eligible as partners in a bank. This integration of private assets and bank capital means that it is often very difficult to distinguish in the balance sheets of private banks between a bank's capital and the partners' money. The capital of most of the banks, as far as it can be identified, was about £10,000, but in many cases it was lower. Profits were mostly fully distributed to the partners and reserves were only built up out of undistributed profits — if at all — after the experience of the 1825/6 crisis. Even in the 1840s it was very unusual to find a bank's capital being augmented by provisions from profits.

The second weak point in the pre-1826 banking system, in the view of the government, was the regular inflation of the money stock (at this time exclusively defined as notes and coin) by the utterly uncontrolled issue of banknotes. This had caused price increases, speculation and finally the crisis. The weaker the capital of a bank, the more it would be inclined to issue a large number of banknotes of low denomination (Pressnell 1956, pp. 225–7, 231; Andreades 1966, pp. 254–5; Clapham 1930, Vol. 1, p. 275).

As a consequence of the crisis — and only three months after it had broken out — the first legislative measure against the inflationary issue of banknotes was taken. This forbade the issue of banknotes under £5 in England (7 Geo IV c.6, 26 March 1826). Instead the circulation of coin was to be revived, in order to put a precious metal reserve 'in the pockets of the public' — an argument that later was to be frequently made against the gold exchange standard. Also the Bank of England's monopoly of joint stock banking was repealed. In future this privilege was to apply only within a radius of 65 miles of the City of London, following the Irish model. However, at the same time, the Bank of England was also empowered to open branches outside London (7 Geo IV, c.46, 26 May 1826). The objective of the reform was to reduce the number of private banks of issue, which had already been considerably lowered by the effects of the crisis. They were to make room for a new type of private issue bank based on shares and with a sounder capital base. At this point, of course, there could be no thought of giving the Bank of England the monopoly of banknote issue. Nevertheless, the intention of the government, which the directors of the Bank of England now supported, was quite obviously to achieve 'a much more complete control . . . over the whole paper circulation' (Clapham 1944, Vol. 2, p. 104, quoting BofE CB) by allowing the Bank of England to set up branches in several major provincial cities. Until 1826 the Bank had already resisted this approach on the part of Peel and Lord Liverpool. At the beginning of the 1820s it had not been willing to be a 'Bank of England' instead of a 'Bank of London' (Palmer) (BPP 1831/32, evidence J.H. Palmer, q.466). Only the pressure of the relationships within the banking system during the 1825/26 crisis, together with some pressure from the government, which threatened to repeal the joint stock bank privilege, caused the directors of the bank to consider seriously the possibility of opening branches outside London.[1]

A further major consideration in the decision to establish provincial branches was the Bank's concern to obtain more deposits. As the safest bank in England, particularly after the many bankruptcies following the crisis, it could expect to be entrusted with holding the assets of many people of private means, anxious after the crisis. As the first bank in England, with a branch network covering the main centres of industry and trade, it could also, by offering favourable transfer conditions, hope to win a number of local banks and trading-houses as customers. In return for the services of the Bank, they would have to maintain a minimum balance on their drawing accounts.

The Bank itself naturally denied any profit interest in setting up its branches. According to Governor Palmer (1832), the cities were chosen

> which . . . would give the best centre[s] of circulation with reference to manufacturing and agricultural districts . . . . The Bank established those Branch Banks with the concurrence of the late Government, without any profit to the Bank of England, the object being to give solidity and strength to the

whole circulation of the country. (BPP 1831/32, evidence J.H. Palmer, qq.511–13)

Despite that statement, it can hardly be doubted that, in selecting suitable cities, the Bank was also motivated by the desire to open up new sources of income by developing discount business, after the previous attempt to achieve this through mortgage lending had failed (Clapham 1941, p. 89; Clapham 1944, Vol. 2, pp. 82–5). The recommendation of the Bank's Committee for Branch Banks, that setting up branches in the provinces would be 'for the benefit of the Bank as well as to the interest of the public and the Government' (Acres 1931a, Vol. 2, p. 428, quoting BofE CB), differs from Palmer's public statement. In fact, the objectives to establish the provincial circulation of the Bank's notes and develop a provincial discount business were identical, in that the one was the prerequisite for the other. This is certainly also the explanation of why the first and third provincial branches to be opened were in relatively unimportant provincial towns like Gloucester and Swansea respectively.

Gloucester was certainly far less important than the other towns and cities, like Liverpool, Manchester, Leeds, Huddersfield and Birmingham, which the Committee for Branch Banks considered. However, in Gloucester the collapse of local private banks of issue had been particularly dramatic and it was urgent to consolidate the local credit market and ensure a supply of means of payment there (Acres 1930a, p. 152; Giuseppi 1966, p. 92). It was also to be expected that the Bank would succeed in attracting a number of the customers of the private banks that had gone down.

Swansea was also a small town, of about 12,000 inhabitants, but it was a port and so a trading-centre, located in the middle of the South Wales coalfield. Here, too, the Bank of England saw a chance of rapidly gaining a foothold, since two of the main banks had collapsed. In view of the opposition in most of the provincial towns to the opening of a Bank of England branch, it was presumably of even greater attraction that the Swansea business communities actually favoured the step. At least it was a great advantage compared with the other Welsh towns, like Cardiff, Newport or Merthyr, which the Committee for Branch Banks had also considered (Acres 1931b, p. 169; Roberts 1958a, p. 85).

All the other Bank's branches were founded 'in a large commercial and manufacturing town surrounded by extensive agricultural objects' (BofE, BBO Misc. Papers, History of Branches C 79/52, undated, c. 1961, quoting contemporary sources). The branches were not necessarily located in regions where, as Clapham said, 'banking was specially weak and sound money desirable . . . as might have been expected from the circumstances of their origin' (Clapham 1930, Vol. 1, p. 276). For even while it was establishing them, the Bank also saw its branches as an instrument of a 'bankers' bank' and ultimately it was more interested in attracting banks rather than private individuals as customers. It preferred to leave filling the gap caused by the collapse of local banks in the 1825/6 crisis, to the provincial bankers themselves, where they could do so. Huddersfield was a typical example of this. As in Gloucester, the collapse of five local banks had caused chaos on the local finance market but, unlike the situation in Gloucester, a joint stock bank had been founded, the Huddersfield Banking Co., to ease the situation (Holmes and Green 1986, p. 8). The Bank of England could therefore refrain from setting up a branch in the medium-sized town of Huddersfield, whereas larger cities like Liverpool, Manchester and Birmingham seemed more appropriate for a 'bankers' bank', 'with banks generally efficient and plenty of business for the Branch Banks to tap' (Clapham 1930, Vol. 1, p. 276).

Although it is difficult to disentangle the various motives that the Bank of England may have had in establishing its provincial branches, it may be assumed that the Bank really did take the step initially 'to give solidity and strength to the whole circulation of the country'. Attracting more deposits and activating discount business were subsidiary to that objective, but, since both these considerations were compatible with it, they probably also greatly facilitated decisions for the directors. Under these circumstances the Bank opened the following provincial branches in the next few years:

Gloucester	19 July 1826
Manchester	21 September 1826
Swansea	23 October 1826
Birmingham	1 January 1827
Liverpool	2 July 1827
Bristol	12 July 1827
Leeds	23 August 1827
Exeter	17 December 1827
Newcastle	21 April 1828
Hull	2 January 1829
Norwich	1 December 1829

The branches were certainly not all as welcome locally as those in Gloucester and Swansea. Those in Manchester, Liverpool and Birmingham, and presumably Bristol[2] as well, were 'acceptable to the mercantile interest' of the town. In Hull, Newcastle and Exeter, however, there was public opposition to a Bank of England branch. In Hull the Lord Mayor, and in Newcastle the Chamber of Commerce, petitioned against the establishment of a branch, while the *Exeter Flying Post* wrote: 'of all men who are sinned against by this uncalled-for interference on the part of the Bank of England none are less deserving it than the bankers of our own city' (quotation from Acres 1930b, p. 81). Unfortunately, it is not known how the local banks reacted to branches in Norwich and Leeds, which, like Newcastle, Hull and Exeter, were set up relatively late. The delay itself may be a sign of local opposition. However, Acres finds technical reasons for the relatively late establishment of these branches: in Leeds delays were encountered in purchasing and fitting out suitable premises, while in Norwich the Bank for a long time could not find a suitable branch agent with the necessary security of £10,000 (BofE, BBO Misc. Papers, History of Branches C 79/52, undated, c. 1944; Acres 1931c, p. 91). The total incapacity of both these branches to interest local banks in rediscounting at the Bank of England over the following decades, however, suggests that there was very strong opposition on the part of at least the local provincial banks. The toast proposed by the Chairman of the Huddersfield Banking Co., which operated in the catchment area of the Leeds branch of the Bank of England, on the occasion of the general shareholders' meeting in 1828, may be symptomatic of this: 'The English Bankers, and may their efforts to resist the encroachments of the Bank of England prove successful' (quoted from Crick and Wadsworth 1936, p. 205).

During the 1820s it was not so much the displacement effect of the Bank's notes which provoked opposition across a broad front from the provincial bankers to the Bank's branches; nor was the branches' discounting practice a real danger to local bankers' lending business, except in Birmingham. At first, the provincial banks were most affected by the function, which the Bank of England now began to exercise in the provinces as well, of being the government's bank. Up to 1822 the collectors of taxes were permitted to invest the money they collected at a profit to themselves before paying it into the government's account. Pressnell has seen this privilege as a major factor in the development of the modern banking system in England. After 1822 the paying-in practice of the tax collectors was supervised, but the taxes were still paid into the provincial banks. From 1827 this privilege was transferred to the Bank of England (7 and 8 Geo IV, c. 53). At first it was limited to those cities where the Bank of England had branches, but in 1831 it was extended to a 25-mile zone. Presumably mainly for these reasons the provincial banks, which had formed a loose collective interest association in 1826, sent letters of protest to the government at the end of 1827 and again in mid-1828, complaining that its privileged position gave the Bank of England a competitive advantage over the provincial banks (Pressnell 1953, pp. 394–5; Thomas 1934, p. 85, n.6).

The Bank of England branch in Exeter did not succeed in establishing itself either as an issuer of banknotes or in normal banking business. This was partly a result of the widespread dislike of the 'newcomer' amongst the branch's potential customers, especially the local banks, but it was also a result of the declining economic importance of the town (Ryton 1984, p. 84; Clapham 1930, Vol. 1, pp. 45–6). The Bank was requested by the Treasurer for the Navy to open branches in Pembroke, Plymouth, Portsmouth and Chatham to facilitate payments for the Naval

Yards, and in May 1834 it moved its Exeter branch to Plymouth. In the same month it also set up a new branch in Portsmouth (Acres 1932, p. 84; Acres 1930b, p. 81).

The last provincial branch which the Bank was to found for some time was established in Leicester. Leicester was a rapidly industrializing town in the Midlands textile region. It was not far from Birmingham, but it offered better access to the other textile centres in the Midlands, like Nottingham and Derby, and to the agricultural hinterland of the East Midlands. Accordingly it perfectly fitted the requirements that the Committee for Branch Banks had drawn up for locations for its branches. The closure of the local bank of issue Clarke, Mitchell & Co. in 1843 also offered a good opportunity for a Bank of England branch. In its recommendation to the Court of Directors the Committee for Branch Banks said:

> It is considered that the consequent withdrawal of a large amount of local notes by the recent failure of the bank of Clarke, Mitchell & Co. offers a fair opportunity to the Bank of England for the extension of their note circulation into that part of the kingdom . . . . The Committee do not contemplate a large profit in the first instance, but they have reason to believe that the Branch will pay its expenses with a surplus and with a fair prospect of increasing profit (BofE CB No. 66, 28 September 1843).

2.2 Branches of the Central Bank

2.2.1 Establishing the Bank of England note, 1826/9–1844

The tasks the provincial branches had to perform necessarily brought them into competition with the local banks (in the discount business) and their London agents (in rediscounting between the banks). For this was the only way to establish the Bank of England note in the provinces. Naturally none of the provincial banks was prepared to consider voluntarily renouncing the issue of its own banknotes without a return service from the Bank of England, since there was competition not only from the Bank, with its privileged position, but also from the new joint stock banks. Although, new joint stock banks were initially slow to be set up, during the first half of the 1830s there was a rapid growth in numbers (see Table 2.1). The Bank of England was bound to endeavour not to intensify the pressure on the provincial banks even further and to enable them to survive without issuing banknotes.

An example is the private bank I. & I.C. Wright of Nottingham. In 1836 it made an agreement with the Bank of England branch in Birmingham to cease its banknote circulation, which was then about £50,000, and only issue Bank of England notes. In return it was granted £10,000 in Bank of England notes free of interest and a credit line with a minimum of £43,000 and a maximum of £50,000 at the Bank of England Birmingham branch. This credit was at 3 per cent, which was

Table 2.1 Joint stock banks in England and Wales, 1826–56

Year	Joint stock banks established		Joint stock banks closed	
	Banks of issue	Non-issuing banks	Banks of issue	Non-issuing banks
1826	6	—	—	—
1827	1	—	—	—
1828	3	2	—	—
1829	4	—	—	—
1830	3	—	—	—
1831	7	1	—	—
1832	10	—	—	—
1833	12	1	—	—
1834	5	3	—	—
1835	35	10	—	—
1836	7	4	4	3
1837	—	—	3	2
1838	—	5	—	—
1839	3	2	—	1
1840	2	—	—	1
1841	1	2	—	1
1842	1	1	—	1
1843	—	1	2	3
1844	—	19	20	—
1845		—	1	—
1846		—	4	1
1847		—	—	2
1848		—	1	1
1849		1	—	—
1850		—	—	1
1851		—	—	3
1852		—	—	1
1853		1	—	—
1854		1	—	—
1855		3	1	—
1856		2	1	2

Note: The table includes London joint stock banks such as the London & Westminster Bank (est. 1834), London Joint Stock Bank (est. 1836), Union Bank of London (est. 1839), London & County Joint Stock Banking Co. (est. 1838) succeeding the Kent, Surrey & Sussex Bank (est. 1836). The establishment of such banks was permitted from 1833. The London joint stock banks were non-issuing banks, since the Bank of England monopoly for the issuing of banknotes inside the radius of 65 miles was still valid.

Source: Select Committee on Bank Acts, BPP 1857, Part 2, App. 21, p. 134.

on average one percentage point below the minimum discount rate for normal customers in London. As security Wrights deposited bills which were payable in London and so credited to its account by the Bank of England on the date they fell due. If the acceptor also had an account with the Bank of England, the whole transaction would be made with two entries in the Bank's books, without banknotes being used at all. Wrights redeemed virtually all its bills payable in London in this way, so it had no difficulty in providing sufficient security for the credits. The margin by which the value of the bills deposited at the Bank of England exceeded the current level of the credit was about 30 per cent to 50 per cent. In this way the Bank of England acted as Wrights' London agent and thereby it was competing directly with the London bill brokers and the private banks that acted as London agents for the provincial banks (BPP 1841, evidence Wright, qq.1589–1599).[3]

Although the costs for the issue of its own notes were only about 2 per cent according to Wright, the banker still saw the agreement with the Bank of England as extremely advantageous to his bank, because he no longer needed to hold gold as a reserve and had 'a feeling of greater security . . . and freedom from anxiety'. With a circulation account he could also obtain credit at 3 per cent in a crisis, when the banks of issue had to pay 7 per cent and more for rediscounting in London (BPP 1841, evidence Wright, qq.1603, 1652; evidence James, qq.1580; BPP 1837, evidence Gilbert, q.2048).

If demand from Wrights went beyond the £60,000 limit (£10,000 interest-free loan and £50,000 circulation account) Wrights were free to fund through a London bank or a bill broker on the London money market, and so acquire Bank of England notes in a way that might well be cheaper. Alternatively, they could also increase their credit line with the Bank of England, but then the additional amount needed would be treated like a normal open account, and Wrights had to pay a negotiated rate of interest. The banks which, like Wrights, did not have a Bank of England branch in their locality, received a further offer from the Bank of England. As compensation 'for the risk and the expense of obtaining notes, there being no branch nearer than Birmingham', the Bank paid Wrights a fixed sum of £350 per year (BPP 1841, evidence Wright, qq.1593). The private bank J.M. Head in Carlisle, which concluded a circulation account agreement with the Bank of England branch in Newcastle in 1836, received seven days' credit on all its bills rediscounted by the Bank of England. However, this was probably a special feature connected with a joint action by the British government and the Bank of England to counteract the circulation of Scottish banknotes in Cumberland. In the case of Head, the Bank of England note was replacing notes from a Scottish bank which the Carlisle bank had previously issued (Crick and Wadsworth 1936, p. 113; Munn 1981, pp. 177–8).

From the early 1830s the Bank of England concluded circulation account agreements with a number of provincial private banks as well as the new joint stock banks. One example is the agreement of 1836 with the Gloucestershire Banking Co. This bank did not have a loan account, like Wrights, rather it had a special discount account with the Gloucester branch of the Bank of England. The discount rate was also 3 per cent. So both classes of circulation account were known as 'three per cent accounts'. The credit line granted to the Gloucestershire Banking Co. was between £100,000 and £115,000.[4] As with Wrights, it also had a non-interest quota of Bank of England notes allocated to it in addition to its 'three per cent account'. In this case the allocation was £42,000, for which only securities (presumably bills, government stock or East India bonds) had to be deposited (Sayers 1957a, pp. 144–5).

The conditions under which the Gloucestershire Banking Co. ceased to issue its own banknotes were therefore more favourable than those given to Wrights. While Wrights received about 20 per cent of the expected circulation largely cost-free, the Gloucestershire Banking Co. had around 40 per cent. The reason for this is presumably that some joint stock banks were opening branches by the 1830s and so had to keep a higher reserve of cash. According to Wright, the advantage of issuing its own notes for a bank was not so much the average amount in circulation (a cost advantage over the Bank of England notes), as that means of payment were always available should demand suddenly rise. As he himself said, Wright therefore endeavoured in his negotiations with the Bank of England to secure that advantage as far as possible (BPP 1847/48, evidence Wright, q.2866). Whether this quota was really held as a reserve, or whether the 3 per cent account, that involved costs, was being appropriately reduced, in other words, used as an additional source of profit, is of course a different matter. All the other details of the agreements between the Bank of England and the two banks were presumably the same. If the note circulation by the Gloucestershire Banking Co. went beyond the limit of £115,000, the bank could also rediscount on the London money market. But quite clearly the Gloucestershire Banking Co. also preferred to increase its borrowing from the Bank of England in such cases, as described above. The reason for this was seen by the Bank England branch agent in Birmingham as that by affirming that it would only rediscount at the Bank of England, the bank intended 'to satisfy the Governor of his anxiety to keep faith with the Bank' (Holmes and Green 1986, p. 26, quoting BofE BBALB).

In addition to the privileged circulation accounts, banks could also apply for an ordinary open account with the Bank of England. An open account would be particularly attractive if the provincial banks wanted to retain greater freedom of choice between the possibilities for rediscounting, as the open account had an upper limit but, unlike the circulation accounts, no lower limit. This meant that better use could be made of the interest differential between the London money market and the Bank of England. The lower limit was usually only £200 and it presumably enabled the Bank of England to recoup the costs of operating the account, like the minimum balance that had to be kept in a drawing account. The upper limit was usually fixed according to the 'legitimate trade' of the applicant and the estimated amount of the partners' capital. The interest rates were generally 4 per cent, therefore higher than those on the circulation account. Often an open account was also used as a preliminary to a circulation account. Since it was difficult to determine the credit lines for a circulation account with banks that had not previously issued banknotes, the Bank of England would first open an open account for them to check the upper level of the bank's circulation of Bank of England notes. Then the amount for the circulation account was fixed accordingly.

The banks in Liverpool made quite different use of their circulation accounts. They discounted only up to the top limit on the account when they could not fund in London at 3 per cent or less. On these occasions the Liverpool banks actually made repeated attempts to extend the credit lines on their circulation accounts. However, when rediscounting in London was cheaper than at the Liverpool branch of the Bank of England, the demand for credit was usually very close to the lower limit of the circulation account, and the banks urged the Bank of England to adapt its interest rates to those on the London money market (Collins 1972a, p. 154).

Lancashire played a special role in every respect. The Bank of England had made greater efforts to gain a foothold here than in any other region. Its concern was not so much the banknote circulation of other banks of issue, whose number was still relatively small, but the fact that local trade bills were circulating as generally accepted means of payment (Ashton 1953, pp. 39–43; Checkland 1954, pp. 129–42; Pressnell 1956, p. 19). So, in return for a circulation account with the Liverpool branch of the Bank of England, the Lancashire banks had to undertake not to issue any more bills as means of payment, as well as ceasing to issue their own banknotes.[5] Nevertheless, the Liverpool branch of the Bank succeeded in concluding more circulation account agreements than any other branch. Of the twenty-six provincial banks that had concluded such agreements with the Bank of England by 1841, seven had a circulation account with the Liverpool branch (see Table 2.2). A further six banks had an open account there in 1838. The Bank of England had therefore succeeded in binding all the local banks (there were thirteen banks altogether in Liverpool in 1840) to its Liverpool branch with either a circulation or an open account and displacing the provincial banknotes altogether (BPP 1837/38, app. 7, p. 122; BPP 1837/38, evidence Turner, qq.335–6; Anderson and Cottrell 1975, pp. 606–7).

The Bank of England Birmingham branch was also fairly successful and by 1841 it had succeeded in concluding circulation account agreements with three out of seven of the local banks. It also had circulation account agreements with a bank in Newcastle-under-Lyme and one

Table 2.2 Number of banks having a 'circulation account' with the Bank of England

Bank of England Branch	Number of 'contract banks' 1835	1838	1841		Feb. 1844	1848
Gloucester	—	1	1	(180,000)	2	2
Manchester	2	3	3	(570,000)	4	4
Swansea	1	1	1	(28,000)	1	1
Birmingham	2	5	6	(382,000)	5	5
Liverpool	4	6	7	(1,035,000)	7	7
Bristol	—	—	—		2	2
Leeds	—	—	—		1	1
Newcastle	—	3	5	(405,500)	7	5
Hull	1	1	1	(20,000)	1	1
Norwich	—	—	—		1	—
Plymouth	—	—	—		3	3
Portsmouth	—	1	2	(45,000)	7	6
Leicester	—	—	—		—	2
London	—	—	—		2	6

Note: ( ) 'circulation account' limit.

Source: 1835 and 1838: BPP 1837/8, App. 8, p. 123.
1841 and 1848: BPP 1847/8, Part 2, App. 22, p. 196.
1844: BPP 1844, Vol. 32, Accounts and Papers: Finance — Bank of England Returns, p. 34.

in Bridgnorth, and open account agreements with a bank in Wolverhampton and one in Bilston. The three contract banks were, as in Liverpool, comparatively young joint stock banks, and they had soon outstripped the old private banks on the local finance market.[6] In 1831 the Birmingham branch could actually afford to turn down an application for a circulation account from a private bank, Attwoods & Spooner (Moss 1982, p. 80). In 1844 the authorized banknote issue of the remaining banks of issue in Birmingham was just £81,000 compared with a Bank of England circulation of around £600,000.[7] However, Birmingham differed fundamentally from Liverpool in that a considerable number of provincial banks of issue were still operating in the neighbouring towns and, although the Bank of England banknote predominated in Birmingham itself, the provincial banknotes were clearly more important as means of payment in the Black Country. Here, in Wolverhampton, Walsall, West Bromwich, Dudley, Stourbridge and Kidderminster, ten provincial banks of issue still had a circulation of about £200,000 in 1844; there were also six provincial banks of issue in towns to the east and south of Birmingham — Coventry, Warwick and Leamington — with a total circulation of about £135,000.

The reason for the initial success of the Birmingham branch of the

Bank of England was presumably that the Bank succeeded in attracting the best and most powerful customers, who had no difficulties in meeting its requirements for security. Since the Bank of England interest rate of 4 per cent in Birmingham was clearly lower than the rate of 5 per cent charged by the private banks (presumably in agreement with each other), which was maximum under the Usury Laws, the Bank initially succeeded in attracting the most lucrative business. The old private bankers had to watch their big customers discount their best bills at the Bank of England, leaving them only bills with a long maturity and acceptances that were not safe enough for the Bank. The Bank had broken into the Birmingham credit market and, with an aggressive competition policy, it was quickly able to take some of the provincial banks' lending business. This meant the end of the oligopoly of the local private banks, which as the branch agent in Birmingham saw it, formed a kind of 'local aristocracy', on the market (Moss 1981, p. 541; see also Holmes and Green 1986, p. 10). Naturally the banks were quick to respond: they took up the fight and lowered their interest rates (Moss 1981, p. 546).[8] All the banks in Birmingham also joined in the campaign conducted by the country bankers against the provincial branches of the Bank of England.

The initial commercial success enjoyed by the Birmingham branch of the Bank of England was therefore ended, and the private banks had more to fear in the way of competition from the new joint stock banks. The Bank of England did not react competitively to the new joint stock banks and its branch agent joined other branch agents who were trying — unsuccessfully — to persuade the Bank in London to adopt a more appropriate market strategy (Moss 1981, p. 546). After the establishment of the first joint stock bank in Birmingham, the Birmingham Banking Co. in the autumn of 1829, the Bank of England's discount business in Birmingham began to drop rapidly (see Table 2.4).

The action by the Bank of England's head office during this phase shows that it did not, at first, have a recognizable strategy for its provincial branches. The rules of the London discount business were simply applied in the provinces, regardless of what effect they might have there, and so in most provincial branches the Bank was uncompetitive from their inception. The local banks actually often left part of the business to it voluntarily, since a Bank of England branch in their neighbourhood brought them considerable advantages (BPP 1831/32, evidence Stuckey, q.1116; evidence Beckett, q.1477; evidence Wilkins, qq.1757 and 1786; S. Jones 1985, p. 33). The pressure on the provincial banknote came initially more from the ban on notes of less than £5. The banknote circulation of the private bank Wilkins & Co. (Brecon and Merthyr) remained extremely stable during the first three years of the existence of the Bank of England branches in Gloucester and Swansea. It was only in 1829 and 1830, when the transitional phase for the £1 notes was over, that this bank's circulation fell to between 70 per cent and 50 per cent of the average for the years 1826 to 1828 (Roberts 1958b, pp. 39–41).

However, after about 1830 the Bank began to see its provincial branches as instruments of a national monetary policy, and a strategy does become clearly recognizable. The Bank of England had to rid itself of the dilemma of not being able to gain a real foothold in most places owing to its restrictive rules, on the one hand, and on the other, to its arousing the opposition of the provincial banks with its relatively low interest rates, as in Birmingham. It solved the problem very skilfully by easing the pressure of competition against the provincial banks and offering its services to them as a bankers' bank at the same time. In this way it did not need to threaten the existence of all the provincial banks, only those which were its particular target, the banks of issue.

The Bank of England had been using circulation accounts and open accounts since the early 1830s as a weapon against the provincial banknotes, and after 1833 banks of issue were on principle excluded from rediscounting at the Bank of England. Only rediscounting 'for the purpose . . . of meeting their notes paid in at . . . the branch banks' was permitted for provincial banks of issue up to 1840. Thereafter, even that exception was no longer permitted (Collins 1972a, p. 150; BPP 1837/8, evidence Curtis, Q 119; BofE BBO Circulars C 79/5, 18 December 1833 and 14 November 1840). The Bank of England welcomed this policy in an internal paper on the occasion of an application from the Towgood & Co. bank of issue in Cardiff for a discount account:

> If the request to discount with you [the Swansea branch agent of the Bank of England] was made merely to uphold their own circulation it cannot of course be admitted, it being a clearly ascertained fact that monies so obtained are not used for country circulation but are transmitted immediately to London to meet the bills due in London drawn in payment of the said circulation — your issue for that purpose becomes therefore substantially a London issue and extends so far the liabilities of the Bank to sudden demands of gold. (Roberts 1958a, p. 150, quoting BofE, Swansea BALB)

The Bank of England was, of course, aware that in excluding the banks of issue from its services as bankers' bank, it was discriminating against them and it felt it necessary to obtain the express approval of the Prime Minister and the Chancellor before introducing the circulation accounts (Clapham 1944, Vol. 2, p. 140). It could be sure of obtaining the approval, since its argument followed exactly the lines of the banking legislation of 1826 and could be seen as its logical development.

The Bank of England was following government policy in other ways than by displacing the provincial banknotes. From the mid-1830s at the latest it had been laying down other criteria, as well as ceasing to issue banknotes, which the individual banks had to fulfil before being granted a circulation account. Some cases are known where the Bank refused to conclude circulation account agreements because it felt that it needed no

Table 2.3 Bank of England branch banknote circulation, 1829–44
(a) (£000)

Year	Glo	Man	Swa	Bir	Liv	Bri	Lee	New	Hul	Nor	Ply	Por	Exe	Lei
1829	48	411	50	178	109	59	54	23	29	—	—	—	18	—
1830	49	904	47	268	212	85	106	35	64	25	—	—	23	—
1831	49	1197	40	357	305	110	157	37	53	40	—	—	27	—
1832	56	1315	49	413	377	113	199	51	51	30	—	—	31	—
1833	49	1527	47	402	523	116	262	50	68	33	—	—	36	—
1834	37	1605	58	353	581	94	230	59	59	25	42	36	35	—
1835	38	1474	69	328	710	85	247	104	52	17	60	62	—	—
1836	82	1560	80	368	829	74	263	123	67	13	64	59	—	—
1837	211	1506	97	432	786	78	212	241	77	12	70	109	—	—
1838	304	1501	100	452	833	75	197	251	80	11	61	127	—	—
1839	340	1476	105	499	800	69	193	338	81	12	56	116	—	—
1840	309	1425	96	526	769	76	164	377	84	11	56	113	—	—
1841	303	1501	82	558	723	79	198	425	79	10	71	189	—	—
1842	278	1604	84	555	778	168	297	498	80	19	255	267	—	—
1843	121	1781	84	605	920	253	326	543	89	56	292	367	—	—
1844	103	2155	96	601	1341	325	322	598	99	66	365	408	—	127

(b) % of total branch banknote circulation

Year	Glo	Man	Swa	Bir	Liv	Bri	Lee	New	Hul	Nor	Ply	Por	Exe	Lei
1829	5	42	5	18	11	6	6	2	3				2	
1830	3	50	2	15	12	5	6	2	3	1			1	
1831	2	50	2	15	13	5	6	2	2	2			1	
1832	2	49	2	15	14	4	7	2	2	1			1	
1833	2	49	2	13	17	4	8	2	2	1			1	
1834	1	50	2	11	18	3	7	2	2	1	1	1	1	
1835	1	45	2	10	22	3	8	3	2	1	2	2		
1836	2	43	2	10	23	2	7	3	2	—	2	2		
1837	6	39	3	11	20	2	6	6	2	—	2	3		
1838	8	38	3	11	21	2	5	6	2	—	2	3		
1839	8	36	3	12	20	2	5	8	2	—	1	3		
1840	8	36	2	13	19	2	4	9	2	—	1	3		
1841	7	36	2	13	17	2	5	10	2	—	2	4		
1842	6	33	2	11	16	3	6	10	2	—	5	5		
1843	2	33	2	11	17	5	6	10	2	1	5	7		
1844	2	32	2	9	20	5	5	9	2	1	5	6		2

Note: Bank of England branches: Gloucester, Manchester, Swansea, Birmingham, Liverpool, Bristol, Leeds, Newcastle, Hull, Norwich, Plymouth, Portsmouth, Exeter, Leicester.

Source: 1829–31: BPP 1837/8, App. 4, p. 120.
1832–44: BPP 1847/8, Part 2, App. 18, p. 189.

Table 2.4 Bills discounted at Bank of England branches, 1831–44
(a) Turnover (£000)

Year	Glo	Man	Swa	Bir	Liv	Bri	Lee	New	Hul	Nor	Ply	Por	Exe
1831	430	1737	470	3206	2626	536	1021	261	373	398			115
1832	298	1217	223	2691	3361	214	699	277	184	38			34
1833	90	1081	121	1591	3104	196	726	71	192	25			6
1834	81	2369	189	1740	6448	189	490	230	142	36			
1835	114	2618	323	1838	7450	135	618	411	178	40	9	90	
1836	622	4868	508	2608	13913	158	862	785	457	25	29	145	
1837	761	4202	331	2479	10436	143	801	1443	519	22	29	189	
1838	603	3717	239	1999	8439	67	635	1302	468	21	24	116	
1839	912	6099	257	2939	11448	65	814	3200	628	17	71	152	
1840	1080	4940	213	2581	8862	45	380	3377	405	19	54	166	
1841	923	5669	180	2593	9404	158	616	3547	332	9	231	620	
1842	674	4439	92	2244	7510	919	982	3771	277	9	540	571	
1843	0	2527	84	1898	5763	607	419	3695	195	8	314	436	
1844	2	2402	69	1677	6047	502	194	2857	263	8	383	440	

(b) 'Bankers' bills' as % of total discounts

Year	Glo	Man	Swa	Bir	Liv	Bri	Lee	New	Hul	Nor	Ply	Por
1835	34	75	73	69	96	0	3	85	13	0	0	0
1836	70	81	78	76	97	0	2	94	57	0	7	0
1837	95	79	66	75	91	0	2	97	52	0	21	37
1838	98	94	70	85	98	0	1	93	39	0	0	19
1839	100	87	60	87	92	0	6	96	46	0	18	44
1840	100	87	61	87	96	0	6	98	46	0	20	80
1841	100	88	33	85	93	94	52	98	42	0	72	86
1842	100	90	22	85	95	98	74	99	38	0	91	88
1843	—	91	35	90	95	100	57	99	22	0	97	87
1844	0	96	48	86	99	100	3	100	9	0	97	85

Note: Bank of England branches: Gloucester, Manchester, Swansea, Birmingham, Liverpool, Bristol, Leeds, Newcastle, Hull, Norwich, Plymouth, Portsmouth and Exeter

Source: BofE, SOC Reports, C 35/2–4;
BofE, SDC Discount Operations of the Bank, C 30/3;
BofE, CB of the respective years.

more banks in that region to circulate its notes, although this stance was only taken in the early 1830s. When applications were turned down thereafter it was mainly because the bank in question did not fulfil other conditions. The Birmingham & Midland Bank, for example, was initially refused a circulation account because its paid-up capital, £30,000 on a nominal equity of £250,000, was regarded as too low. After about a year of negotiations the Birmingham & Midland Bank finally agreed to reduce its nominal equity to £120,000 and increase its paid-up capital to £60,000, following which it was allowed a circulation account (Holmes and Green 1986, pp. 18–21).

The success that the Bank of England enjoyed in these negotiations shows clearly how attractive a circulation account must have been to a provincial bank. It may therefore be assumed that the circulation accounts contributed very largely to the success of the Bank in displacing the circulation of provincial banknotes in Birmingham and the circulation of bills in Lancashire, even if displacement in the latter case had probably started even before the Bank of England branches were opened (Checkland 1954, p. 141; BPP 1837/8, evidence Turner, qq.287–95). Further evidence of this may be seen in that in the Bank's main centres of activity in the provinces — Manchester, Liverpool and Birmingham — between 75 per cent and 95 per cent of the discount business was bankers' bills and not traders' bills (see Table 2.4).

An even better indicator is the share of the bills discounted at 3 per cent, that is, the rediscounting by contract banks, in the provincial branches' discount business. In 1831, when only three banks had circulation accounts in Liverpool and Birmingham, the share was still 12 per cent (although it was 33 per cent in Birmingham); in 1832 it had risen to 47 per cent (Birmingham 56 per cent and Liverpool 75 per cent) and by 1833 to 56 per cent. After 1834 this accounted for more than half the entire discount business in the three most important Bank of England branches (Liverpool 80 per cent, Birmingham 58 per cent and Manchester 57 per cent). In that year these three branches handled just on 90 per cent of all the discount business conducted by the provincial branches. At the end of the 1830s, when the contract banks were distributed between all the provincial branches, the share of the circulation accounts in the provincial branches' total discount business was up to 80 per cent (1838) (BofE, SDC Reports C 35/2; BofE, SDC Discount Operations of the Bank). Not least for that reason the circulation accounts also had the side-effect of compensating for the decline in the normal commercial banking business. Finally, by better control of the provincial banks' funding, the Bank could adapt their banknote circulation to the national requirement, which it regarded as paramount, of securing convertibility. According to a statement by the Bank of England branch agent in Liverpool, the agent had to orient the credit he granted to the 'periodical returns of the Bank of England' and 'the state of the foreign exchanges' (BPP 1837/8, evidence Turner, q.273).[9] The circulation accounts were the best way to combine all three requirements.

However, the high share of the discount business handled through circulation accounts is also an indication that the strict rules regarding the quality of the bills were a great handicap to non-banks. For, in addition to the name of the discount customer, every bill had to bear the names of two persons classified by the Bank as sound. The Bank took these rules extremely seriously and applied them very strictly, and often several bills from a package handed in for discounting would be returned. The currency of a bill had to be no longer than three months. At a time when foreign trade bills were generally for six months, this constituted a serious obstacle to many potential Bank of England customers. However, after 1835 the Bank eased this requirement slightly by accepting 'bills of Government, the East India Co. or other approved bills of exchange' with a maturity of up to six months as security for loans on bills of between one and three months. This change particularly helped the Swansea branch, where the mining companies in South Wales generally only had six months bills to offer, which the Bank of England would not accept. Moreover, a bill on principle must represent a 'bona fide trade transaction'. All bills which were even suspected of being accommodation bills were rejected: that was the case generally for bills of every kind of broker and 'railway contractors' (BofE BBO Circulars C 79/5, 23 July 1835; BPP 1831/2 evidence Dyer, q.4178; BPP 1841 evidence James, qq.1431, 1438, 1509; Roberts 1986, p. 72; Roberts 1958a, p. 234; Collins 1972a, p. 150). Governor Palmer wrote to the branch agent in Liverpool on this in 1831:

> To discount any other than negotiated bills would in fact be lending a banker capital to lend to his customer, in other words to help him to create capital, rather than circulate capital already in existence — which latter alone is legitimate business. (Collins 1972a, p. 151 quoting BofE Liverpool BALB; see also Roberts 1958a, p. 232, n.7 and n.10)

The situation was quite different in the West Riding of Yorkshire, another industrial district. The Leeds branch of the Bank of England was the only provincial branch where more traders' bills than bankers' bills were discounted. Two reasons can be identified for this. First, the branch manager had excellent contacts with the local business world (Hudson 1986, p. 189), which would explain the very high absolute number of traders' bills. Second, and more important, the business with the local banks was unusually small. Until 1838 not a single bank in the region had concluded an agreement for an open account and it was not until 1842 that the first, and only, agreement was concluded for a circulation account at the branch,[10] by the Yorkshire District Bank, a joint stock bank which operated fifteen branches, a very high number for the time. The bank was reorganized in 1843 and its successor, the Yorkshire Banking Co., characteristically resumed the issue of banknotes; only the Sheffield branch, which had been made independent in the course of the reorganization and now operated as the Sheffield Union Bank, maintained a circulation account with the Bank of England in Leeds. In this the Bank of England lost one of its most important contract banks, as the banknote quota of the Yorkshire District Bank before its collapse had been £100,000 (Hudson 1986, p. 304 n.22). While the successor bank was allocated an authorized issue of £122,500 under Peel's Act, the Bank of England Leeds branch was left with only the Sheffield Union Bank at this time as contract bank and its quota was only £20,000 (BofE, BBO Bank Note Composition C 79/26).

Hudson assumes that the relatively slight importance of provincial banknotes in Yorkshire was the reason for a certain reserve on the part of the Bank of England in Leeds. But it can hardly be said that the provincial banknotes were of slight importance in Yorkshire; in the last quarter of 1836 at least £750,000 of private banknotes were circulating there, £400,000 in the West Riding, in addition to £1 million of banknotes from joint stock banks. This made Yorkshire the county with the highest circulation of provincial banknotes in the whole of England (BPP 1841, app. 24, p. 312; evidence Gilbert, q.940; Hudson 1986, p.190).[11] In 1844 the circulation of the provincial banks of issue located in the catchment area of the Bank of England Leeds branch was also still extraordinarily high:

- Leeds: six banks of issue with an authorized issue totalling £269,275;
- Bradford: in addition to two branches of banks of issue in Leeds, three banks of issue with a total of £82,052 authorized issue;
- Halifax/Huddersfield: in addition to the branch of a bank of issue in Leeds, four banks of issue with a total of £147,787 authorized issue;
- Sheffield: four banks of issue with a total authorized issue of £130,607;
- York: in addition to the branch of a bank of issue in Leeds, three banks of issue with a total authorized issue of £218,322. (Banking Almanac 1845, Banking Directory)

If one also takes into account that in Yorkshire, especially in the West Riding, bills were circulating as means of payment, as they were in Lancashire (BPP 1831/2, evidence Burgess, q.5331), it is more likely that the Bank of England was very keen to gain a foothold in the West Riding. Unfortunately, the starting conditions for its branch in Leeds have so far not been researched and consequently we can only put forward an alternative hypothesis here. The most probable explanation for the relatively slight success of the Leeds branch in replacing the provincial banknotes with Bank of England notes (see Table 2.3) would seem to be a certain reserve on the part of the provincial banks to the Bank of England, rather than *vice versa*. One indication of the extraordinarily great interest shown by the Bank of England in doing business with the banks in the West Riding is certainly the special position of the Yorkshire District Bank, which was given a circulation account even before it ceased to issue its own notes in 1841 'with the view to the gradual withdrawal of their issue' (BofE, BBO Circulars C 79/5, 30 July 1841).

Thanks to this circulation account agreement with the Yorkshire District Bank, discount business at the Leeds branch did in fact increase (see Table 2.4) and, as a consequence, the circulation of Bank of England notes also increased noticeably in Leeds in 1842 (see Table 2.3). Nonetheless, Leeds remained the branch with the biggest non-bank credit business. Most of the traders who had discount accounts with the Bank of England Leeds branch were large merchant houses of first class standing, with capital estimated by the Bank of England to be at least £25,000. The rule on capital, and the requirement of a minimum balance of £200 to be maintained on a Bank of England account, however, excluded most of the textile producers in the region right from the start. Manufacturers were therefore a minority among the customers, even of the Leeds branch (Hudson 1986, p. 189, quoting BofE Leeds BALB).

A second and extremely effective way of displacing the provincial notes was to make quarterly advances available from the provincial branches. Quarterly advances had been introduced in London to alleviate the effects of the tax payments on the government accounts with the Bank of England. Since these funds accumulated in the Bank until the interest was paid on the national debt, only the Bank of England was in a position to increase the liquidity of the market. From 1829 it met that need by giving special credits with maturities of only a few days. At the beginning of the 1830s, once the practice had become established in London, the Bank decided to offer quarterly advances in its branches in Manchester, Liverpool and Birmingham and, a little later, at its other branches (BofE, BBO Circulars C 79/5, 5 June 1834 and 4 June 1835). The shortage of means of payment and a slow circulation of banknotes was also felt in the provinces at the quarters, mainly by the banks which issued only Bank of England notes. While banks of issue could avoid the stringency by issuing more notes, the non-issuing banks found it difficult to acquire Bank of England notes, if they did not want to use Bank of England credits with normal maturities, as London banks and bill brokers also suffered from the liquidity shortage and were thus not very inclined to help their provincial customers. By introducing quarterly advances the Bank of England eliminated an important competitive disadvantage suffered by its contracts banks against the banks of issue.

The privileged circulation accounts and quarterly advances also countered a central concern that had caused some agitation among the provincial banks in the 1820s. Since the provincial banks had not been able to induce the Bank of England to withdraw from the provinces, they had very quickly demanded, as an alternative, that they should have the same status as the London banks (Moss 1981, p. 545). Whether intended as a strategy or not, the different treatment by the Bank of banks of issue and those provincial banks that had agreed to cease issuing their own banknotes drove a wedge between the two. This split the front that had been fairly united right across the country in opposition to the banking legislation of 1826 and the Bank of England's provincial branches.[12]

In addition to the discount accounts, which had been almost exclusively a source of funding for the provincial banks since the beginning of the 1830s, the drawing accounts also contributed very largely to the spread of Bank of England notes in the provinces. At a time when even banks that already had several branches only covered markets that were very close together, the safe and rapid transfer of larger amounts of money constituted a major problem. None of the provincial banks was in a position to link regions where there was a surplus of capital seeking investment with regions where there was a shortage of capital. That could only come directly through the credit market. The Bank of England could usually only satisfy a small part of the rapidly growing demand for funds, as its interest rates on normal discount accounts were usually above the London market rate, but it could very greatly facilitate payments transactions. Its branch network linked many major industrial and trade centres in different parts of the country. This also brought the Bank customers in places where its branches could not compete with the local banks in the lending business.

The advantages of a drawing account with the Bank of England were considerable. Instead of paying out banknotes, every customer could also have special bills issued for a term of up to twenty-one days. Since these bills were issued on a specific person and a specific date, they were an ideal substitute, obviating the risk of theft of banknotes. During the mid-nineteenth century very many customers made use of this possibility. The circulation of these bills was almost £100,000 in the 1830s and around £250,000 in the 1840s. Most of them (at times more than 80 per cent) were, however, issued by only two branches, Manchester and Liverpool (BPP 1847/8, Part 2, App. 16, p. 186). Only when the communications system improved in the second half of the century did the importance of these bills decline.

The great advantage of a drawing account was in the rapid, cheap and safe transfer of sums of money. If neither the sender nor the recipient of a transfer had an account with the Bank of England, the costs were 0.25 per cent plus postage. The same rate was charged by the provincial banks to their customers. If only the recipient had an account with the Bank of England, only the postal charges had to be borne, and if both sender and recipient were customers of the Bank, the transaction was entirely free of charge. Naturally the provincial banks could not offer such a service at this time, and so non-banking firms also made use of the possibility of lowering their transfer costs through a Bank of England account, in so far as they were in a position to satisfy the Bank's minimum requirements. The provincial banks that were non-issuing banks were compensated for this competitive disadvantage by the Bank of England in that they were allowed to transfer free of charge in any case (Collins 1972a, p. 146; S. Jones 1985, p. 33). These special conditions were of particularly great value, since most bills were already payable in London at this time. As an example we only need recall how I. & I.C. Wright made use of their circulation account. These advantages made the drawing accounts very good instruments against the provincial banknotes.

The Bank of England was equally restrictive in granting drawing accounts to banks as it was in granting circulation accounts. Since the early 1830s banks of issue in general had been excluded from holding drawing accounts. The only exceptions were banks operating in a town at great distance from the nearest Bank of England branch.[13] One such exception was the private bank Wilkins & Co. in Brecon (Roberts 1958b, p. 47). For most provincial banks the practice was applied which the banker S. Lloyd of Birmingham could still well remember in 1875. His bank was denied a drawing account as long as it had a licence to issue banknotes. While the Bank of England would exchange every Bank of England note that had been issued outside Birmingham for gold, even if the holder was not a customer of the Bank, this service was on principle denied to the local banks of issue, for the Bank of England was not legally bound to exchange their notes.[14]

The Bank of England could be quite generous at times in allowing drawing accounts to non-banks, if it saw this as a way of increasing the circulation of its own notes. We can take as an example the practice of allocating drawing accounts in Manchester and Liverpool in the early 1830s. Then the circulation of notes in Lancashire was still relatively small, for reasons already outlined above. In addition to the bills, which were still very popular, traders and manufacturers in Manchester were increasingly using notes issued by the Bank's Manchester branch for payments to importers in Liverpool. However, this caused mainly a one-way flow of the Bank's notes from Manchester to Liverpool, and created considerable problems for the Bank as it had to return the Manchester notes paid into its Liverpool branch to Manchester at its own expense. Each banknote was marked with its place of issue and could only be reissued there. To reduce the costs of transporting the notes back from Liverpool to Manchester and to discourage the use of bills, which were also circulating as means of payment, the Bank permitted drawing accounts to be opened in Liverpool and Manchester on an unusually large scale. Since drawing accounts enabled traders and producers to transfer money largely free of charge, as both the sender of the payment in Manchester and the recipient in Liverpool had accounts with the Bank of England, the Bank hoped that this would achieve its aim (Collins 1972a, p. 147).

As Table 2.3 shows, Manchester was the most important issuer of Bank of England notes of all the Bank's branches. Soon after the branch was set up four of the seven local banks had opened drawing accounts, including Jones Loyd, one of the biggest and most successful banks in the whole of England at the time (S. Jones 1985, p. 34). Some of the eight joint stock banks that were subsequently established in Manchester also opened accounts with the Bank of England, but the Bank initially only succeeded in inducing some of the Manchester joint stock banks to cease issuing their own notes. One reason for this may be the refusal on the part of the Bank to conclude a circulation account agreement with a second bank in Lancashire after its agreement with the Bank of Liverpool in 1831. The Director of the Bank of Manchester, Dyer, admitted in

1832 that his bank had been refused a circulation account because the Bank of England saw no need to concede such an account in Manchester as Manchester was 'full of Bank of England notes' anyway. According to Dyer the Governor of the Bank was 'looking to the interests of the Bank of England', as Dyer felt he had every right to do (BPP 1831/32, evidence Dyer, qq.4134, 4144).

Clearly the Bank of England felt that the drawing accounts granted in Manchester were sufficient to establish the circulation of its notes in that city. By 1832 all the banks in Manchester were in fact obtaining the cash they needed through the Bank of England, if they did not issue their own notes. They funded on the London money market and had the amount transferred by their London agent from Threadneedle Street to Manchester. Cassels, Director of the Northern & Central Bank of England, a bank of issue that did not have a drawing account, said that such an account with the Bank of England was a great competitive advantage (BPP 1836, evidence Cassels, qq.1628–9).

So unlike in most other provincial cities, the Bank of England did not need to make great concessions to the banks in Manchester. The dislike of the banks of issue on the part of the general public was so great that citizens' committees were actually formed in Manchester to protest against the banks that were considering issuing only their own notes. And, as elsewhere, only banks that had agreed not to issue their own notes were allowed a drawing account with the Bank of England. The account of the Bank of Manchester, the first joint stock bank in Manchester, was closed again when the bank applied for an issue licence in 1834 (Thomas 1934, p. 133; S. Jones 1985, p. 35).

By the beginning of the 1840s there were no joint stock banks left in Manchester issuing notes. The Northern & Central Bank of England and the Commercial Bank of England, which had stated that the issue of banknotes was to be one of their most important tasks when they had been established in 1833 and 1834 respectively, only operated for three and six years. The Imperial Bank and the South Lancashire Bank, both founded in 1836, also survived for only a very short time. The Manchester & Liverpool District Bank, which too had proclaimed the issue of banknotes to be one of its major functions on its establishment in 1829, ceased to issue notes in Manchester as early as 1832 and in its other branches in 1834.[15] The Bank of Manchester, which had issued its own notes from 1834, also gave up in 1841, and subsequent banks — the Manchester & Salford Bank and the Union Bank of Manchester — made agreements with the Bank when they were founded in 1836. The last provincial bank of issue in Manchester was a branch of the National Provincial Bank of England, the only joint stock bank, apart from the Bank of England, which then had a branch network extending beyond one or two counties. But it too ceased to issue notes in Manchester in 1843 (S. Jones 1978b, p. 108).

Since the Bank of Manchester had to cease payments in 1842 and could reopen only in 1852, there were just three joint stock banks left in Manchester in 1844: the Manchester & Liverpool District Bank, the Manchester & Salford Bank and the Union Bank of Manchester (S. Jones 1978a, p. 177). They also had their head offices there. All three had circulation accounts with the Bank of England before Peel's Act was passed. Unlike the situation in Liverpool or Birmingham, however, in Manchester it seems that the drawing accounts were the attraction that induced the local joint stock banks to do business with the Bank of England. At any rate, the relatively slight importance of the Bank of England's (re)discounting business in Manchester, in comparison and its predominant position as an issuer of banknotes, suggests this (see Tables 2.3 and 2.4).

With its circulation accounts, quarterly advances and drawing accounts, the Bank succeeded in achieving a relative increase in the provincial circulation of its banknotes between 1830 and 1844 (see Figure 2.1). It is striking that this growth was only marginally disrupted by cyclical factors. The stagnation of 1839 and 1840 was presumably due mainly to the unusually high interest rates charged by the Bank of England and the restrictions it imposed on the granting of credit. This was in sharp contrast to the relatively stable economic situation at home and must be regarded solely as reaction to the outflow of gold abroad. A banking crisis in Belgium and France had caused a rapid rise in the demand for gold in these countries and, since the beginning of 1839, the Bank of England had been forced to use the range of instruments at its disposal to reduce the 'money stock' (Clapham 1944, Vol. 2, pp. 166–7). The shortage of Bank of England notes in the provinces was thus not a result of lack of demand, but of deliberate steering of the 'money stock' by the central bank. Moreover, the demand for credit had risen rapidly in the English provinces as well. The total amount of bills handed into provincial branches of the Bank of England for discounting had risen from £17.6 million in 1838 to £26.6 million in 1839. This was not a sign of growing economic activity, rather it was the expression of a greater need for liquidity on the part of both banks and non-banks. This is very evident in the credit granted by Threadneedle Street — £1.5 million for 1838 and £15.1 million for 1839. The explanation of the differences in the development of the demand for credit and the circulation of Bank of England notes must be seen in that customers, who previously had met their need for notes by rediscounting on the London money market and transferring the amount to their Bank of England account at one of the provincial branches, were now rediscounting directly at the Bank of England. The Bank's key rate was noticeably lower almost throughout the entire year 1838/9 than the interest rates on the London money market. Since these transactions were carried out very largely for liquidity reasons, the balance could remain with the Bank of England and no additional need arose for Bank of England notes.[16]

The growth in the circulation of notes by each of the Bank of

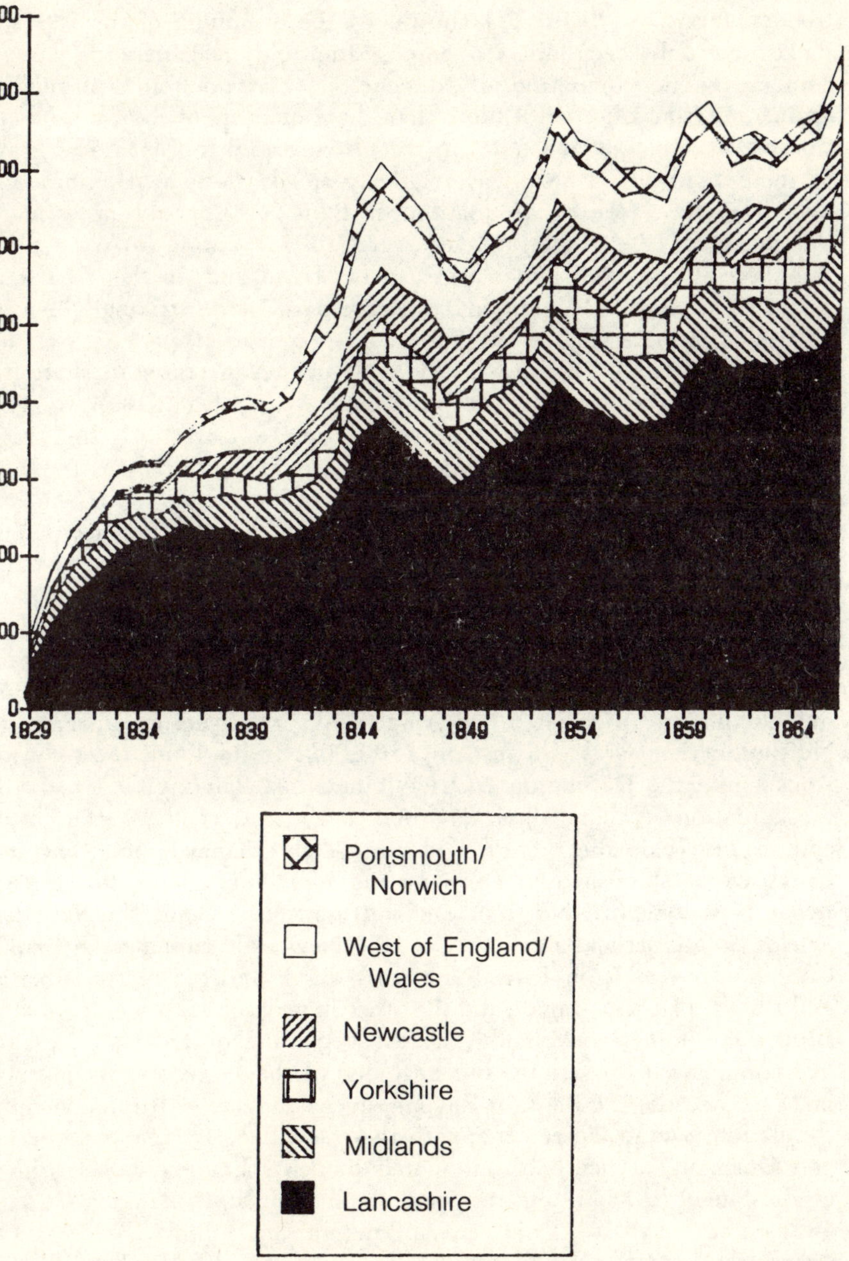

Figure 2.1 Bank of England bank banknote circulation, 1829–66 (£000)

Source: see Table 2.3 and BofE, BBO Annual Statistical Reports (C 79/20 and C 79/21).

England's provincial branches was certainly not as even as the overall trend suggests. As Figure 2.1 shows, by the beginning of the 1830s the Bank had only been able to gain a foothold in Lancashire and the Midlands. The circulation of Manchester, Liverpool and Birmingham branch notes accounted for more than three-quarters of the entire circulation of Bank of England notes in the provinces up to 1836. The growth at these branches, which was relatively steady, largely determined the overall picture for the circulation of Bank of England notes in the provinces. In 1843 these branches were still accounting for 61 per cent. But there were some sudden leaps in the trend and, in this regard, the branches in Newcastle and Gloucester are particularly striking. Newcastle succeeded in increasing its share from 2 per cent to 10 per cent over only seven years from 1834 to 1841, while Gloucester increased its share from 1 per cent to 8 per cent in only three years, from 1835 to 1838; however, again within only three years from 1840 to 1843, this was to fall back from 8 per cent to 2 per cent (see Table 2.3).

Presumably the Bank of England branch in Newcastle, along with Hull and Exeter, had encountered the greatest initial opposition (see section 2.1). Measured against the economic importance of Newcastle, the circulation of Bank of England notes was extremely low at the beginning of the 1830s, at less than £50,000. The Newcastle branch made its major breakthrough at the end of 1836, after a new agent had taken over in April (McCord 1979, p. 61). During the second quarter of 1836 the circulation of notes by private banks of issue in Durham and Northumberland was still just on £500,000. In addition, the only joint stock bank, the Darlington District Joint Stock Banking Co., had notes in circulation totalling about £75,000 at the end of 1836. But, by the end of the year, the picture had completely changed. Six joint stock banks were established in Durham and Northumberland during 1836, five in Newcastle (the North of England Joint Stock Bank, the Newcastle, Shields & Sunderland Banking Co., the Newcastle Commercial Banking Co., the Newcastle-on-Tyne Joint Stock Bank and the Northumberland and Durham District Bank), and the other in neighbouring Sunderland (the Sunderland Joint Stock Bank). By the beginning of 1837 all six banks had commenced operations, but only one of them was still issuing notes in 1844, because the Bank of England agent had succeeded in concluding circulation account agreements with the other five. The Northumberland and Durham District Bank circulated Bank of England notes from its establishment in 1836, and the Sunderland Joint Stock Banking Co. after 1838. The Newcastle Commercial Banking Co. followed in 1840, the Newcastle Joint Stock Banking Co. in 1841 and the North of England Joint Stock Banking Co. in 1842 (BofE, BBO Circulars C 79/5, 30 July 1841, 13 April 1842 and 7 November 1842; BPP 1837/8, App.8, p. 123). The circulation of notes by private banks of issue, therefore, dropped rapidly from about £350,000 in the fourth quarter of 1836 to about £180,000 during the first three quarters of 1840. The reasons for this are easy to identify. Either the private banks lost a large part of their business to the new joint stock banks or they were absorbed by them. Finally, the largest private bank in Newcastle (Lambton & Co.) also ceased to issue its own notes in 1840 in return for a Bank of England circulation account (BofE, BBO Circulars C 79/5, 30 July 1841). These successes made the Bank of England Newcastle branch the third most important rediscounting branch from 1839 and, from 1843, it was in second place, before Manchester and Birmingham. It was also acting as a clearing house for the local banks in the 1840s, that is, around twenty years before Threadneedle Street (Clapham 1944, Vol. 2, p. 215).[17]

The development of the banknote circulation by the Gloucester branch of the Bank of England, which also deviated greatly from the general trend, is also first an example of a successful attempt to step up the circulation of Bank of England notes, and second it is an indication of the change in the attitude of the Bank to its provincial branches, which became very evident after 1844. The ninefold increase in the circulation of Gloucester branch Bank of England notes is almost exclusively due to an agreement with the Gloucestershire Banking Co., which had been founded in 1831. At the end of 1836 the branch agent in Gloucester made an arrangement with that bank for a circulation account for a minimum amount of £100,000 (see p. 12 above). Very probably the actual demand on the part of the Gloucestershire Banking Co. was considerably higher (see Sayers 1957a, pp. 145–6) and the rise in the circulation of Bank of England notes in Gloucester from £38,000 in 1835 to £211,000 in 1837 must be seen as almost exclusively due to the activities of this bank. In 1838 the Gloucestershire Banking Co. succeeded in obtaining a further increase in the amount of its circulation account, in return for ceasing to circulate its own notes in a branch outside Gloucestershire. Other increases were agreed in 1839 and 1840. In 1842 the total amount of Bank of England notes circulated by the Gloucestershire Banking Co. had reached £250,000. The circulation of Bank of England notes by the Gloucester branch had thus risen by almost exactly the same amount that had been put in circulation by the branches of the Gloucestershire Banking Co.

In the 1840s, however, relations between the Bank of England and the Gloucestershire Banking Co. deteriorated. By 1840 the Bank of England was no longer willing to agree to a prolongation of the agreement on the old conditions, as it was then clear that changes would be made to the banking legislation that would be to the disadvantage of the banks of issue in the provinces, and it no longer seemed necessary to force the circulation of Bank of England notes at the Bank's expense. The negotiations came to nothing and the Gloucestershire Banking Co. began to issue its own notes again at the beginning of 1843. However, in the spring of 1844 the average amount of these in circulation was only £155,900, about £100,000 below its former circulation of Bank of England notes. Clearly many customers of the Gloucestershire Bank Co.

were no longer prepared to accept any other than Bank of England notes, and this is presumably also the explanation of why the circulation of Gloucester branch Bank of England notes never fell back to its 1835 level, although it did decline rapidly in 1843. It is also striking that the decline in the circulation of Bank of England notes in Gloucester was largely compensated by an almost parallel rise in neighbouring Bristol, so that the circulation of Bank of England notes in the West of England was relatively stable from 1838. The same is also observable in other regions. In Lancashire the rise in the circulation of Liverpool branch Bank of England notes was largely at the expense of the circulation of notes by the Manchester branch, and a similar situation is evident after the establishment of the Leicester branch in 1844 for the Midland circulation of Bank of England notes (Ziegler 1989, graph 2, p. 24).

Despite the relative rise in the circulation of Bank of England notes in the provinces up to the beginning of the 1840s, it cannot be said that by then the Bank of England had either displaced the provincial banks or enjoyed a monopoly of banknote issue. According to official figures, published in the first half of 1841, 287 private banks and 91 joint stock banks were still issuing their own notes. The circulation of notes by private banks was between £5.8 million and £6.8 million and that of the joint stock banks between £3.4 million and £4.0 million (BPP 1841, App. 13b, p. 282). Then the Bank of England maintained a total circulation of £16.7 million, with the help of its forty-three contract banks (private and joint stock banks) (BPP 1841, App. 23b, p. 311), but only around £4 million of these were circulated in the provinces.

In view of the low number of branches that the Bank of England maintained in the provinces, it is hardly surprising that the importance of its banknotes varied greatly from one region to another. Near the main provincial branches of the Bank, the circulation of banknotes by provincial banks was generally low, particularly in Lancashire. But in Warwickshire only £140,000 joint stock banknotes and £160,000 private banknotes were in circulation in 1836. In the Eastern counties on the other hand, the Bank of England notes were clearly of less importance. In Lincolnshire, for instance, a region that was as yet not greatly industrialized but nevertheless prosperous, around £550,000 notes issued by provincial banks were in circulation in 1836. Apart from the obvious displacement effect of a Bank of England branch, the country banker Seebohm saw a great demand for local banknotes in an area that was thinly populated and hardly industrialized as one of the main reasons for the survival of the provincial banknote. Why these remained in demand for so long in mainly agricultural regions he did not, however, explain (BPP 1875, evidence Seebohm, qq.7615–6). The fact in itself is striking,[18] however, for there were certainly regions in which the Bank of England notes were unsuccessful for a long time, despite branches of the Bank being in the vicinity.

Some Bank of England branches were unable for a long time to throttle the circulation of provincial banks' notes. In Somerset and Gloucestershire, two neighbouring counties each with a Bank of England branch (Bristol and Gloucester), well over £1 million banknotes[19] issued by provincial banks were circulating in 1836, as compared with around £150,000 by the two Bank of England branches. The relation did change in favour of the Bank of England notes a short time later, when the Bank concluded its agreement with the Gloucestershire Banking Co. Nonetheless, the issue by provincial banks authorized in the Bank Charter Act of 1844 within the catchment area of the Bank of England branches in Gloucester and Bristol was still more than twice as high as the circulation of notes by these two Bank of England branches. In view of that situation, it is hardly surprising that, just twenty years after Lord Liverpool's first reform and attempt to displace the circulation of notes by provincial banks, a further step was taken towards a monopoly for the Bank of England.

2.2.2 The Bank and the 1844 Regulation Act

The effects of Peel's Bank Charter Act of 1844 (7 and 8 Vict., c.32) on the provincial banks of issue were at first much more far-reaching than the changes felt in London. The most important part of the Act for the provinces was the limit on the issue of banknotes by all issuing banks in England and Wales. No bank was allowed to extend its issue beyond the legally fixed maximum amount, independent of its note cover reserves. Not even the Bank of England was now free to determine the level of its banknote circulation itself. Its position as the central bank of issue was, however, acknowledged in that the amount it could issue was regulated by the gold holdings of the Issue Department. Since an active policy of buying and selling gold was also made difficult by legislation, the possibilities for the Bank to regulate the issue were minimal.

The situation was rather different for the circulation of banknotes. With both the Banking Department liabilities and the Issue Department gold stock being constant, the Bank of England's circulation depended on the relation between the cash reserves of the Banking Department and 'Securities'. Fluctuations in the gold holdings of the Issue Department would therefore inevitably have effects on the Bank's credit policy, and withdrawals of gold from the Issue Department would almost inevitably lead to a reduction in the cash reserves of the Banking Department, which could only be countered by a more restrictive credit policy and/or by selling investments. In this way the money stock (which those who had drawn up the Bank Charter Act saw as only notes and coin) was to be quasi-automatically regulated by the foreign exchanges. It was the declared aim of the Act to prevent the provincial banks of issue from filling the 'gap' between the supply of credit and the demand for credit, opened through the contraction of the circulation of Bank of England notes, by increasing the circulation of their notes and so undermining the adjustment process. To this end the upper limit for the issue by any individual issuing bank (apart from the Bank of England) was calculated according to the average of the circulation of notes during the months February to April 1844.

The provincial banks naturally felt this regulation as a serious attack on their freedom of action and their profit interests. However, their lobbying only succeeded in a slight easing of Peel's original draft. At first Peel wanted to make the average for the last two years the basis for calculating the upper circulation limit, but in the depressed first half of the 1840s the circulation of provincial notes had been clearly lower than during the 1830s, so that the new regulation would have meant a slight increase in the quotas. Moreover, the issuing banks had to observe their quota for only four weeks on average, so that exceeding this slightly once or twice would not automatically involve sanctions. Nevertheless, the average circulation of banknotes by the provincial banks would necessarily be lower than the law permitted, as the banks would always have to hold notes in reserve against a sudden increase in demand. What looked like stability policy from a macro-viewpoint, would be a considerable destabilization for the provincial banks at the micro-level in a tight money market, owing to the extremely inflexible credit policy. However, since priority was clearly being given to the balance of payments in monetary policy, the personal approaches which some bankers made to the Prime Minister or the Chancellor of the Exchequer, in the hopes of being permitted a higher quota, were not very successful (Sayers 1957a, p. 146).

From about 1841, sensing that the coming legislation would strengthen its position as central bank of issue, following two Parliamentary Committees of Inquiry which had considered the problem of the 'Banks of Issue', the Bank of England was no longer prepared to make concessions to the banks of issue like I & I.C. Wright or the Gloucestershire Banking Co. Even in negotiations on the renewal of an existing agreement, the Bank was no longer prepared to continue the contract under the old conditions (again as described above, in the case of the Gloucestershire Banking Co.). After Peel's Act was passed in the middle of 1844 and came into force in September of that year, the Bank actually went further. The Act had made provisions regarding provincial banks which ceased to issue notes. It laid down that all agreements between the Bank of England and those banks 'which have ceased to issue their own Bank Notes' no longer applied from the end of 1844 (Bank Charter Act 1844, in: Gregory 1964, Vol. 1, pp. 129–47). Compensation of

> one Pound per Centum per Annum on the average amount of Bank of England Notes issued by such Banker respectively and actually remaining in circulation . . . shall be paid by the Governor and Company of the Bank of England out of their own Funds. (Clause 23)

Consequently, the contract banks were no better off than the banks that were currently issuing notes. They, too, were to have 'One Pound per

Centum per Annum on the Amount of Bank of England Notes which shall be issued and kept in circulation by such Banker', if they ceased to issue their own notes (Clause 24). So they were free to choose between ceasing to issue their own notes under the new conditions or maintaining their issue. The contract banks, on the other hand, for which this regulation would generally mean a massive deterioration compared with the old circulation accounts, could not resume the issue of notes. New licences were, on principle, no longer to be given (Clause 10).

Both the Bank of England and the government had expected a rapid end to the circulation of provincial banknotes. In Peel's own words, the objective of the legislation was 'to increase the controlling power of a single bank of issue' (Hansard, Vol. 74, 1844, 6 May 1844). It was not so much the decision not to issue new licences, or the limit on the circulation of banknotes by the remaining banks of issue, that gave rise to this expectation, but a further regulation which was also aimed against the provincial banks of issue. This stated that: 'it shall not be lawful for any Company or Partnership now consisting of only six or less than six Persons [private banks] to issue Bank Notes at any time after the number of partners therein shall exceed six in the whole' (Clause 11) [joint stock banks]. Consequently a new joint stock bank could not take over quotas of any constituent bank, let along cumulating quotas, nor could existing joint stock banks increase their quota by taking over another bank of issue. Moreover, every joint stock bank, as soon as it opened a branch in London (or, to be more precise, within the 65-mile zone) would have to cease its banknote issue altogether. The ban on the issue of banknotes was therefore no longer limited to the 65 miles around the City of London. The best-known example of the effect of this was the return of the licence of the National Provincial Bank of England in 1866, after it had opened a branch in London. The National Provincial Bank had a banknote quota of almost £450,000, and so it was the first of the large banks of issue to take such a step.[20]

Peel's Act was not only to enforce a monetary policy oriented to the balance of payments, it was also designed to induce the banks of issue voluntarily to cease to issue banknotes. This objective was wholly in the interests of the Bank of England. In 1875 its Deputy Governor, E.H. Palmer, said in answer to the question of whether he still regarded the 65-mile zone as meaningful:

> Assuming, as I do, that the most perfect form of a fiduciary currency is one uniform in its expression, and of unquestionable convertibility, and believing that the intention of the Bank Acts of 1844 and 1845 was to promote the establishment of such a currency for the whole country, I imagine that such a purpose would be inconsistent with removing from issuing banks any of their disabilities pending the final settlement of the currency question.

And to the question 'Then you do not consider that the disabilities and restrictions are important in themselves, but that they are important as bringing pressure to bear upon the issuing banks to induce them to surrender their issues?' he answered briefly and succinctly, 'Exactly so' (BPP 1875, evidence Hodgson and Palmer, pp. 7472–3).

The provincial banks adjusted to the new situation at different speeds. Some at first proved remarkably inventive at utilizing the upper limit as far as possible without running liquidity risks. First, the entire risk could be shifted onto a competitor bank, as in the case of the Gloucestershire Banking Co. and the County of Gloucester Bank. The former issued banknotes of the County of Gloucester Bank each time it passed its upper limit, instead of its own or Bank of England notes. A second possibility was to issue bills with very short maturity dates, which were then very like banknotes. The bills did not bear the name of the bank but the names of individuals, generally the partners in the bank. In this way the private bank of Storey & Thomas (Shaftesbury) was able to keep its average banknote circulation only a few pounds below its authorized limit (Sayers 1957a, p. 149). However, these were exceptions. Most of the banks of issue began to change into deposit banks. The larger joint stock banks limited their banknote issue to a few branches, generally in agricultural regions far from the nearest Bank of England branch, and operated the others as 'pure' deposit banks.

For the contract banks, that is, the banks that had already given up their own issue in order to maintain a circulation account with the Bank of England before Peel's Act came into force, the degree to which they were affected by the new legislation was determined by the extent to which they depended on the circulation account. If they had already started to attract sufficient deposits before 1844, through a branch network beyond their immediate locality, and only needed to balance fluctuations in demand through the London money market, they could, like the Manchester & Liverpool District Bank (BPP 1875, evidence Cooke, q.6713) actually do without a 'three per cent account' with the Bank of England. For it was uneconomical for a deposit bank to continue utilizing a loan at 3 per cent from the Bank of England of about the same amount as its former circulation of banknotes and, for these banks, the increase in the interest rate for circulation accounts from 3 per cent to 4 per cent was of no significance.

For the smaller banks of issue the end of the old agreement and the new rules on compensation, however, must have been a heavy blow. 'Soon after the Act of 1844 was passed the Bank of England said: "There is an end of the agreement"', as I.C. Wright stated about three years after Peel's Act came into force and around six years after his enthusiastic appeal for cooperation between the provincial banks and the Bank of England (BPP 1847/8, Part 3, evidence Wright, q.2864). The Bank was no longer prepared to negotiate in any way; it withdrew the non-interest banknote quota — Wrights was certainly not the only case of this — and raised the interest rate on the circulation account from 3 per cent to 4 per cent.[21] In keeping with the legislation the remuneration was, instead, raised from £350 to £500 to meet the requirement for compensation to the amount of 1 per cent of the former banknote circulation. Wright's negotiating position was, of course, extremely unfavourable. He could not, as the Gloucestershire Banking Co. had been able to do shortly before, threaten to resume issuing notes. Since Wright had not issued any banknotes between February and April 1844, on account of his agreement with the Bank of England, this possibility was not available to him in future either.

However, not all the banks had so weak a negotiating position as Wright, and they were not all dependent on the goodwill of the Bank of England. Five Liverpool banks still succeeded, after the Act was passed, in winning from the Bank of England a circulation account on almost the old conditions, instead of the compensation prescribed in the Act. Under these agreements they were able to discount specific amounts at 1 per cent under the Liverpool Bank Rate — the Liverpool Commercial Bank up to £70,000, the Liverpool Union Bank and Barnes & Co. £100,000 each, the Liverpool Borough Bank £120,000 and the Bank of Liverpool £200,000. The interest rate was, however, at least 2½ per cent, and at most 4 per cent (BofE, CB No. 67, 9 January 1845, 6 February 1845 and 13 March 1845; BofE, BBO Bank Note Composition C 79/26). The reason for this success was presumably that the banks were among the seven contract banks that had concluded a circulation account agreement with the Liverpool branch of the Bank of England before 1844. The non-interest bearing minimum balances and the rediscount lines for these banks were probably major factors in making the Liverpool branch by far the most profitable of the provincial branches maintained by the Bank of England. The same probably applies to the success of the Birmingham & Midland Bank, which was able to rediscount £42,000 on similarly favourable conditions (Holmes and Green 1986, p. 25).

The same Liverpool banks were able to win further major concessions from the Bank of England in 1848. They wanted the discount rate of the Bank of England Liverpool branch to be used no longer as the basis for calculating the interest rate on the circulation account, but rather the London Bank Rate. The London Bank Rate had generally been clearly below the old 4 per cent mark ever since Peel's Act came into force in September 1844. The Liverpool banks did not obtain what they wanted, but they did achieve a compromise. Interest rates were to be three-quarters of a per cent below the London Bank Rate, and be at least 3 per cent and at most 4½ per cent. Although the maximum and minimum rates were higher than under the old agreement, this was an improvement, since ¾ per cent below the London Bank Rate was then more than 1¼ per cent below the discount rate of the Liverpool branch of the Bank of England, compared with 1 per cent before.

Most of the banks succeeded in adjusting to the different circumstances. The issue of banknotes was playing only a minor role for most by the 1850s, although not many contemplated giving up their issue

Table 2.5 Lapsed country bank issues, 1844–74

Cause	Private banks Number	Private banks Amount (£)	Joint stock banks Number	Joint stock banks Amount (£)
Amalgamated	26	388,129	8	182,392
Arrangement with BofE	12	104,992	—	—
Opening of London office	—	—	1	442,371
Bankruptcy	31	532,531	2	48,101
Closed (other reason)	10	84,741	7	169,589
No reason named	6	82,592	—	—
	85	1,283,035	18	842,453

Source: Select Committee on Banks of Issue, BPP 1875, App. 16, p. 553.

licence. Of the 207 private banks and 72 joint stock banks in 1844, 122 private banks and 54 joint stock banks still had a licence to issue banknotes in 1874, and their authorized issue was about £6.5 million. As Table 2.5 shows, the banks that did cease to issue banknotes were mostly smaller banks (private banks) and the reasons were generally far from voluntary. Half of these banks were closed altogether and another third were absorbed by larger banks. At most, eighteen (or 6 per cent of all the issuing banks in 1844) ceased entirely voluntarily to issue banknotes during those thirty years. Only a single major provincial bank of issue, the National Provincial Bank of England, preferred to extend its activities to London and so renounced its issue licence. Its authorized issue alone was 26 per cent of all the other 102 banks. Consequently it cannot be said that there was a gradual erosion of the issue rights. Only directly after the Act was passed, between 1844 and 1848, did £423,000 worth of issue rights cease: in the mid-1860s around three-quarters of a million of private issue lapsed (1864–8), mainly as a consequence of the National Provincial Bank of England and the conversion of Lloyds Bank into a joint stock bank in 1865 and its takeover of some smaller banks shortly after (altogether £108,000). Between 1868 and 1875 the reduction in the private issue was only another £320,000 with the actual circulation of provincial banknotes stabilised at about £5 million after 1867 (*Bankers' Magazine*, Vol. 34, December 1874, p. 949).

Peel would hardly have been satisfied with this result after thirty years (see BPP 1875, evidence Hodgson and Palmer, q.7555).[22] However, his Act had achieved its main objective. A monetary policy by the Bank of England oriented to the balance of payments could no longer be undermined by the provincial banks and, in 1870, the Bank of England came to terms with the provincial banks of issue. The Court of Directors formed a Special Committee on Discount Accounts to Banks and in 1871 permitted a number of issuing banks to discount at the appropriate Bank of England branch (BofE CB No. 93, 12 January 1871, 16 February 1871; CB No. 94, 7 December 1871).

Table 2.6 Merger activity in British banking, 1870–1913

Year	Number of firm disappearances	Authorized issue	Year	Number of firm disappearances	Authorized issue
1870	0 (0)	£6.73m	1890	16(12)	£4.83m
1871	2 (1)		1891	21(18)	
1872	4 (4)		1892	11 (7)	
1873	4 (4)		1893	16 (6)	
1874	6 (6)		1894	10 (8)	
1875	5 (5)	£6.52m	1895	3 (3)	£4.32m
1876	4 (2)		1896	20 (6)	
1877	8 (5)		1897	9 (6)	
1878	12(10)		1898	10 (6)	
1879	4 (3)		1899	9 (6)	
1880	4 (4)	£6.07m	1900	15 (7)	£2.96m
1881	3 (2)		1901	9 (7)	
1882	3 (3)		1902	15 (7)	
1883	8 (5)		1903	8 (7)	
1884	6 (4)		1904	7 (7)	
1885	2 (2)	£5.85m	1905	5 (4)	£1.82m
1886	2 (2)		1906	6 (5)	
1887	4 (4)		1907	8 (7)	
1888	11 (8)		1908	5 (3)	
1889	16(12)		1909	8 (7)	
			1910	3 (3)	£1.17m
			1911	4 (4)	
			1912	2 (2)	
			1913	4 (3)	

Note: ( ) number of disappearances because of mergers.

Source: Capie and Rodrik-Bali 1982, table 1, p. 283.

Although no changes were made to the legislation, the decline in the issue of banknotes by provincial banks did accelerate from the end of the 1870s, as more and more provincial banks (deposit and issuing banks) lost their independence and were linked with one of the large joint stock banks with its head office in London, or themselves opened a branch in London, which then quickly became the bank's head office. In both cases the banks of issue lost their issue licence. The process of concentration and centralization in the English and Welsh banking sector had begun in the mid-1860s, but it was interrupted for a time after the 1866 crisis, and it was only at the end of the 1870s that a London and provincial bank was formed when the North Wilts Banking Co. (head office in Melksham, Wiltshire) merged with the Hampshire Banking Co. (head office in Southampton) to form the Hampshire & North Wilts. Banking Co. Shortly afterwards the bank opened a branch in London, and from 1878 was called the Capital & Counties Bank.

The demise of thirty-three independent banks from 1875 to 1879 (see Table 2.6) did not cause a major concentration in deposits, but the circulation of provincial banknotes fell again noticeably for the first time for a decade by about £500,000. The merger activity slowed down again in the 1880s for a time, but accelerated towards the end of that decade, and from the 1890s a clear concentration in bank deposits is also evident (Capie and Rodrik-Bali 1982, Table 3, p. 286). At the same time the banks built up a dense branch network (usually by converting former independent banks) (Sykes 1926, p. 113; Nevin and Davis 1970, pp. 72, 74–5). It was the birth of the modern high street banks in England.

The most spectacular case of the establishment of a large bank during the 1880s was the merger of Lloyds Banking Co. (head office in Birmingham), then the second largest provincial bank, with both its London 'sister', the private bank Barnetts, Hoare, Hanbury & Lloyd and another London private bank, Bosanquet, Salt, Whatman, Harman, Salt & Bosanquet in 1884. Another bank in Birmingham moved to London in 1891 when the Birmingham & Midland Bank merged with the Central Bank of London to form the London & Midland Bank (now the Midland Bank). A year before, the Manchester & Salford Bank merged with the London private bank Williams, Deacon, Thornton & Co. and Parr's Bank (head office in Warrington, Lancashire), had combined with the London private bank Fuller, Banbury & Nix. The concentration in the British banking sector reached another peak when Barclay's Bank was established in 1896 by the merger of eighteen Quaker country banks and the London private banks Barclay, Bevan & Tritton and Gosling & Sharpe. Only the London & Westminster Bank kept aloof from the race for new branches for a time. Between the spectacular takeover of Loyd Jones in 1864 and the 'marriage of elephants' with the London & County Bank in 1909 it did not take over a single bank. It was only towards the end of the nineteenth century that the London & Westminster Bank began to build up a branch network that extended outside London (Gregory 1936, p. 284; see also Nishimura 1971, Table 2, pp. 84–5).

It was not the restrictions of Peel's Act, but the concentration wave around half a century later that finally displaced the provincial banknote. By around 1900 it was only a marginal feature, accounting for just 7 per cent of the circulation of banknotes in England, at about £2 million. In 1911 only eleven private and eleven joint stock banks still had the right to issue banknotes, for a total of £1.17 million.

2.3. Branches of a commercial bank

2.3.1. The commercial decline begins

The change in the relations between the Bank of England and the provincial banks naturally also had repercussions on the Bank's provincial

Table 2.7 Bills discounted at Bank of England provincial branches, 1835–74 (yearly average)

Decade	'Bankers' bills'			'Traders' bills'		
	Mean (£000)	% of total discounts	Standard deviation	Mean (£000)	% of total discounts	Standard deviation
1835–1844	17,800	88	21	2,500	12	39
1845–1854	12,400	75	26	4,100	25	40
1855–1964	13,800	58	31	9,900	42	15
1865–1874	12,900	59	32	8,800	41	14

Source: BofE, SDC Reports, C 35/2–4.

branches. On the one hand, the branches profited from the restriction on the issue of banknotes by provincial banks, being able to continue increasing the circulation of their own notes, albeit no longer at a steady pace. On the other hand, banking business in the narrower sense, that is, lending and deposits business, began to stagnate for the branches and, in some cases, it actually declined. Most striking was the decline in bill discounting during the first decade after Peel's Act compared with the decade before. During the boom and the ensuing crisis demand for bill discounts had at first risen markedly, but after 1848 came seven 'lean years', with discount turnover clearly below 20 million a year (see Table 2.7).

The reason for this decline in the demand for credit at the Bank of England branches generally, and by the local banks in particular, was the *de facto* end of the situation that had put the provincial banks and trading houses on a par with the London credit market. This found expression in a number of ways. First, interest policy remained extremely rigid in the provinces in contrast to London. While the discount rate in London was lowered from 4 per cent to 2½ per cent immediately after Peel's Act came into force, and the Bank's rates in London very largely followed market rates over the next few years, interest rates of the provincial branches began to move only three to six months later. Unlike before 1844, when the high share of 3 per cent circulation accounts in discount turnover had pushed the average interest rate of the provincial branches down below the London rate, the interest rates of the provincial branches were now clearly above London rates. However, it is difficult to judge how much higher interest rates in Liverpool or Birmingham, for instance, actually were, in comparison with those at the head office, as those published from March 1845 were minimum rates which applied only to first class bills.

The Bank itself endeavoured to keep its lending in the provinces within limits. The branch banks' office Circular of 1847 states: 'The term 'first class' is . . . applicable only to those names which would be considered here [London], as coming under that class; names locally so ranked in the district merely, being excluded' (BofE, BBO Circulars C 79/5, 17 June 1847). Up to, and into, the 1847 crisis the minimum rate in Manchester and Liverpool was about half a percentage point above Bank Rate. The difference for the other branches was, if anything, rather greater. Interest rates at the branches in Gloucester, Norwich, Swansea, Plymouth and Portsmouth were actually still 4 per cent, even during the low-interest phase from 1844 to 1846, and they did not drop below 3½ per cent at the branches in Hull, Leicester and Bristol (BPP 1847/8, Part 2, app.15, p. 184). Around 1850 the interest rate at all the branches for first class bills was presumably one-quarter, three-quarters for second class bills and for third class one and a quarter percentage points, above the London Bank Rate. The difference between second and third class was not defined, it was left to the agent to decide in individual cases (BofE, BBO Circulars C 79/5, 28 March 1850).

Under such circumstances the contemporary statements on the actual difference between the Bank of England rates in the provinces and in London naturally differed greatly. Governor Morris said in 1848 that the difference was one quarter of a percentage point, while the Director of the Bank of Liverpool, Hodgson, spoke of a difference of one percentage point. P.H. Muntz, an entrepreneur in the iron industry in Birmingham, also said that the rates for the Bank of England Birmingham branch were between half (bank paper) and one percentage point (general commercial paper) higher than the rates of the Bank of England in London (BPP 1847/8, Part 1, evidence Morris and Prescott, qq.3574–8; evidence Hodgson, q.155; evidence Muntz, q.1265).

The gradation of interest rates to the disadvantage of local bills and the deterioration in the conditions for circulation accounts meant that the provincial Bank of England branches lost much of their attraction, both for traders and for the local banks. The unwillingness of the Bank of England to negotiate evoked a reaction from some smaller banks. The discount account of the private bank Biddulph Bros. & Co. (Carmarthen), for example, was closed altogether in 1844 (Roberts 1958a, p. 235). Unfortunately we can only assume that the changes in the conditions for the circulation account were the main reason. They certainly were in the case of the private bank I. & I.C. Wright (Nottingham). I.C. Wright stated before the Parliamentary Committee of Inquiry 'On Commercial Distress' in 1848 that the increase in the interest rate on his circulation account from 3 per cent to 4 per cent had forced him to repay his loan from the Bank of England (see section 2.2.1) and had, instead, to rediscount on the London money market. Here he had recently been able to obtain credit for 2½ per cent instead of 4 per cent. Clearly Wrights were now using the Bank of England, or its branch in Leicester, only for transferring the payments by its agent in London to Leicester, where it could collect Bank of England notes as it needed them (BPP 1847/8, Part 3, evidence Wright, qq.1877, 2963).

However, it was not only the interest rates that annoyed the provincial banks. Two measures by the Bank which were felt as extremely hostile were, admittedly, not of long duration, but by temporarily introducing fees for transfers (see BofE, BBO Circulars C 79/5, 7 December 1844, 20 December 1844) and refusing to meet the greater need for credit on the part of the provincial banks in the spring of 1847 (BPP 1847/8, Part 1, evidence Hodgson, qq.513–20; evidence Muntz, qq.1259–64), the Bank made them very aware of the change in its perspective. It had once more become a London bank, and it was not making any efforts to disguise the change in its attitude to the provincial banks. Deputy Governor Prescott commented before the Committee of Inquiry 'On Commercial Distress' on the difference in its treatment of customers in the provinces: 'In the country where we employ agents we are not able to allow them the same discretion as we can exercise in London' (BPP 1847/8, Part 3, evidence Morris and Prescott, q.536).

Although all the provincial branches felt the reaction from their old customers, some experienced a real break in their business. The closure of the Bank of England branch in Gloucester can probably be seen as due entirely to this change in the attitude of the Bank of England to the provincial banks. Around 1840 the Gloucester branch was not only the fourth most important issuer of banknotes, it was fifth among all the branches in the discount business. When the Gloucestershire Banking Co. resumed issuing its own notes, it became clear that the entire credit business of the Gloucester branch had depended on the circulation account agreement with this one bank. From 1843 the branch had practically no credit business at all (see Table 2.4), and up to 1848 only bills to the amount of a few thousand pounds were discounted there, compared with around a million in 1839–40.

Gloucester was an extreme case, but it was not the only one. In Portsmouth, where the seven contract banks had ensured a brief upswing in the credit business at the beginning of the 1840s, there was no demand for credit from the banks during the ten years after Peel's Act and, even in Manchester, the rediscounting business of the banks fell after the 1847/8 crisis to the level of the early days of the branches. For all the Bank of England branches credit business in the 1850s had fallen to below the level of 1844.

However, this development was not in any way dramatic for the Bank of England Directors. The end of the provincial banknote was expected in the near future and, once the Bank was divided into an Issue Department and a Banking Department, they no longer depended on what the provinces could bring. With the philosophy that the Banking Department, which was also responsible for the branches, was to be conducted as a normal commercial bank, the Bank concentrated entirely on its London business. After the reform of the discount business in the autumn of 1844, its earnings in London were higher than those on the branches' discount business almost every year. Between 1831 and 1844 the reverse had been the case.

The Bank no longer needed to force its banknote circulation in the provinces at its own expense, although it probably could have easily achieved a monopoly at one step. The banks of issue could not see why they should have to take a loan with fixed upper and lower limits at 4 per cent from the Bank of England as 'compensation' for ceasing to issue their own banknotes, when they could rediscount far more cheaply — at the Bank of England itself — in London. If the Bank had been prepared to keep to its old principle and ensure that the provinces did not have worse conditions for credit than London, it could certainly have reached agreements with the provincial banks of issue within a very short time.

Characteristic of the attitude of the Bank was its reaction to an enquiry from Pares' Leicestershire Banking Co., directly after the interest rates in London were lowered, in September 1844. According to the branch agent Turner, this joint stock bank of issue was prepared to renounce its issue licence, if it could rediscount at the Bank of England Leicester branch at the London Bank Rate. The answer from the Deputy Governor to the enquiry was:

> This facility is limited to London . . . . It is impossible to offer any opinion as to the course which the Court may at any future time determine on. It will, however, be open to Pares, whether issuers or not, to avail themselves to the London rate through the medium of their agents or bill-brokers here. (BofE, LBALB Out No. 1, 18 September 1844, In No. 1, 19 September 1844)

The reasons for this disinterest on the part of the provincial branches are easy to identify. First, greater operations on the London money market and long-term loans to railway companies and local authorities were more profitable than discounting bills that were of inferior quality by London standards and paid interest at only a fixed rate of 3 per cent. Second, the bank could not, in view of the new cover requirements, play the role of 'lender of last resort' for the banking system. London banks did not on principle rediscount with the Bank of England. They had to keep their portfolios so liquid that it was not necessary. If many provincial banks did not behave in a similarly 'sound' fashion, their demand should at least reach the Bank through the buffer of the London money market. When this buffer really proved inadequate, in the crisis of 1857, and the pent-up demand on the market looked likely to jeopardize the convertibility of sterling, the Bank actually went so far as to interrupt the contact with the market even further and exclude the discount houses from discounting bills. Thereby the Bank of England was 'teaching' the market, the discount houses in London and the provincial banks to keep their portfolios as liquid as possible, since under existing conditions they could no longer rely on a possibility of funding.

From the standpoint of the shareholders, who wanted high dividends, the decision by the Bank of England not to rediscount for provincial banks was not to be regretted. The increase in the earnings in London soon proved far greater than their decline in the provinces, and the endeavours on the part of the Bank to make its provincial branches more competitive were only half-hearted. At the beginning of the 1850s it did introduce a certain flexibility in interest rates by authorizing its branch agents to apply special rates for 'principal customers' of their branches,[23] but a real revival in the discount business is apparent only during the boom in the mid-1850s. Whether the alignment of the interest rates for first class bills in the provinces to the London Bank Rate in 1854, as a number of agents had fiercely demanded (BofE BBO Circulars C 79/5, 10 July 1854), played a part in this is unlikely, as, in contrast to the 1830s, the increase in bill discounting at the Bank of England provincial branches was not in bankers' but traders' bills (see Table 2.7). However, these accounted for only a small percentage of the first class bills.[24]

Although bankers' bills still comprised a larger share than traders' bills on average for the years 1855 to 1874, at 58 per cent, the Bank of England's provincial branches were certainly no longer acting as the 'bankers' bank' during this period, since not only the quantity, but also the quality — that is, the nature of the borrowing by the banks — had changed completely. Before 1844 the circulation accounts, with their lower limit, had ensured a certain stability in the demand for credit by the provincial banks. Owing to the predominance of bankers' bills before 1844, the fluctuations in demand on the part of traders were not of such importance, and the growth in the discount business could proceed relatively steadily.

However, the end of the circulation accounts after the 1850s also put an end to the stability of demand for credit from banks, and thereafter they went to the Bank of England only to meet their peak demand when London money market rates were rising. If demand for credit in London was slight and interest rates low, demand from the provincial banks at the Bank of England also dropped, to levels considerably below the figures for comparable years before 1844. When interest rates were rising (1857 and 1864–6), on the other hand, demand certainly reached the level of 1836 and 1839, so that the fluctuations in the 1850s and 1860s were much more serious than before 1844. The situation was different for traders' bills. They fluctuated only slightly. During the 1850s turnover rose steadily to between £8 and £10 million, a level that was maintained throughout the 1860s and during the boom at the beginning of the 1870s.

The fluctuations in bankers' bills during the 1850s and 1860s were so extreme that, although these bills accounted for a very much smaller share, they caused major swings in the overall level of bill discounting at the Bank of England provincial branches. This was particularly the case for branches with an above-average share of bankers' bills. The Manchester branch discounted bills at on average £4.5 million a year between 1861 and 1870, of which £3.1 million were bankers' bills and £1.4 million traders' bills. The standard deviation was 40 per cent. This extremely high figure can be seen as being due exclusively to the above-average share of bankers' bills, where the standard deviation was 46 per cent, while it was only 25 per cent for traders' bills. The situation in Birmingham was similar, where £2.5 million (1861–70) a year was discounted on average, of which at least £2 million were bankers' bills and only £0.5 million traders' bills. The standard deviation was 35 per cent.

In Liverpool, the branch with by far the largest discount turnover at £7 million a year (1861 to 1870), bankers' bills also accounted for around 70 per cent, but the standard deviation was only 25 per cent. Here demand from both bankers and traders had proved fairly stable, compared with the other branches. However, there were evident differences in the fluctuation of bankers' and traders' bills in Liverpool as well. The standard deviation for Liverpool traders' bills was 16 per cent, and for bankers' bills 33 per cent. One reason for the relative stability in Liverpool could be that the most important local joint stock banks had kept their circulation accounts after 1844, while the banks in Manchester preferred to take the compensation payment.

The situation was quite different in Leeds. This was the only branch (apart from Bristol, where the credit business was much smaller) to be a traders' branch even at the end of the 1830s, when traders' bills accounted for 98 per cent of its discount business. Altogether Leeds was, however, still behind Liverpool, Manchester, Birmingham, Newcastle and even at times Gloucester at that time. In the 1860s Leeds moved up to be the third most important branch in the discount business — behind Liverpool and Manchester, but in front of Birmingham and Newcastle. In traders' bills it had actually overtaken Liverpool and Manchester. Traders' bills accounted for about two-thirds of the total at this time for Leeds and the standard deviation was correspondingly low, at only 17 per cent (1861–70). The situation in Leicester was similar during the 1850s and into the early 1860s, before the branch started to decline (Ziegler 1989b, pp. 13–14). At that time the discount business in Leicester amounted to about 5 per cent of the total for all the provincial branches, putting Leicester in seventh place among the eleven provincial branches. Here too the share of traders' bills was above the average, at 45 per cent (1853–62) and the standard deviation correspondingly low at 14 per cent.

The role played by bankers' bills for the Newcastle branch was particularly interesting. During the 1850s the branch had moved up to second place, behind Liverpool, in the provincial branches' credit business. In the early years of the decade it was actually ahead of Liverpool, as it had clearly proved more able to keep the downslide in the banks' rediscounting business within limits than any of the other branches. After the crisis of 1857, however, the discount business (or to be more precise, rediscounting for banks) collapsed completely in Newcastle following a number of spectacular bank failures. In 1855 and 1856 bankers' bills at the Newcastle branch had accounted for 29 per cent and 26 per cent respectively of all the provincial branches. From 1862 to 1864 they accounted for only 1 per cent to 2 per cent. With the exception of 1866, almost only traders' bills were discounted in Newcastle after 1862. Leaving out the crisis year 1866, the standard deviation was only 14 per cent (1862–71). But in 1866 the demand from the banks rose again rapidly, from £17,000 in 1865 to £1,200,000 in 1866, and Newcastle could demonstrate, more than any other branch, how destabilizing bankers' bills were in the discount business of the provincial branches. Including 1866 the standard deviation over the entire period was 27 per cent, for traders' bills 15 per cent and bankers' bills 170 per cent.

The Directors of the Bank of England will certainly have appreciated the relative stability of the discount business at their branches in Leeds and Leicester, for these two ensured stable earnings when interest rates were low, demand in London and at the other branches also slight, and the Directors had difficulties in maintaining dividend payments. On the other hand, Leeds and Leicester put only slightly greater pressure on its cash reserve in times of crisis, when the Bank was facing intense demand on the market.

Unlike Threadneedle Street, the credit business in the provinces was almost exclusively in the form of bill discounting. While the earnings on business in lombard loans sometimes accounted for up to one-third of interest income on short-term investments in London, lombard loans accounted for very little of the business at the provincial branches, especially advances on stocks and bonds. Since it had begun to operate in the provinces, the Bank of England had been endeavouring to maintain some distance from certain practices of many provincial banks. Contrary to what the textbooks said (see Rae 1850, p. 18; Rae 1903, pp. 33–5; *Bankers' Magazine*, Vol. 35, May 1875, Suppl. p. 151), it had become quite usual for many provincial banks regularly to prolong nominal short-term loans (see Cottrell 1980, pp. 211–36; Mathias 1973, pp. 136–7; Hudson 1986, pp. 220–7; Collins and Hudson 1979, p. 73; Ollerenshaw 1988, p. 68; Roberts 1986, pp. 68, 73, 79). As early as 1829 the branch agents had been made aware that loans (specifically bills discounted, but the same will certainly have applied to advances) were

> presumed to be occasional accommodations. Discounts are effected by the Bank not to enable manufacturers to hold but to dispose of their goods — to give facilities to actual traders and not to encourage the increase of manufacturers which the present state of the market evidently proves to be unnecessary. (Roberts 1958a, p. 233, quoting BofE, Swansea BALB)

The currency of a loan from the Bank of England was therefore at most thirty days and it could be renewed only once.

Loans in the form of overdrafts were strictly forbidden in the provinces, contrary to a widespread practice. The Leicester branch agent instructed a customer on 'sound banking' only a month after the branch was opened:

> The Bank on principle declines to make such advances [on open account] — being fully satisfied that the banker ought not to find capital for his customers, and that however in particular cases an advance might benefit a careful man of good character and steady habits, the system of making advances was in the long run injurious alike to the banker and to his customer. (BofE, LBALB Out No. 1, 1 February 1844)

It was particularly 'injurious to the Bank of England' to cover credits that often only consisted of the agreement that the credit lines must not exceed 10 per cent of the annual turnover on the account (Hudson 1986, pp. 225, 227; Collins and Hudson 1979, p. 75).

The third and most difficult obstacle to a more active lombard business for the provincial branches was the fact that the Bank accepted only paper that could be traded on the London Stock Exchange. The provincial banks on the other hand had had to accept highly illiquid securities, since there were no alternatives (see Collins and Hudson 1979, p. 77; Cottrell 1980, pp. 214, 222–3; Roberts 1986, p. 79). As additional cover, each credit from the Bank of England had to be approved by the branch banks' office in London, and the branch agents' letter books clearly show the extent of this business. In Leicester, for instance, a loan on stock was given only once in the second half of the 1860s. It had a term of thirty days and was renewed once. East India bonds were deposited as security, at a margin of 140 per cent (BofE, LBALB Out No. 8, 8 February 1869, 12 March 1869; In No. 2, 9 February 1869, 13 March 1869). With such conditions it is hardly surprising that these credits were virtually never requested. Loans on bills were of rather greater importance, but they were not a significant source of income for the Bank. During the 1850s and 1860s there was demand for credit in the form of loans on bills of exchange to the amount of 10 per cent to 25 per cent of the bills discounted, but the credits were so short term that the interest earnings were only 5 per cent to 10 per cent of the discount business. Most of them were either credits to local banks at quarter end or bridging loans for funding on the London money market. To be able to compete with the London banks, the provincial branches often sent bills payable in London to the head office of the Bank of England, which then sold the bills on commission for the customer on the London money market. Until the transaction was complete the customer was given a bridging loan by the Bank of England and, in this way, the Bank was able to put bills on the London money market for its provincial customers without the bills bearing the endorsement of the Bank of England (Collins 1972a, p. 148). This enabled the Bank's customers to discount in London at London rates.

With the strict rules on lending against stocks and bonds and the specific nature of lending against bills, it was impossible for the Bank to earn much directly on the lombard business. In quantity the lombard business was so small that the branch banks' office did not even feel it necessary to calculate the annual average for the amounts outstanding before 1887. The only figure given for the 1860s is £250,000 for the provincial branches for the accounting year 1867/8 (BofE, BBO C 79/27, Annual Advances in Profit and Loss Accounts and Averages). But the provincial branches held bills to the value of on average £3,279,000 in the calendar year 1867 in their portfolios (BofE SDC Reports C 35/4, Average Amount Held in Bills Under Discount: Branches).

Presumably on considerations of principle, lending against stocks and bonds was not regarded as a very desirable branch of the lending business, while lending against bills was not an independent branch of it. It was rather a special service which the Bank provided to make the other services it could offer more attractive. The bridging loans for funding were part of the range of transfer payments services offered to the provincial banks by the Bank of England. In particular, they helped to make the provincial banks more competitive against the London banks and bills brokers, that is, they secured the lucrative business as London agent. In return the customers had either to pay a commission on the turnover on their drawing account or maintain a minimum balance. The quarter-end credits were a service offered by the Bank of England in its function as the government's bank. The shortage of means of payment had been artificially brought about by the Bank, and therefore it had to try to counteract this as far as possible. Otherwise its position as the government's bank might be jeopardized.

Deposits at the provincial branches, originally one of the motives for setting up the branches, developed as unsatisfactorily as bill discounting after Peel's Act was passed, and the Bank did not progress beyond the promising beginnings in the 1820s and early 1830s. Unlike the commercial banks, the Bank of England did not pay interest on deposits in the provinces. Even before 1844, therefore, its provincial branches were probably largely dependent on the balances which the provincial banks had to maintain either as reserves or as minimum balances for a drawing account. The deterioration in the relations between the Bank of England and the provincial banks after 1844 must have had its effects here too. While the amount that flowed to the banks generally as deposits multiplied at this time, the drawing account balances maintained at the Bank of England provincial branches remained relatively stable in the 1860s and 1870s, at about £2 million. Up to the mid-1870s that was enough only to cover the provincial branches' assets in the depression year of 1868. Apart from a few exceptions, they were, therefore, dependent on transfers from London (see BofE, General Ledgers ADM 7 of the respective years). The disproportion between assets and liabilities was particularly marked for the Leeds, Bristol, Hull and Leicester branches. Of the provincial branches that had a lending business of note, only the Newcastle branch had a relatively satisfactory deposits base after 1858 (see Table 2.8). Nor did the establishment of local clearing houses (first

Table 2.8 Average amount of deposits at the Bank of England provincial branches, 1853–75 (£000)

Year	Man	Swa	Bir	Liv	Bri	Lee	New	Hul	Ply	Por	Lei	Aggregate amount
1853	525	32	101	370	132	59	86	44	60	83	30	1,522
1854	383	40	69	304	144	61	72	37	49	67	30	1,226
1855	360	30	97	314	125	52	70	34	51	74	36	1,242
1856	360	40	109	286	120	61	71	36	48	76	39	1,244
1857	389	33	101	308	118	63	86	36	42	69	38	1,283
1858	449	31	168	445	138	69	423	70	47	85	48	1,973
1859	511		161	473	125	78	441	82	58	81	41	2,054
1860	511		137	434	109	86	341	81	61	81	50	1,892
1861	509		125	480	107	85	357	54	58	73	50	1,893
1862	659		144	656	118	103	324	64	68	81	55	2,270
1863	503		125	617	109	100	334	53	69	76	52	2,039
1864	383		100	422	91	91	306	42	57	69	51	1,612
1865	418		114	423	91	190	238	50	52	83	50	1,709
1866	527		298	518	102	142	259	57	63	78	58	2,102
1867	496		333	797	126	190	298	70	64	79	58	2,513
1868	521		273	987	154	167	356	74	73	91	55	2,752
1869	509		182	840	147	157	292	75	78	87	57	2,424
1870	533		154	742	136	147	292	69	94	94	64	2,325
1871	524		169	754	139	155	315	80	99	88	55	2,378
1872	512		243	685	136	141	334	83	91	72		2,303
1873	530		208	573	148	130	509	103	88	64		2,253
1874	533		208	577	148	130	427	100	84	57		2,264
1875	625		236	567	154	122	462	93	75	58		2,391

Source: BofE, BBO Annual Statistical Reports: Average Deposits, C 79/21.

at the beginning of the 1870s in Manchester and Newcastle, a little later in Liverpool and Birmingham, and then in the 1890s in Leeds, Sheffield, Leicester and Bristol) have any noticeable effect on deposits at the provincial branches.[25]

The negative development in the lending business did not at first affect the figures for most of the provincial branches, and presumably all of them, like the contract banks, received a credit of 1 per cent of their average banknote circulation. This relic of Bank of England policy in the 1830s, which was actually contrary to the spirit of a commercial bank, remained, remarkably, in force until the mid-1870s. Until then, most of the provincial banks remained in the black, and it was not a coincidence that the three branches that were closed between 1849 and 1859 had in common not only that their deposit and/or bill discounting business was declining at an above-average rate, but also that their banknote circulation was shrinking. This was particularly striking in the case of the Gloucester branch, but Swansea also experienced a relative decline in its banknote circulation at the same time as a fall in its discounting business.[26]

The situation was rather different when the Leicester branch was closed. This branch had been opened only in 1844, much later than the other branches. By then the Bank of England no longer needed to incur the costs of opening another branch in order to force the circulation of its banknotes. Peel's Act had not yet been passed, but it was clear that new legislation of this kind was coming when the decision to set up a branch in Leicester was taken. In fact, after an initial start-up phase the lending business of the new branch proved very satisfactory; however, it did not obtain any deposits. Since around nine months had elapsed between the closure of the Clarke Mitchell bank (see Section 2.1.4) and the opening of the Leicester branch, customers of Clarke Mitchell had moved to other banks. Customer deposits at the Leicestershire Banking Co., for instance, rose from £306,000 to £412,000 over 1843 (Crick and Wadsworth 1936, p. 256). The Leicester branch of the Bank of England was therefore dependent on resources from London right from the start.

As an issuer of banknotes it was very successful, but on balance its issue of notes did not lead to the hoped-for increase in the total circulation of Bank of England notes, only to a corresponding decline in the circulation of Birmingham branch Bank of England notes (Ziegler 1989b, Graphs 1 and 2). The private bank I. & I.C. Wright in Nottingham, for instance, which had been circulating only Bank of England notes since 1836/7, naturally obtained its notes after 1844 from the nearest Midland's branch, the new one in Leicester. In the town the three local banks had inherited almost all of the Clarke Mitchell business. The circulation of Leicestershire Banking Co. notes actually almost doubled during 1843, rising from £48,000 to £82,000.

While this development might possibly have been foreseen by the Bank of England, its Directors were disappointed in their expectation that the local banks would soon give up issuing their own notes after the new legislation came into force and at least open a drawing account with the Bank of England. The legislation, which came into operation nine months after the Leicester branch was opened, had exactly the opposite effect. The banks in Leicester (the joint stock banks Pares Leicestershire Banking Co. and Leicestershire Banking Co. and the private bank Paget & Co.) did not come to the Bank of England, rather they kept their issue licences for decades. The upper limit fixed in 1844 for the banknote circulation of these three banks together was £180,000.[27]

Both the contract banks of the Leicester branch were located outside the town. I. & I.C. Wright was in Nottingham and Robinson & Bradhurst in Mansfield (Nottinghamshire). These two banks circulated about £80,000 in Bank of England notes. However, they gave up their circulation accounts soon after Peel's Act was passed and contented themselves with the compensation payment laid down in the Act. After charges were introduced for transfer payments for Wrights, this old customer also left the Bank of England, which certainly had an effect on its drawing account balances. Although the Leicester branch lost this customer only a few months after it was founded, its profitable lending business, and particularly the relative stability of this thanks to the high share of traders' bills, took it through the lean decade after 1844, during which three other branches fell victim.

When the Leicester branch was finally closed in 1872 its role as issuer of Bank of England notes played no part in the decision the Directors took. For the first time financial accounts were drawn up for a branch without the credit for banknote circulation, and it became clear that the Leicester branch had been in the red as a commercial bank since at least 1853. The deterioration of this situation during the depression in the late 1860s finally brought the decision to close the branch (for more details see Ziegler 1989b, pp. 17–19). In this case, as in that of the branches in Gloucester and Swansea, the function that the Leicester branch had played as a base for the Bank in the provinces (to circulate banknotes and handle government payments) could be taken over by a neighbouring branch. The Birmingham Branch could resume this role without great difficulty, as it had before the Leicester branch was set up. That was not possible for the branches in Portsmouth, Plymouth and Hull, and so although their operating results were similar — if not worse — than those in Leicester, they were able to survive.

2.3.2 The crisis in bill discounting

The crisis of 1866 was a major break in the evolution of payments habits and consequently of the money market as well. The collapse of the Overend Gurney discount house came as a total surprise to a number of provincial banks. The traditional function of the London money market as turntable for the reallocation of resources between the regions no longer seemed very reliable. At the same time the provincial banks were far less dependent than formerly on rediscounting through the London money market, due to the effects of the depressions of the late 1860s and the mid-1870s on the demand for credit. From the mid-1870s, therefore, most of the provincial banks experienced a noticeable rise in deposits in comparison with the demand for credit (discounts and advances). This development was encouraged in that the terms for bills had shortened, for various reasons, since the 1860s (Nishimura 1971, pp. 26–43, Tables 25 and 26, pp. 106–7; Collins 1984, pp. 53–4).

With the resultant improvement in liquidity the provincial banks incurred less risk in granting their customers current account credit, instead of discounting bills, and the competition between the banks, even in small towns, often forced them to meet their customers' wishes for the more flexible current account loans. Once they had become accustomed to receiving credit as an overdraft, instead of having bills discounted, the customers in turn began to pay with cheques instead of bills. Since most

Table 2.9 Average amount held in bills at Bank of England provincial branches, 1853–70 (£000)

Year	Man	Swa	Bir	Liv	Bri	Lee	New	Hul	Lei	Aggregate amount
1853	185	18	239	655	56	545	577	63	192	2,569
1854	166	47	350	653	61	529	649	54	174	2,743
1855	261	82	368	779	83	521	848	53	127	3,181
1856	516	105	302	714	109	505	939	47	129	3,416
1857	780	119	312	867	150	704	990	98	181	4,255
1858	259	95	198	656	116	509	376	63	165	2,583
1859	465		277	724	182	453	324	112	159	2,755
1860	909		338	1077	268	472	413	135	163	3,822
1861	638		288	872	260	392	410	156	137	3,205
1862	379		221	735	244	510	356	161	143	2,808
1863	620		285	856	145	513	382	133	163	3,164
1864	864		421	983	135	462	336	119	149	3,526
1865	895		503	1251	258	717	378	127	115	4,284
1866	870		563	1318	281	778	459	142	109	4,536
1867	461		306	986	199	631	312	164	96	3,179
1868	355		252	518	150	560	296	216	57	2,419
1869	620		275	584	133	601	257	210	94	2,799
1870	596		318	669	185	607	268	240	72	2,968

Note: Aggregate amount includes the branches at Portsmouth and Plymouth.

Source: BofE, BBO Annual Statistical Reports: Average Amount of Bills, C 79/21.

of the provincial banks were now linked directly with the London bankers' clearing house through their London agents, cheque payments were by far the easiest method for them (Holland 1910, p. 210; Nevin and Davis 1970, p. 69). So the bill was displaced as a means of payment. In the provinces this process was accelerated when local clearing houses were set up in some provincial cities as well at the beginning of the 1870s. According to Nishimura, the decline of the domestic bill began after the boom in the first half of the 1870s. Although he cannot produce any reliable figures for the total of domestic bills drawn per year during the 1870s and 1880s, his estimates confirm the assumptions of contemporary bankers that such bills were in short supply on the money market (Nishimura 1971, Table 15, p. 53 and Table 17, p. 54).[28]

The Bank of England was already feeling this development in the provinces in the 1860s. The number of its discount customers dropped from around 800 at the beginning of the decade to 430 towards its end. The cyclical upswing in the 1870s brought another slight increase to 470 discount customers, but thereafter the number dropped to 214 in the mid-1880s (BofE, SDC Reports C 35/4). However, the decline in the

Table 2.10 Bills discounted at Bank of England provincial branches, 1870–89

Year	'Bankers' bills' £m	Index	'Traders' bills' £m	Index	Total discounts £m	Index
1870	12.6	87	8.4	88	21.0	87
1871	10.6	73	8.5	89	19.2	80
1872	12.4	85	7.9	82	20.3	84
1873	11.7	81	7.9	82	19.6	81
1874	8.8	60	7.6	79	16.4	68
1875	8.9	61	6.4	67	15.3	63
1876	6.8	47	5.6	58	12.4	51
1877	5.2	36	4.7	49	9.9	41
1878	6.7	46	4.2	44	10.8	45
1879	4.7	32	4.1	43	8.7	36
1880	4.3	30	4.1	43	8.4	35
1881	4.0	28	3.2	33	7.2	30
1882	3.6	25	2.7	28	6.3	26
1883	3.8	26	2.5	26	6.4	26
1884	3.4	23	2.6	27	6.0	25
1885	3.1	21	2.2	23	5.3	22
1886	2.9	20	2.0	21	4.9	20
1887	2.9	20	1.5	16	4.5	19
1888	3.4	23	2.6	27	5.9	24
1889	6.4	44	4.2	44	10.6	44

Note: Index: 1865–9 yearly average = 100

Source: BofE, SDC Reports, C 35/4.

number of discount customers was not yet evident in turnover in the discount business in the 1860s, and after the breaks during the late 1840s and early 1850s, turnover had more or less stabilized. Certainly the fluctuations can be regarded as due to the cyclical situation (see Table 2.9).

The diminishing attraction of the Bank of England branches as lenders is then clear from the boom in the early 1870s, when the increase in demand was extremely moderate compared with earlier cyclical upswings. As Table 2.10 shows, not even the average level of the second half of the 1860s was reached, when there were two boom years and two depression years, representing approximately the average for a business cycle. When the cyclical downswing phase began in the mid-1870s, banking business for the Bank of England branches worsened dramatically. After 1874 the demand for credit fell drastically, and in the mid-1880s turnover in bill discounting fell to its lowest level since 1829. Bankers' and traders' bills were equally affected, with bankers' bills only falling more strongly on occasions in the 1870s (1874, 1876 and 1878/9).

A better measure of the discount business than the sum of the bills

Table 2.11 Average amount held in bills at Bank of England provincial branches, 1870–89 (£000)

Year	Liv	Man	Leeds	Bir	New	Bri	Hull	Aggregate amount
1870	669	596	607	318	268	185	240	2,969 (86)
1871	625	448	539	290	296	188	315	2,768 (81)
1872	693	462	478	275	261	187	309	2,682 (78)
1873	641	462	575	181	327	174	223	2,589 (75)
1874	703	255	443	159	283	167	255	2,271 (66)
1875	606	344	275	112	204	185	194	1,926 (56)
1876	510	195	240	88	166	224	268	1,701 (49)
1877	403	250	202	139	151	82	249	1,489 (43)
1878	362	400	173	173	131	88	178	1,456 (43)
1879	342	353	192	155	137	73	113	1,376 (40)
1880	272	200	168	153	141	48	142	1,133 (33)
1881	298	137	143	142	73	42	120	960 (28)
1882	273	70	87	100	71	61	84	753 (22)
1883	324	104	80	87	87	32	69	789 (23)
1884	350	100	82	84	84	10	73	790 (23)
1885	240	83	64	70	80	9	69	632 (18)
1886	242	59	61	99	53	7	56	590 (17)
1887	210	42	53	61	76	10	52	517 (15)
1888	315	73	86	76	68	7	59	697 (20)
1889	579	429	168	98	65	2	130	1,483 (43)

Note: ( ) 1865–9 yearly average = 100.

Source: BofE, BBO Annual Statistical Reports (C 79/21 and C 79/22).

presented for discounting is the average stock of bills in a portfolio during a year. For with such quantities fluctuations in the unlapsed currency of the bills (or the currency of the discount loans) can have an effect. The total index for all branches in Table 2.11 does not show any marked deviation from Table 2.10 — the correlation coefficient between the two flows is extremely high at $r = 0.993$ — but the shorter terms certainly made themselves felt in some years. The development during the early 1870s is particularly striking. Thanks to the boom more bills were discounted, but the stock of bills in the portfolio of the Bank was already beginning to fall from 1871. This divergence can only be due to a shortening of the average unlapsed currency of bills discounted. Probably shortage of liquidity forced some customers (mainly banks, no doubt) to (re)discount bills which under normal circumstances they would have kept until they fell due. Since it was evident that the shortage of liquidity would be only temporary, the banks no doubt chose bills which had only a short term left to run. An important indicator in support of this hypothesis is that traders were already discounting less at the Bank of England provincial branches in 1872 and 1873, while the sum of bankers' bills was higher during these years than in 1871. This supposition is also supported by the trend in London, where the average term of the bills discounted is known. There too it was shorter in 1872 and 1873 than in 1871 (BofE, SDC Reports C 35/4).

While the declining trend in the number of provincial bills in the Bank of England's portfolio from 1870 to 1887 does not, on aggregate, show any breaks, the fluctuations in the individual branches were extremely high and anything but uniform. The rise in the demand for credit at the Leeds and Newcastle branches, for instance, in 1873 (+ £163,000) was compensated by a decline in Birmingham and Hull (– £180,000) at the same time, while the strong fall in the following year was caused mainly by a drop in Manchester. Many other examples can be seen in Table 2.11. The decline at the individual branches also differed. The stock of bills held at the Manchester branch in 1887 was just 7 per cent of the average stock for the years 1865–9. In Leeds it was 8 per cent, in Birmingham 16 per cent and in Newcastle also 16 per cent in 1886. The Liverpool and Hull branches fared better, and their lows in 1887 were 23 per cent and 31 per cent respectively. Hardly a branch had an individual trend over the longer term that corresponded to the general trend. The reasons for this are unfortunately not clear, but they are presumably local.

Although the causes of the crisis in bill discounting and the changes in payments habits, affected all the banks in the provinces and in London, the Bank of England was more strongly affected than other banks. With its strict rules on the terms and quality of bills or acceptances, it was at a competitive disadvantage right from the start, and with the rising demand on the market for first class bills of exchange, this was increasingly felt as time went on. Moreover, the Bank was too inflexible, with its Bank Rate functioning as key rate, to be a serious competitor. The Bank's bill portfolio therefore declined much faster than the total amount of bills in circulation.

It is extremely difficult to calculate the Bank of England's market share owing to lack of data, but a calculation using Nishimura's figures suggests a decline of just 3 per cent in 1870 to about 0.6 per cent in 1887. Although these figures contain more than one factor of uncertainty, the trend is still so clear that one must assume a faster decline in bill discounting at the Bank of England than at other banks. Examples from individual banks confirm this hypothesis. For banks that were not yet expanding during the 1870s and 1880s,[29] the decline in the discount business was between 20 per cent and 30 per cent. The stock of bills both at the Bank of England provincial branches and at the head office reached its low in 1887, with falls of 85 per cent (provinces) and 84 per cent (London) from the second half of the 1860s.

Although the discount business in London and the provinces was largely parallel between the end of the 1860s and the end of the 1880s — the correlation coefficient for the stock of bills in the provincial branches and London was r = 0.895 — there were great differences, particularly in the 1870s. While the boom at the beginning of the 1870s did not have a noticeable effect on any of the large provincial branches, London during the first half of the 1870s was clearly above the average for the second half of the 1860s; indeed, in 1873 it actually regained the level of 1866. The following decline, especially in 1876 and 1877, was then more drastic in London than in the provinces. The introduction of the private discount rate in London enabled the discount office to improve its activities slightly in 1878, while the provincial branches stagnated. Only in the 1880s did the development run largely parallel, although London was not yet profiting from the general economic improvement in 1889. The strong rise in the demand for credit at the branches in Manchester, Liverpool and Hull cannot, however, be explained solely by the cyclical upswing, as changes in the regulations affected the provincial branches here (see pp. 62–63 below).

The decline in the importance of the discount business, both in London and in the provinces, naturally had considerable influence on whether the Bank could pay a dividend regarded as satisfactory. Since the mid-1870s the discount business at the branches had not only been insignificant for the Banking Department's gross earnings (see Table 2.12), it was not even sufficient to cover running costs for the provincial branches, most of which had been showing a loss in their accounts after 1875 (see Table 2.13). The earnings by the branches in Liverpool (£3,800 on average for the years 1875/6 to 1888/9), Manchester (£2,650) and Newcastle (£1,650) were not nearly enough to compensate for the losses suffered by the other branches.

The effect of the decline in the discount business on the losses suffered by the branches cannot unfortunately be shown statistically, since the accounts were drawn up at the end of August for each year, while the discount figures relate to the calendar year. However, there can be no doubt that interest income on the bill discount business was the most important source of income, as after 1876 the branches no longer received a credit for their average banknote circulation. The decline in the discount business therefore accounted for a considerable part of the losses that the branches had suffered since the 1870s. However, the deposit business was also seen as playing an important role after the basis for calculation changed in 1875, because interest on 'London Money Used at Branches' was shown as expenditure in the accounts. Conversely, a branch whose stock of deposits exceeded its lending business was credited with interest for 'Branch Money Employed in London' (BofE, BBO Profit and Loss Account Averages C 79/27).

Some branches were therefore able to reduce the effect of the decline in the discount business by increasing their deposits — the Newcastle branch did relatively well in this compared with Leeds or Hull, for instance. The lending business for these three branches was roughly comparable between the mid-1870s and the end of the 1880s, but while

Table 2.12 Share of gross profits provided by interest on bills at the provincial branches, 1870–89

Half-year ending	Interest on bills (£) (a)	Banking dep. gross profits (£) (b)	Col. (a) as % of Col. (b)
Feb. 1870	39,000	696,200	6%
Aug. 1870	51,300	756,100	7%
Feb. 1871	42,000	744,600	6%
Aug. 1871	40,000	716,600	6%
Feb. 1872	38,600	744,800	5%
Aug. 1872	51,100	803,200	6%
Feb. 1873	57,100	836,800	7%
Aug. 1873	61,800	869,200	7%
Feb. 1874	50,900	823,900	6%
Aug. 1874	42,800	766,800	6%
Feb. 1875	35,200	753,200	5%
Aug. 1875	33,300	772,600	4%
Feb. 1876	29,500	741,900	4%
Aug. 1876	26,900	740,000	4%
Feb. 1877	15,000	792,900	2%
Aug. 1877	18,500	779,800	2%
Feb. 1878	19,900	771,100	3%
Aug. 1878	19,000	789,100	2%
Feb. 1879	44,700	950,100	5%
Aug. 1879	16,600	798,300	2%
Feb. 1880	13,500	758,300	2%
Aug. 1880	16,500	795,100	2%
Feb. 1881	14,800	782,800	2%
Aug. 1881	13,400	792,600	2%
Feb. 1882	17,600	836,700	2%
Aug. 1882	13,700	850,500	2%
Feb. 1883	14,500	869,300	2%
Aug. 1883	15,600	844,500	2%
Feb. 1884	11,300	844,500	1%
Aug. 1884	9,700	816,100	1%
Feb. 1885	11,900	813,900	1%
Aug. 1885	8,900	867,200	1%
Feb. 1886	7,400	827,500	1%
Aug. 1886	7,000	849,100	1%
Feb. 1887	8,800	842,800	1%
Aug. 1887	7,000	827,000	1%
Feb. 1888	8,300	836,900	1%
Aug. 1888	6,400	902,100	1%
Feb. 1889	17,200	902,700	2%
Aug. 1889	15,900	850,600	2%

Source: BofE, Stock Estimate (ADM 19), Profit and Loss Accounts.

Table 2.13 Profits and losses of Bank of England provincial branches, 1875/6–1889/90 (£)

Year	Man	Bir	Liv	Bristol	Leeds	New	Hull	Ply	Port
1875/76	−752	−2,555	+4,331	−1,217	−218	+133	−259	−1,954	−1,478
1876/77	−689	−4,963	+8,529	−19,783	−2,748	−1,855	−187	−4,418	−3,293
1877/78	+1,704	−2,929	+4,762	−3,581	−4,021	−213	−918	−3,039	−3,010
1878/79	+15,178	−4,232	+11,623	+8,251	−2,483	+5,210	−1,623	−1,826	−2,877
1879/80	+1,915	−2,711	+3,361	−1,812	−5,276	+1,606	−2,153	−3,347	−3,265
1880/81	+2,276	−2,917	+9,082	−3,725	−5,451	+663	−2,983	−2,424	−3,514
1881/82	+4,420	−1,228	+3,570	−1,119	−5,515	+3,316	−2,033	−1,682	−2,618
1882/83	+3,750	−2,544	+7,368	−16,058	−5,167	+3,646	−2,622	−1,314	−2,441
1883/84	+1,162	−3,490	−3,701	−1,605	−6,001	+78	−3,709	−1,967	−3,082
1884/85	+1,556	−2,506	−1,717	−3,544	−6,256	+1,428	−4,179	−1,714	−3,016
1885/86	−2,385	−2,390	−6,374	−4,408	−7,897	−899	−4,791	−2,182	−3,130
1886/87	+3,149	−395	+4,044	−3,628	−6,979	+3,270	−3,759	−1,051	−2,751
1887/88	+4,307	−3,018	+2,452	−3,134	−7,960	+3,744	−3,800	−1,089	−2,546
1888/89	+1,566	−783	+6,065	−5,244	−7,852	+3,157	−3,879	−1,175	−3,361
1889/90	+5,848	+6,459	+15,677	−3,341	−6,944	+6,727	−3,073	−1,139	−3,142

Note: (+) profits, (−) losses.

Source: BofE, BBO Annual Statistical Reports (C 79/22)

Table 2.14 Average amount of deposits at Bank of England provincial branches, 1875–1913 (£000)

Year	Man	Bir	Liv	Bri	Leeds	New	Hull	Ply	Por	Aggregate amount
1875	625	236	567	154	122	462	93	75	58	2,391
1876	559	223	643	148	141	389	101	74	62	2,340
1877	561	229	640	147	156	350	118	70	66	2,336
1878	621	246	678	172	139	441	123	75	61	2,556
1879	790	292	985	875	186	604	160	162	77	4,130
1880	760	270	962	297	180	625	151	142	70	3,457
1881	693	266	1,138	267	176	499	121	130	68	3,359
1882	592	234	912	215	146	545	136	117	69	2,966
1883	584	204	839	203	154	540	117	107	74	2,824
1884	590	212	876	203	153	575	113	123	72	2,917
1885	598	250	851	198	135	549	108	111	71	2,870
1886	619	255	820	133	120	560	116	140	72	2,895
1887	642	277	711	186	117	532	106	153	70	2,794
1888	641	303	756	192	126	496	115	132	63	2,825
1889	623	326	837	165	142	512	122	132	59	2,918
1890	612	326	759	182	140	518	120	133	56	2,846
1891	667	450	891	198	163	623	118	131	57	3,299
1892	760	416	930	199	191	587	111	120	61	3,375
1893	714	371	938	206	201	561	115	128	71	3,304
1894	728	366	933	184	247	608	109	126	84	3,385
1895	1,108	395	1,019	199	327	642	98	142	83	4,014
1896	1,208	449	1,074	212	367	710	113	136	80	4,350
1897	1,291	477	989	219	409	688	118	136	84	4,411
1898	1,322	447	917	229	489	720	123	148	86	4,477
1899	1,360	391	892	230	424	725	134	169	88	4,413
1900	1,331	400	1,041	218	379	751	127	142	93	4,483
1901	1,344	368	1,008	226	391	717	119	133	96	4,403
1902	1,354	362	870	207	419	642	157	155	102	4,268
1903	1,321	321	829	200	436	717	170	180	104	4,278
1904	1,223	342	808	199	420	680	136	216	103	4,127
1905	1,341	427	940	234	407	679	155	231	97	4,511
1906	1,247	443	938	247	469	751	146	306	94	4,641
1907	1,264	499	1,033	249	489	722	142	365	100	4,863
1908	1,422	491	1,123	246	479	778	143	349	96	5,127
1909	1,594	502	1,181	252	469	686	140	342	96	5,262
1910	1,479	509	1,085	270	491	658	146	333	100	5,071
1911	1,532	521	1,157	290	488	636	161	325	104	5,214
1912	1,589	537	1,196	291	394	714	158	351	114	5,344
1913	1,544	565	1,251	284	383	707	164	334	112	5,344

Source: BofE, BBO, Annual Statistical Reports (C 79/22 and C 79/23)

Newcastle had had a good stock of deposits for some time (see Table 2.14) and was actually able to improve this further, deposits had been stagnating on a low level in Leeds and Hull since the early 1870s. The good overall results in 1878/9 were only partly due to the discount business, and the rise in deposits at the provincial branches, from £2,556,000 on average for the year 1878 to £4,130,000 on average for 1879, was equally important. While the increase in profits for the Manchester branch, from £1,704 in the financial year 1877/8 to £15,178 in 1878/9, was certainly due to the rise in the discount business in the calendar years 1878 and 1879, the branch in Bristol owed its profit of £8,251 in 1878/9 to the increase in the average stock of deposits from £147,000 in the calendar year 1877 to £875,000 in 1878. Between 1882 and 1890 deposits at all the branches remained relatively stable, and the record loss of £34,500 in 1885/6 and the good result for 1889/90 were due mainly to the fluctuations in the discount business.

2.3.3 The new upswing in lending 1889–1913

The break in the development of the Bank of England's provincial branches at the end of the 1880s was no less important than that in the mid-1840s, but, unlike 1844, the new phase in the Bank's policy to the provinces during the quarter-century before the First World War was hardly registered by the general public. Even histories of the Bank of England deal with it only briefly. From 1889/90 the provincial branches on balance showed consistently a profit (see Table 2.15). The majority of them (Leeds, Hull, Bristol, Portsmouth and Plymouth) remained in the red up to and during the depression of the mid-1890s, but the profits earned by the branches in Liverpool, Manchester, Birmingham and Newcastle were at times so huge that they not only compensated for these losses in the first half of the 1890s but brought a considerable surplus on balance. From the second half of the 1890s the branches in Leeds, Bristol and Hull also showed a profit, as did even the Plymouth branch from 1905/6. During this time the provincial branches made an important contribution to the gross earnings of the Banking Department.

Interest income on the discount business generally accounted for between 3 per cent and 7 per cent, and interest income on the lombard business a further 4 per cent to 12 per cent of the Banking Department's gross earnings (see Table 2.16). Only during the depression in the mid-1890s did the interest income on the discount business drop for a time almost to the level of the 1880s. Nevertheless, the drop in the discount business for the provincial branches in the mid-1890s cannot be compared with the break ten years before. Between 1890 and 1903 the average holding of bills in the provincial branches' portfolios did not fluctuate nearly so strongly (with one exception in 1899) as appears from the interest income. During the depression years 1893 and 1894 the bill holding was clearly higher, at £1.8 million, than during the depression

Table 2.15 Profits and losses of Bank of England provincial branches, 1889/90–1912/13 (£)

Year	Man	Bir	Liv	Bri	Leeds	New	Hull	Ply	Por
1889/90	+5,848	+6,459	+15,677	−3,341	−6,944	+6,727	−3,073	−1,133	−3,142
1890/91	+9,469	+5,069	+20,900	−2,302	−7,028	+10,508	−3,072	−1,634	−2,712
1891/92	+7,709	+10,192	+24,668	−2,925	−5,533	+5,769	−1,668	−3,126	−3,062
1892/93	+5,339	+7,849	+30,036	−2,195	−4,700	+6,174	−3,989	−3,386	−3,695
1893/94	+5,845	+9,074	+21,895	−1,939	−2,703	+4,590	−4,124	−3,403	−3,783
1894/95	+5,926	+2,840	+7,679	−418	−174	+374	−4,608	−3,238	−3,867
1895/96	+6,947	+93	+5,139	+1,266	+3,827	+7,151	−3,306	−3,023	−4,309
1896/97	+18,580	+9,652	+18,610	+4,108	+9,820	+13,216	+8,195	−3,105	−4,037
1897/98	+28,294	+2,715	+19,066	+5,079	+11,817	+13,504	+4,797	−2,503	−3,491
1898/99	+35,109	+8,103	+18,239	+5,181	+16,017	+18,366	+4,453	−1,853	−3,110
1899/00	+40,199	+9,547	+25,374	+5,543	+26,739	+26,523	+8,942	−1,515	−3,260
1900/01	+36,488	+5,826	+21,264	+5,328	+12,515	+27,752	+11,122	−1,013	−3,271
1901/02	+31,467	−516	+14,836	+636	+8,107	+15,037	+1,327	−1,648	−3,337
1902/03	+31,740	−700	+23,368	+197	+15,986	+20,120	+4,487	−1,304	−3,662
1903/04	+35,416	+1,368	+27,732	−256	+15,417	+18,566	+6,657	+255	−3,129
1904/05	+26,661	+1,120	+18,171	+1,253	+7,951	+13,655	+3,190	−136	−3,033
1905/06	+40,337	+4,944	+57,247	+4,382	+18,706	+23,626	+1,745	+1,165	−3,136
1906/07	+48,568	+8,670	+91,307	+7,408	+26,988	+26,919	+3,810	+3,324	−2,714
1907/08	+38,712	+5,582	+70,437	+2,853	+16,561	+18,782	+3,540	+3,340	−3,505
1908/09	+22,287	+2,309	+13,045	−1,419	+3,439	+11,740	−1,825	+2,584	−3,523
1909/10	+31,371	+4,993	+36,786	+2,115	+16,909	+18,452	+1,526	+3,170	−3,386
1910/11	+34,316	+4,569	+38,402	+1,418	+17,334	+15,304	+951	+2,706	−3,081
1911/12	+34,152	+5,029	+34,142	+1,721	+15,290	+14,195	+2,506	+3,533	−2,875
1912/13	+43,087	+6,902	+50,257	+4,286	+32,490	+17,934	+4,614	+3,096	−2,505

Note: (+) profits, (−) losses.
Year beginning March and ending February of the next year.

Source: BofE, BBO Annual Statistical Reports (C 79/22 and C 79/23).

Table 2.16 Share of gross profits provided by interest on bills and advances at the provincial branches, 1889–1911

Half-year ending	Banking dep. gross profits £	Interest on bills £	%	Interest on advances £	%	Interest on total short-term sec. %
Aug. 1889	850,600	15,900	2	16,000	2	4
Feb. 1890	905,000	28,000	3	44,200	5	8
Aug. 1890	863,300	35,100	4	44,500	5	9
Feb. 1891	921,000	44,600	5	62,000	7	12
Aug. 1891	921,500	44,100	5	45,100	5	10
Feb. 1892	856,100	31,100	4	45,600	5	9
Aug. 1892	905,200	25,700	3	32,800	4	6
Feb. 1893	824,900	23,000	3	38,700	5	7
Aug. 1893	913,200	26,700	3	52,400	6	9
Feb. 1894	829,400	22,900	3	49,100	6	9
Aug. 1894	937,400	20,500	2	37,600	4	6
Feb. 1895	801,600	11,500	1	32,300	4	5
Aug. 1895	712,700	15,600	2	35,900	5	7
Feb. 1896	788,600	16,200	2	38,800	5	7
Aug. 1896	809,400	17,600	2	50,100	6	8
Feb. 1897	868,400	26,900	3	80,400	9	12
Aug. 1897	874,000	30,500	3	64,800	7	11
Feb. 1898	872,200	23,600	3	78,800	9	12
Aug. 1898	928,700	39,600	4	95,400	10	14
Feb. 1899	893,300	37,300	4	110,600	12	16
Aug. 1899	960,200	50,500	5	89,700	9	15
Feb. 1900	1,026,300	50,600	5	104,200	10	15
Aug. 1900	1,047,800	41,300	4	84,600	8	12
Feb. 1901	1,098,400	35,500	3	96,700	9	12
Aug. 1901	1,047,900	39,900	4	88,700	8	12
Feb. 1902	1,059,600	30,800	3	73,100	7	10
Aug. 1902	1,016,800	35,700	4	61,000	6	10
Feb. 1903	1,056,200	31,200	3	72,300	7	10
Aug. 1903	1,014,600	37,800	4	75,200	7	11
Feb. 1904	1,083,900	35,600	3	81,400	8	11
Aug. 1904	962,600	50,700	5	75,400	8	13
Feb. 1905	985,500	41,200	4	62,900	6	11
Aug. 1905	987,000	51,400	5	57,000	6	11
Feb. 1906	1,193,000	66,900	6	80,100	7	12
Aug. 1906	1,149,500	81,500	7	84,300	7	14
Feb. 1907	1,293,000	71,200	6	100,000	8	13
Aug. 1907	1,212,800	114,000	9	73,900	6	15
Feb. 1908	1,244,400	97,200	8	75,700	6	14
Aug. 1908	1,102,300	76,400	7	42,300	4	11
Feb. 1909	1,073,500	38,200	4	38,800	4	7
Aug. 1909	1,090,700	57,800	5	44,000	4	9
Feb. 1910	1,064,400	57,800	5	58,400	5	10
Aug. 1910	1,164,700	60,000	5	58,300	5	10
Feb. 1911	1,132,600	55,100	5	58,500	5	10
Aug. 1911	1,104,400	73,400	7	48,100	4	11
Feb. 1912	1,107,400	38,800	4	57,900	5	9

Source: BofE, Stock Estimates (ADM 19), Profit and Loss Accounts.

in the preceding cycle, in 1886 and 1887, when the provincial branches did not have on average £0.6 million in provincial bills in their portfolios. The poor interest earnings in 1894 and particularly 1895, when the discount business had actually already improved, is mainly due to the extremely long period of low interest rates, which was unique in English financial history.

However, this trend in the discount business cannot be explained solely by cyclical factors. The rise in the demand for discounting in 1889 was certainly partly due to the general improvement in the domestic economy, but the rise in demand was so rapid that other causes were at work. First, the conditions had to be created for the cyclical impulses to be felt at all. After all, the Bank had been suffering from an almost unbroken decline in its discount business since about 1870, and during this previous period a cyclical upswing had at best halted the declining trend. Moreover, conditions were needed to prevent the Bank of England being the first to feel the decline in the demand for credit during a downswing, as had been the case until then on account of its inflexible interest rates.

It was no doubt in reaction to devastating half-yearly results (see Table 2.12) that the Directors extended the application of the private discount and lombard rates to the provincial branches at the beginning of 1888 (BofE, CB No. 110, 26 January 1888). From then on the branch agents could offer their customers private discount rates that could be adapted relatively well to market rates, depending on the standing of the borrower and the quality of the bills, since they were fixed individually. This reform probably not only opened the way to the increase in demand in 1889–91, but also prevented a fall in the discount business during the following depression years comparable to the fall in the 1880s. The number of discount customers proved extremely stable between 1893 and 1896 in the provinces, as the interest rates could be adapted individually, although the declining trend continued in London. The private discount rule also applied there, but market rates in London were so low that the Bank was not a serious competitor, although its rates were at times considerably below the official minimum discount rate of 2 per cent. In the provinces, on the other hand, interest rates never dropped to the level they reached in London in the mid-1890s. The competition from the savings banks prevented deposit rates from falling to the London level, and so lending rates could not fall so far either. The Bank of England, which did not have to pay interest on deposits and did not have any means of investing funds in London, could underbid its competitors in the provinces on occasion.

As in the past, the increase in the discount business for the provincial branches was in the main limited to but a few. While the business stagnated in Newcastle and actually continued to decline slightly in Birmingham, bill holdings in Liverpool rose from £280,000 on average for the years 1880–8 to £1,117,000 on average for 1890–1903, and in

Table 2.17 Average amount held in bills at the Bank of England provincial branches, 1890–1913 (£000)

Year	Liv	Man	Lee	Bir	New	Bri	Hul	Aggregate amount	
1890	1,067	507	134	89	96	11	131	2,047	(59)
1891	1,371	742	160	78	118	5	155	2,641	(77)
1892	1,486	347	132	66	79	—	181	2,307	(67)
1893	1,287	186	112	59	72	3	100	1,829	(53)
1894	1,177	141	244	73	59	19	76	1,801	(52)
1895	1,500	254	304	75	62	58	92	2,354	(68)
1896	1,173	495	372	87	167	66	237	2,606	(76)
1897	1,383	401	438	68	187	78	238	2,797	(81)
1898	1,164	480	504	93	185	59	184	2,671	(77)
1899	1,696	437	767	70	178	44	191	3,391	(98)
1900	634	495	530	79	121	42	178	2,050	(59)
1901	778	401	438	65	89	42	191	2,135	(62)
1902	881	577	383	56	111	29	199	2,252	(65)
1903	785	590	361	33	93	16	161	2,056	(60)
1904	1,261	988	466	55	185	72	201	3,243	(94)
1905	1,981	1,005	485	32	310	57	229	4,121	(119)
1906	2,015	1,107	625	40	227	15	207	4,254	(123)
1907	2,721	915	581	39	234	17	184	4,705	(136)
1908	2,121	957	596	40	289	12	235	4,263	(124)
1909	2,767	771	673	26	277	11	223	4,768	(138)
1910	1,436	686	773	37	322	29	202	3,504	(102)
1911	1,847	779	873	23	324	33	163	4,058	(118)
1912	1,188	549	729	77	44	19	143	2,764	(80)
1913	1,018	505	824	66	3	3	175	2,614	(76)

Note: ( ) 1865–9 yearly average = 100.

Source: BofE, BBO Annual Statistical Reports (C 79/22 and C 79/23).

Manchester over the same period, from on average £75,000 to on average £450,000. With their increase of £1,265 million these two branches alone accounted for almost the whole rise in the bill holdings of all the branches over the same period, from £760,000 to £2,350,000 (see Tables 2.11 and 2.17).

The situation was quite different with regard to the lombard business, which was very much a secondary activity for all the provincial branches up to the end of the 1880s. With the strict rules on the terms for the loans and the quality of the securities, almost unchanged since the 1830s, lombard business was conducted almost only with banks, and even then only at a few branches. Although loans on bills had become very much more important in the 1870s than they had been in the two decades before, and accounted for up to 75 per cent of the turnover after the decline in the discount business from the end of the 1870s, it was not

Table 2.18 Average amount of advances granted at Bank of England provincial branches, 1887–1913 (£000)

Half-year ending	Liv	Man	Lee	Bir	New	Bri	Hul	Aggregate amount
Aug. 1887	79	43	22	208	51	1	4	430
Feb. 1888	106	42	48	234	25	1	4	470
Aug. 1888	137	46	21	256	33	1	8	503
Feb. 1889	230	63	28	287	56	1	76	757
Aug. 1889	435	132	28	464	98	2	55	1,227
Feb. 1890	709	179	25	656	292	19	51	1,947
Aug. 1890	934	206	32	768	290	82	55	2,342
Feb. 1891	889	282	18	847	494	140	62	2,746
Aug. 1891	849	326	40	999	321	125	61	2,728
Feb. 1892	800	295	46	976	375	130	105	2,676
Aug. 1892	821	311	67	904	314	148	106	2,680
Feb. 1893	1,026	285	111	974	303	158	110	2,981
Aug. 1893	1,234	418	149	981	331	156	58	3,332
Feb. 1894	875	433	269	1,003	286	155	63	3,100
Aug. 1894	811	450	381	871	299	171	42	3,037
Feb. 1895	863	436	352	719	313	185	37	2,917
Aug. 1895	936	495	377	766	299	208	22	3,112
Feb. 1896	1,118	526	450	833	389	278	33	3,649
Aug. 1896	1,464	586	568	881	457	280	450	4,704
Feb. 1897	1,292	548	521	972	495	346	614	4,818
Aug. 1897	1,108	624	699	897	739	415	562	5,061
Feb. 1898	1,443	675	1,019	823	475	462	471	5,489
Aug. 1898	1,709	1,356	932	836	583	502	469	6,397
Feb. 1899	1,038	1,468	1,009	827	628	493	504	5,978
Aug. 1899	1,016	1,292	989	747	571	500	639	5,764
Feb. 1900	655	977	596	523	740	400	668	4,575
Aug. 1900	659	994	583	471	692	364	774	4,541
Feb. 1901	621	988	435	441	793	343	882	4,527
Aug. 1901	766	1,097	437	390	956	335	819	4,841
Feb. 1902	776	1,068	429	252	626	243	362	3,786
Aug. 1902	1,119	835	444	215	640	205	144	3,616
Feb. 1903	931	736	599	161	621	161	268	3,488
Aug. 1903	1,086	769	694	178	763	77	406	3,995
Feb. 1904	992	756	529	188	591	93	452	3,651
Aug. 1904	952	837	709	216	769	236	435	4,175
Feb. 1905	752	718	579	242	624	323	354	3,609
Aug. 1905	1,109	726	479	269	459	260	365	3,694
Feb. 1906	1,367	637	511	282	694	276	79	3,879
Aug. 1906	1,300	750	554	289	678	365	111	4,088
Feb. 1907	1,318	549	499	274	539	349	133	3,705
Aug. 1907	1,165	579	437	272	324	323	159	3,316
Feb. 1908	1,080	462	356	231	287	322	161	2,967
Aug. 1908	1,043	500	368	226	172	280	135	2,786
Feb. 1909	950	376	368	274	199	316	152	2,707

Table 2.18 contd.

Half-year ending	Liv	Man	Lee	Bir	New	Bri	Hul	Aggregate amount
Aug. 1909	935	423	458	276	289	353	209	3,021
Feb. 1910	890	356	505	260	462	313	192	3,050
Aug. 1910	903	404	536	254	547	245	136	3,102
Feb. 1911	855	441	450	246	320	233	145	2,761
Aug. 1911	1,098	493	518	218	210	226	122	2,956
Feb. 1912	944	406	472	229	362	234	198	2,916
Aug. 1912	889	377	404	193	549	231	196	2,909
Feb. 1913	983	390	377	175	476	225	150	2,831
Aug. 1913	944	465	702	184	438	194	171	3,153
Feb. 1914	1,041	370	467	144	431	194	209	2,918

Source: BofE, BBO Annual Statistical Reports (C 79/22 and C 79/23).

nearly sufficient to stop the decline in interest earnings. During this period lombard loans on bills might have been an alternative for borrowers to bill discounting, because, thanks to the improvement in their liquidity, the provincial banks were not, as a rule, so dependent on rediscounting in the late 1870s as in preceding decades. When there was a temporary need for funding, lombard loans on bills had the advantage that the term of the loan could be adjusted to the expected duration of the liquidity shortage, so they were preferable for seasonal, that is, foreseeable, fluctuations in the demand for credit at the banks.

In the 1880s lombard loans on bills dropped back to almost the level of the 1850s and 1860s, and during the depression in the mid-1880s interest income was actually below £1,000 per banking half-year on average. Thereafter, lombard loans against bills remained an insignificant factor in the lending business of the Bank of England's branches right up to the First World War, despite an increase in turnover in the early 1900s. The increases in turnover in the lombard business for the branches from the beginning of the 1890s were almost exclusively due to the increases in advances on stocks and bonds, although this type of lending was also a marginal activity until the end of the 1880s.

Lombard business was of such slight significance in the provinces that the branch banks' office did not even think it necessary to calculate its size regularly until towards the end of the 1880s. Since the office showed a figure only on the flow of advances in the provincial branches' portfolios from the banking half-year (March to August) 1887, its size in earlier decades can only be estimated from the half-yearly balances. On this basis an average annual amount of about £300,000 may be assumed between the end of the 1860s and the beginning of the 1880s, with a very much higher amount likely in exceptional years (for instance after the collapse of the City of Glasgow Bank, which caused a hitherto underestimated liquidity crisis for the English provincial banks, see Collins 1989, pp. 504–7).

During the 1880s the picture was unfortunately uneven, and up to 1887 an estimate is risky. We have reliable data after 1887, which show that the level of the advances was then only slightly above that estimated for the 1870s (see Table 2.18). The upswing started in the lombard business in the second half of 1889, almost parallel to the movement in bill discounting, and according to the February balance sheet for 1890 the income on the lombard business was outstripping that on discounting (see Table 2.16). The increase in the amount of advances was not, like that in bill discounting, limited to a few successful branches; almost all the branches were able to increase this area of their activity during the 1890s several times over. Even the 'smaller' branches, Hull and Bristol, where advances were virtually unknown up to 1889, caught up with their larger counterparts around the turn of the century.

This development became possible when the Bank of England's Directors permitted their branch agents more scope in handling their lending business in 1888. In addition to greater flexibility over interest rates, the main factor was the relaxation of the old rule that only 'London securities' could be used as cover for advances.[30] In view of the strict ban on overdrafts, which was still in force, this was necessary to enable the branches to compete with the provincial banks in the normal banking business. It can be seen from a list of the borrowers from the provincial branches how successful they were in the normal lending business (BofE, CB No. 116, 8 March 1894). The total loans were to:

29 employees of the Bank	£70,000 (= 2 per cent)
309 private customers	£1,600,000 (= 37 per cent)
90 traders and merchants	£1,100,000 (= 24 per cent)
46 stock brokers	£1,300,000 (= 30 per cent)
14 corporations	£250,000 (= 6 per cent).

Certainly it could no longer be said that the Bank was 'the bankers' bank'. Only a single bank had taken up a loan from a Bank of England branch, for £20,000 (= 0.4 per cent). After the phase of co-operation between the Bank of England and the provincial banks in the 1830s had given way to a relatively uneventful coexistence following Peel's Act, from the late 1880s most of the provincial branches, chief among them Birmingham, were increasingly fierce and successful competitors of the commercial banks.

Only the third activity in the provincial branches' banking business was not initially affected by the reform of 1888. Up to and including 1890 the stock of deposits remained constant from the early 1880s at the level of about £2.8 million to £2.9 million. Only after the Baring crisis was there a slight increase, by about £0.5 million, with another increase of around £1 million after the turn of the century. Following the 1907 crisis the stock of deposits at the provincial branches rose strongly, reaching a level of at least £5 million before the First World War. However, this increase was very much smaller than the rise in the lending business and the relationship between deposits and lending changed accordingly (see Table 2.19). While the provincial branches were able to send funds from deposits to the head office in the 1880s for the purchase of colonial and corporation bonds, the flow soon reversed after the reform of the lending business in the provinces. As in the 1850s and 1860s, the provincial branches were again dependent on funds from London (see BofE, General Ledgers, ADM 7).

Thanks to the reform, which was only to make the provincial branches more competitive in normal banking business, the income on lombard and discount business for the provincial branches developed into a major factor in ensuring an adequate dividend payment by the mid-1890s. But in 1893/4, just when the stability of the provincial branches' lending business seemed for the first time to be lessening the shortfall in income on the lending business in London, some of the old restrictive rules were reincorporated in the regulations. The reason for this was the discovery of speculation on the part of the Bank's chief cashier, Frank May, and the ensuing investigation of the lending practice in London and the provinces.

Directly after the scandal the Court of Directors set up a committee of inquiry to make a careful examination of the lombard business, first in Threadneedle Street. The examination revealed inadequate cover for a number of loans and, in January 1894, the Court decided on a stricter version of the guidelines for advances. About the same time the Committee for Branch Banks was instructed to examine the lombard business at the branches, and here too the cover proved to be inadequate in some cases, although the extent could not be compared with the situation in Threadneedle Street.[31] Only the Birmingham branch had accepted securities which the inspectors felt were inadequate. They were 'speculative and rather doubtful', they said. The high share of securities 'of a purely local character' was a particular cause for concern, although the Directors had to admit that so far no losses had been incurred (BofE, CB No. 116, 8 March 1894, 3 May 1894). Only two accounts did not have adequate cover. Nevertheless, a provision of £31,000 was made for losses on 'bad debts' in Birmingham.

Before the Committee for Branch Banks had presented its report, the Court of Directors decided, as a first measure, to bring the Regulations to Govern Advances to Customers at Branches into line with the rules that applied in London (BofE, CB No. 116, 1 February 1894). Branch agents were no longer allowed to accept as collateral securities that could not be traded on the London Stock Exchange. To ensure that this regulation was observed, all securities had to be sent to London. The only exception was securities deposited by stock brokers for short-term loans. Moreover, the approval of the Deputy Governor was again necessary for every loan.

Table 2.19 Credit/deposit ratio at Bank of England provincial branches 1870–1913, (%)

Year	Liv	Man	Leeds	Bir	New	Bri	Hull	Total
1870	(90)	(112)	(413)	(206)	(92)	(136)	(378)	(128)
1871	(83)	(85)	(348)	(172)	(94)	(135)	(394)	(117)
1872	(101)	(90)	(339)	(113)	(78)	(138)	(372)	(116)
1873	(112)	(87)	(442)	(87)	(64)	(118)	(217)	(115)
1874	(122)	(48)	(341)	(76)	(66)	(113)	(250)	(100)
1875	(107)	(55)	(225)	(47)	(44)	(120)	(209)	(81)
1876	(79)	(35)	(170)	(39)	(41)	(151)	(265)	(73)
1877	(63)	(45)	(129)	(61)	(43)	(56)	(211)	(64)
1878	(53)	(64)	(124)	(70)	(30)	(51)	(145)	(57)
1879	(34)	(45)	(103)	(53)	(23)	(8)	(71)	(33)
1880	(28)	(26)	(93)	(57)	(23)	(16)	(94)	(33)
1881	(26)	(20)	(81)	(53)	(15)	(16)	(99)	(29)
1882	(30)	(12)	(60)	(43)	(13)	(28)	(62)	(25)
1883	(39)	(18)	(52)	(43)	(16)	(16)	(59)	(30)
1884	(40)	(17)	(54)	(40)	(15)	(5)	(65)	(27)
1885	(28)	(14)	(47)	(28)	(15)	(5)	(64)	(22)
1886	(30)	(10)	(51)	(39)	(9)	(4)	(48)	(21)
1887	40 (30)	13 (7)	70 (45)	93 (22)	23(14)	5 (5)	52 (49)	34 (19)
1888	65 (42)	20 (11)	88 (68)	114 (25)	26(16)	4 (4)	86 (51)	47 (25)
1889	139 (69)	94 (69)	136(118)	199 (30)	50(13)	7 (1)	148(106)	104 (51)
1890	260(141)	122 (83)	114 (96)	273 (27)	182(19)	66 (7)	159(109)	162 (72)
1891	246	156	123	235	75	66	199	162
1892	262	85	116	242	66	82	262	153
1893	249	85	155	285	68	77	139	154
1894	216	80	247	239	60	108	106	140
1895	250	69	218	222	63	150	122	142

Table 2.19 contd.

Year	Liv	Man	Leeds	Bir	New	Bri	Hull	Total
1896	238	88	250	203	90	182	679	169
1897	269	81	315	195	114	237	642	184
1898	274	142	304	206	109	244	545	198
1899	283	115	370	179	114	215	628	205
1900	122	112	274	135	103	180	802	147
1901	154	131	183	105	117	147	665	153
1902	221	101	142	68	115	101	255	136
1903	220	102	223	68	108	51	348	138
1904	261	133	263	83	130	166	434	173
1905	343	125	241	72	138	140	290	174
1906	354	140	246	72	110	150	224	176
1907	372	114	201	58	74	135	242	164
1908	278	98	201	59	61	127	266	136
1909	311	73	246	59	94	135	302	149
1910	213	75	278	56	114	100	234	127
1911	248	80	278	48	97	91	201	134
1912	178	59	284	49	78	86	201	105
1913	161	60	369	40	62	69	220	105

Note: Discounts plus Advances:Deposits.
( ) Discounts:Deposits.
Discounts and Deposits are based on yearly data.
Advances are based on yearly data ending February of the next year.

Source: See Tables 2.11, 2.14, 2.17 and 2.18.

However, this more restrictive policy on the part of London towards the provincial branches was never put into effect, and by the summer of 1894 the effects of the 'May scandal' had evaporated and the majority of the Directors had swung round again. One of the rare cases where a controversial discussion between the Directors was actually recorded in the Court minutes is the discussion on an application from the Newcastle branch agent in June 1894 on 'whether the Bank should discount or advance upon Bills drawn in the United Kingdom and accepted, payable in London, by an acceptor having only a foreign residence'. These were bills 'drawn against exports to European ports of coal, coke, machinery etc., which represent an important proportion of the best business of the port . . . . The Scotch banks take them freely, but not so the bankers and brokers in London.' The Committee for Branch Banks could not agree on this question and presented it to the Court for decision, without a recommendation. On the one hand it recognized that the business did not constitute an 'undue risk', but the adoption of business practices determined by the competition of the commercial banks contravened the principle that had only just been reaffirmed, namely that the provincial branches should follow London business practices. Remarkably, the majority of the Court approved the application from Newcastle despite these basic objections (BofE, CB No. 117, 21 June 1894).

A glance at the business trend at this time will explain the change in attitude. The discount and lombard business in London was in a serious crisis. Despite a key rate of 2 per cent and a share of around 11 per cent of the discount business handled at the private discount rate (compared with 5 per cent in the previous year), between the beginning of May and 21 June 1894, when this decision was taken, only £270,000 had been discounted (£3.3 million in the same period of the previous year), and around £100,000 in lombard loans given (£5.4 million in the same period of the previous year). The Directors had to find a means of compensating this, for a revival of the business in London was not to be expected over the medium term. The provincial branches proved relatively resistant to the trend, unlike London, and were clearly to be made even more resilient by giving the agents a largely free hand. For the rest, the practice adopted by the branch banks' office to the Birmingham branch shows that since 1894 the requirement that only 'London securities' should be accepted as cover had been little more than a formality. But, although at least the Birmingham branch was accepting bonds from local firms, with the support of the branch banks' office and with the knowledge of the Court of Directors (BofE, CB No. 117, 3 May 1894), the rules for the lending business in the provinces did not initially change.

In another way, however, the branches profited from the principle that their business was to be conducted like that of the head office. This was particularly the case with the relaxation of the regulations on the terms of the loans, that were mainly designed for London. The regulation of

February 1895, under which bills for up to 126 days could be regularly discounted and bills with a term of up to six months with the approval of the Governor (BofE, CB No. 117, 14 February 1895), presumably greatly suited at least the branches in Liverpool, Manchester and Newcastle, because until then they had suffered from being able to discount only bills with a term of at most ninety-five days. In their case it was the regulations on the term of the bills, rather than the criteria for their quality, that had been the main disadvantage in competition with the local commercial banks and, as a result, the branch agents had often ignored the regulations.

However, the Directors were not able to bring themselves to liberalize fully the bill lombard business. The new regulation of the autumn of 1895, under which loans for ninety-five days maximum could also be given against bills with a term of up to six months (BofE, CB No. 118, 5 September 1895) was clearly not sufficient to ensure a revival of the business in the provinces, unlike London. The doubling in the lombard business during the next two to three years was almost exclusively due to advances against stocks and bonds. This will certainly have been helped by the regulation of July 1894, under which advances 'for regular and valued customers and after careful consideration' could be prolonged frequently enough for these credits to 'assume a continuous character' (BofE, CB No. 117, 19 July 1895).

The long depression caused the Bank to look to the provinces with an attention it had not shown for decades. Unlike the winter of 1893/4, the Directors showed some understanding for the business practices of the branch agents. A report 'On the Business Conducted at the Branches' in July 1896 reached a positive assessment of the practice on the whole, which was really contrary to the 'spirit' of the 1894 rules (BofE, CB No. 119, 30 July 1896). Of course some criticisms were made — for instance, that interest rates were frequently too low, the cover for the credits still insufficient in some cases and the 'class of securities' often rather 'poor'. Altogether, however, the Committee concluded that 'the loans are well secured as a whole with a little risk of loss'.

Six months later the Committee for Branch Banks presented a report on the way the 1894 rules were working (BofE, CB No. 119, 4 February 1897). However, they did not, interestingly enough, go into the possible discrepancy between the 'spirit' of the rules and current practice. Possibly the members of the Committee did not wish to provoke those Directors who wanted the provincial branches to operate on London principles by calling that into question. The Committee for Branch Banks was pragmatic and it did not touch the substance of the rules, it only recommended further relaxation on certain individual points, such as ceasing to insist on the burdensome transfer of all securities to London and greater flexibility on interest rates (BofE, CB No. 119, 4 November 1897).

The fruits of this policy were the enormous increase both in the lombard and the discount business (and of course in interest earnings) in the second half of the 1890s. As during the years 1889–91, the provincial branches were able to benefit from the cyclical upswing of 1896–1898/9, but this time at a higher level. The lombard business reached its peak in mid-1898, when the August balance sheet showed an increase in business of 110 per cent from the August balance sheet of 1894, which had been affected by the depression and restrictive application of the rules. The discount business reached its peak in 1899 with an increase of 90 per cent over 1894. In February 1899 a profit of £150,000 could be transferred from the provincial branches' credit business to the accounts. That was 16 per cent of the Banking Department's gross earnings (see Table 2.16).

The decline in the provincial branches' lending business that began in 1899 and was clearly visible in 1900 was not, unlike the situation in the mid-1890s, due to a decline in domestic economic activity. On the contrary, the cyclical indicators for gross domestic product and net investment suggest that the cycle only reached its peak in 1899/1900.[32] Business in London was also still expanding. The decline in the lending business for the provincial branches was therefore exclusively due to a decision by the Court of Directors of February 1899 to require branch agents to reduce loans that had come to be of a long-term nature, although the instruction was tempered by stating that not too much pressure need be put on the borrowers. The main reason for this measure was given as the current situation on the stock market (BofE, CB No. 121, 16 February 1899). Naturally this meant the London Stock Market.

The situation on the London Stock Market at the time is evident from the Money Market Report on 11 February 1899 in *The Economist*:

> No fresh feature has developed itself in the market during the past week. Money has been in very strong demand in connection with the Stock Exchange settlement. In certain departments, such as those for American securities and South African mines, that has been heavy almost, if not quite, beyond precedent, and all around there appears to have been a broadening out of business on the Stock Exchange. Even though special arrangement had been made, the Stock Exchange Clearing House has again been unable to cope with the work thrown upon it, and consequently as a fortnight ago, large advances have had to be obtained from the Bank . . . . With trade expanding, with business on the Stock Exchange developing with unexpected rapidity, with a number of new loans getting ready to be launched . . . bankers are consequently right in being chary of tying up their funds at the rates now current. (*The Economist*, 11 February 1899, p. 191)

So the Bank was preparing for an increase in demand on the market as the spring went on; its current situation was anything but a cause for concern. The gold stock held by its Issue Department was rising slightly and, together with the seasonal inflow of deposits, it would be more than enough to meet a rise in demand for credit. Altogether the main items in the balance sheet were about the same as in the previous year.

As the year went on the demand for credit did rise, as *The Economist* had predicted. It is particularly evident from the development of the lombard loans against stocks and bonds in Threadneedle Street that the decision by the Court to reduce long-term lending was directed mainly at the provinces and not London. The normal advances on securities (unlike the short-term Stock Exchange 'advances on floaters') did rise in Threadneedle Street in the 1898/9 half-year accounts but only to on average £3.8 million compared with on average £3.5 million in the 1898 half-year, as this balance sheet (drawn up as per 28 February) would naturally not yet be greatly affected by the increase in demand. But in the 1899 half-year accounts the amount had risen to an average of £4.6 million. Turnover in lombard loans on bills and 'advances on floaters' was rather higher in the 1899 half-year than in 1898/9. Only the provincial branches' advances on stock declined over this period, from £6.4 million on average for the banking half-year 1898 to £6.0 million in 1898/9 and £5.8 million in 1899 (see Table 2.18).

A week after the decision by the Court of Directors to reduce advances that were tending to become long-term, the Special Committee sent a memorandum to the branch agent in Birmingham, requesting him to raise his interest rates for these loans (BofE, BBALB In No. 15, 22 February 1899). Three months later all the branch agents were instructed by London to avoid granting new loans on account of the low gold reserves in the Issue Department and the continued pressure on the reserves, and to increase their interest rates further for the tendentially long-term loans; if possible these loans should be reduced, especially if the cover was 'Industrials' (BofE, BBALB, in No. 15, 7 May 1899).

Only after the outbreak of the Boer War at the end of 1899 did the branch managers have to cut their lending to such an extent that the lombard business virtually broke down for the provincial branches (see Table 2.18), and then Threadneedle Street also felt the restrictions. The decline in the advances against securities in London and the provinces by 25 per cent[33] did not, however, visibly benefit the central bank reserves. It formed a buffer for the enormous increase in demand on the money market (the brokers' loans, that is, lombard loans on bills and advances on floaters, were the indicator of this), as stock brokers and discount houses sought to fund at the Bank of England to meet the tighter money situation (the issue of government stock to finance the war in South Africa).

Although the provincial branches' lombard business did not recover from this decline, their lending business remained a major factor in the Banking Department's accounts (see Table 2.16) in the last decade before the First World War, despite the restrictive application of the rules. The fears expressed by the Principal of the branch banks' office in 1904 did not materialize (BofE, Edye Report G 15/39). The Bank did not return to the conditions of the 1880s, when its portfolio structure was very similar to that of an investment trust. On the contrary, better co-operation with the commercial banks paid off in that five out of the eight most important provincial banks again began to rediscount regularly at the Bank of England. In the cities where bills were still (or once more) playing an important role as a means of payment, the discount business for the Bank of England branch from about 1904 to 1905 rose clearly above the level of the second half of the 1890s. The average holding of bills in the provincial branches' portfolios was almost twice as high as during the preceding five years, thanks to the revival in business in Liverpool and Manchester and to a lesser extent in Newcastle and Leeds (see Table 2.17).

In the cities where bills had been replaced by cheques as a means of payment and book credits as an instrument for loans, an expansion in the discount business was not possible. The conditions were also very unfavourable for a renewed expansion in the lombard business. The only incentives were the interest rates at which the provincial branches would give lombard loans. 'Trading customers' had to pay only a quarter to a half per cent above Bank Rate (discount rate) for their loans. While the Bank endeavoured to keep the lombard rate between 3 per cent and 4 per cent in times when the discount rates were very low, in keeping with the practice of the provincial banks, when London rates were very high ('owing to international reasons'), it did without the premium and in exceptional cases would actually lombard below Bank Rate (BofE, BBO Special Reports No. 607b). The strict ban on overdrafts and the restrictive rules on securities were, however, a major obstacle to more active lombard business. In 1911 the ban on overdrafts, which dated from 1894, was modified for the chief cashier in London to the extent that overdrafts up to £100 were no longer subject to approval (BofE, CB No. 134, 6 July 1911). Whether this also applied to the provinces is, however, doubtful, for it is not mentioned in the new version of the regulations for the branches a year later (BofE, CB No. 135, 18 April 1912).

The change in the rules in 1912 did not affect the strict refusal to accept local securities either. Although in London 'securities not quoted at London Stock Exchange' were still not acceptable, the rule for the branches was: 'No advance on securities officially quoted on any of the recognised Exchanges, not even for sole and valued customers, until after special reference to the Governor' (BofE, CB No. 135, 18 April 1912). This rule corresponds precisely to the account given by the Governor of the Bank of England to the US National Monetary Commission: the Bank granted advances 'on the various classes of marketable securities, quoted on the London Stock Exchange, with the exception of mining shares; also with discretion good securities not so quoted, when their value can be ascertained' (Gregory 1964, Vol. 2, p. 311). The flexibility of the concept of 'value' is evident from the example of the Birmingham branch during the 1890s.

3

The limits to central bank policy

The central bank policy measures employed by the Bank of England and the development of central bank techniques have been the subject of numerous works on the international gold standard before the First World War. Most of them draw basically on Sayers' *Bank of England Operations*, which appeared in 1936 and, judging by the sources available at the time, gives an almost complete survey of the development of central bank policy in England between the Baring crisis and the First World War. Sayers bases his account mainly on contemporary periodicals (*The Economist* and *Statist*) and the major older works, Bagehot's *Lombard Street* (1873), Palgrave's *Bank Rate and the Money Market* (1903) and Withers' *The Meaning of Money* (1909).

The first analytical evaluation of almost all the sources in the Bank of England archives that are relevant to the subject was presented by J. Clapham in 1944. His evaluation of the minutes of the Court of Directors and the Committee of Treasury as well as other sources is a valuable addition to Sayers' work, because Clapham examines the question of the development of central bank policy over a very much longer period than Sayers. The quality of both works is evident from the fact that Sayers can deal with the quarter-century before the First World War in his great three-volume monograph of 1976 on the Bank of England in only sixty-five pages. Apart from a short eleven-page section on business policy, this is largely a summary of what he had to say in 1936 and of Clapham's work of 1944. So it is not surprising that Collins drew mainly on these works by Clapham and Sayers for the section on the Bank of England in his recent history of British banking (Collins 1988, Ch. 6, pp. 167–97). In view of the state of research on this question, there seems to be little point in repeating the results in detail here.

There is much less clarity on the question of the predominance of central bank policy considerations over the Bank of England's interests as a commercial bank. I have considered this question in detail elsewhere, and it is not necessary to repeat my arguments here. This chapter is therefore concerned with the question of what was actually understood by a central bank before the First World War. Was it to be a switchboard for the gold standard as a kind of monetary free trade system, or an agency for the emergent 'intervention state'? Although this problem is seldom thematized, most authors see central bank policy as explicit in the system of the international gold standard, the 'rules of the game'. In so far as the Bank of England acted largely according to these rules, it could not conduct counter-cyclical policy and, to that extent, *ipso facto* it could not be an agency for the emergent intervention state, for its monetary policy would necessarily have a pro-cyclical effect. Comparatively little attention is paid in this context to Sayers' argument that partial deviations from the rules of the game derived from the 'tenderness towards home trade and industry'. Sayers is drawing here on the comment by the Governor of the Bank of England, Cole, in 1911, quoted on p. 2 above. Sayers comments: 'Though nothing can be proved from the statistical evidence, the available figures are at least consistent with what the Bank said it was doing and with what the contemporary commentators said it was doing' (Sayers 1976, Vol. 1, p. 43; see also Dutton 1984, pp. 174–6).

The only evidence Sayers offers in interpreting such comments as an indication of a responsibility that goes beyond the rules of the game is the more cautious handling of Bank Rate after the 1890s. The following chapter outlines the state of development of central bank policy to the provinces during the three different periods, first, under the 'Palmer Rule', second, during the credit crises under Peel's Act, and third, in the calmer period after 1866. Particular attention will be paid to the reasons for the application of different measures in the range of central bank policy instruments with regard to 'tenderness towards domestic industry and trade'.

3.1 From the 'Palmer Rule' to Peel's Act

The decision by a government to define the currency of a country in terms of a certain relation to a precious metal required the legislature and the banking system to observe certain rules. The legislature had to lay down in law the obligation to purchase and exchange gold, and instruct a certain institution, such as the Treasury or a central bank of issue, to perform this task. Moreover, the trade in gold, especially imports and exports of gold, could not be subject to any restrictions. The banking sector also had to operate a payments-balance oriented policy, that is, the inflow and outflow of gold could not be compensated by the creation of money or its destruction. During the nineteenth century this function of steering the money supply was transferred to a central bank of issue in most gold standard countries, and the bank then had to ensure that the amount in circulation always corresponded to its currency reserves, so that the effect of payments balance disequilibria on economic activity was strengthened or at least made possible.

The need for regulation naturally applied mainly to the outflow of gold. There might be many reasons for a gold outflow. First, the domestic economic activity might be overheated so that gold had to flow out to compensate for surplus imports of goods. Great Britain had a chronic trade balance deficit throughout almost the entire later period under consideration, and this could be so increased that it could no longer be compensated by the invisibles on current account, such as net earnings by the merchant navy and the reflows from capital investments overseas. Second, a crisis abroad could cause arbitrage operations against London, as the gold flowed to the financial centre which had the highest interest rate. Third, capital exports could be far in excess of interest earnings and reflows. In all these cases the contraction of the central bank reserves would drive interest rates up, so that both the level of interest rates in London made the arbitrage operations unprofitable (with effects on the balance of payments) and the issue of bonds became too costly for borrowers overseas. In addition, the increase in the interest rate level would dampen the domestic cycle (with effects on the trade balance) and so throttle goods imports. Moreover, the deflationary effect on the price level should increase goods exports and possibly replace imported goods. In so far as the level of interest rates in the provincial industrial centres could be influenced by the London level, one can certainly say this was cyclical steering.

However, in this case the recessionary effects of monetary policy would also occur, if the domestic activity was anything but overheated — for instance, when independent developments overseas made it seem necessary to raise interest rates in London. In such a case the result would be not so much an inflow of gold from abroad, but more that gold would flow from domestic circulation to London (together with deposits at commercial banks). This could cause sudden leaps in interest rates in the provinces, even if the level was generally slack, and these sudden leaps would frequently counteract the trend in interest rates that was needed for the economic recovery. A monetary policy by the central bank oriented consistently to the balance of payments, however, did not on principle exclude consideration for these problems. How great the scope was for the central bank depended mainly on the legal framework — the scope the legislature was prepared to allow the central bank at all. For the Bank of England this scope was relatively great after the reintroduction of sterling convertibility following the Napoleonic Wars. However, Peel's Act of 1844 greatly restricted it, and the possibilities for a counter-cyclical monetary policy were much more limited before the First World War in England than they were for the central banks in comparable European countries.

During the 1830s the Bank of England's central bank policy was determined by what is known as the 'Palmer Rule' of 1832. This was a policy outlined by Governor Palmer of the Bank during his period in office (1830–3) and presented to a Parliamentary Committee of Inquiry. Under Governor Palmer and his three successors, the Bank expressly avoided competition with the commercial banks and aimed actively to expand lending only if the market needed support. This was to prevent restrictive effects from the 'rules of the game' of the gold standard, particularly if the Bank of England's gold holdings were to be reduced temporarily by other than cyclical causes. Instead of immediate recourse to measures to protect the gold reserves, the aim was to increase goods exports (that is, to pursue a policy oriented to the trade balance as well) and replenish the gold holdings over the medium term (see BPP 1831/2, evidence Palmer, qq.72–96, 561–74; BPP 1840, evidence Palmer, qq.1368–9, 1426–1435; BPP 1847/8, Part 3, evidence Palmer, q.838; Fetter 1965, pp. 149–51; Horsefield 1949, pp. 143–58). Naturally this policy must never be taken so far as to jeopardise the convertibility of sterling. This purpose was also served by the policy of excluding all the factors that could undermine the Bank's monetary policy. So the Palmer Rule was an attempt at a compromise between acting as lender of last resort and as guardian of the gold standard.

These two objectives required different measures, and naturally during the 1830s there were frequent conflicts between them. It was difficult for the Bank to identify the point where the contraction of the gold reserves was no longer of a temporary nature and the restoration of balance of payments equilibrium required a cautious policy to protect the gold reserves. If the Bank reacted too late, it had to put on the emergency brakes. This inevitably caused credit restrictions for the commercial banks, and in the extreme case could spark off a financial crisis. As Levy-Leboyer was able to show, the Bank did fail to recognize the crucial point in time twice at the end of the 1830s (in 1837 and at the beginning of 1839), and he sees this as the reason for a reorientation on the part of the Bank. The pragmatic directors decided for one of the two objectives and after the 1839 crisis oriented their policy exclusively to the convertibility of sterling (Levy-Leboyer 1982, pp. 85–93).[1] Thereafter trade balance disequilibria ceased to be a problem to the bank, as long as they could be compensated by other factors in the payments balance. What mattered was only to remove payments balance disequilibria. What effects the measures to balance the payments had on the trade account was of minor importance, as long as they secured equilibrium in the payments balance. The separation of the Bank into two departments introduced in Peel's Act, and the related quasi-automatic protection of convertibility were therefore welcomed by the majority of the directors. Therefore the Bank, if only to ensure the liquidity of the Banking Department, had to counter the withdrawal of gold with credit restrictions. But this was done only indirectly, to maintain confidence in gold convertibility (Goodhart 1972, p. 206, Dornbusch and Frenkel 1984, p. 260; Collins 1988, pp. 180–1). Holders of Bank of England notes did not need to fear for convertibility in view of the low fiduciary issue. The Bank was much more concerned about the convertibility of deposits, that is, exchanging book money for cash.

Limiting the fiduciary issue of banknotes after 1844 meant that the banking system was no longer in a position to adapt the growth in the money supply to cyclical fluctuations. The possibilities for the provincial banks of issue to have a compensatory effect were even more restricted than for the Bank of England (see section 2.2.2). If they had reached the top limit of their issue, they initially tended to turn down any further requests for credit rather than control demand by varying interest rates.[2] In the view of the majority of contemporary economic historians, the prospects of being able to expand the money stock (defined as notes and coin) if demand for credit rose, could undermine the 'salutary effect' of contracting the money supply. In the words of Lord Overstone, the quotas imposed for issues by all the banks of issue were to 'compel both the public and the Bank to form a more definite estimate of the true limits of the resources of the Bank' (BPP 1857, evidence Overstone, q.3646). The clear limits to which the Bank of England was subject with regard to supporting commercial banks with liquidity problems, were to induce the commercial banks to cut down their lending in good time and comprehensively, in the interests of their own liquidity. If they did not do this, and even if only because their asset structure did not permit it, the inevitable result would be that the bank would have to cease payments. This is precisely the reason for the 'almost pathological concern with liquidity' on the part of the English banks which Cameron complains of (1982, p. 106). It was to be left to the market to ensure order, while the state saw its task as preventing an inflationary price development induced by the fiduciary banknote issue with an effect directed at throttling the import of goods.

A petition against Peel's Act by 'Merchants and Traders of London' describes the direct effects of the Act on the policy of the Bank of England and its indirect effects on the credit supply in the provinces as follows:

> It is in the nature of mercantile dealings, when duly supported, to rectify, within a reasonable time, any temporary inequality which temporarily disturbing causes may produce; on which account it is essential that the power of giving temporary aid, if called for by the mercantile body at such periods of emergency, should exist. It has recently become apparent that the Bank of England is restrained by legislative enactment from giving such facility, if called for. The establishment has been compelled, by the operation of the existing law, to refuse discounting commercial bills of the first credit, having not more than three months to run. The fact of such refusal, together with the knowledge of the ground on which it was made, produced such a degree of consternation and disturbance of public confidence throughout the country, that commercial bills could only be discounted at all to a very limited extent, and at rates of interest hitherto unknown in this country. One consequence was the immediate suspension of the executing of orders for manufacturers for distant markets, at the very moment when there was an obvious policy in facilitating exports of British production. (quoted from Gregory 1964, Vol. 2, p. 4)

The provincial banker Wright, who preferred to cut down his lending if funding under 5 per cent was not possible rather than charge 'exorbitant interest rates', described the effects on the clothing firms in Nottingham during the 1847 crisis as follows:

> They could not execute orders. In many cases they could not get their bills discounted. I speak from experience. Customers used to come for increased assistance, and I said: 'No, the law forbids me now. You must turn out your hands. I cannot assist you any longer, under the law of 1844'. (BPP 1847/8, Part 3, evidence Wright, q.2920)

So Wright thought the central bank should have other priorities in its monetary policy. In answer to the question whether he thought it advisable not to reduce banknote circulation if there were an outflow of gold he said:

> Certainly, it is desirable that it should not be lessened but rather that it should be increased under such circumstances, because the amount of circulation out is no criterion of the wants of the country . . . . The question is whether it is desirable to preserve what is called 'convertibility' or to ruin the country. (BPP 1847/8, Part 3, evidence Wright, qq.2935–6)

Naturally, the Bank of England did not see 'preserving convertibility' and 'ruining the country' as acceptable options; to the Bank the first was the way to prevent the second. Critics like Wright were not taken seriously by the Bank of England. It was assumed that they merely wanted to escape the consequences of their own excessive speculation. G.J. Goschen, a director of the Bank of England and later Chancellor of the Exchequer, said in 1865, only a year before the third suspension of the cover requirements:

> It is not too much to say that in many quarters it was hoped that the Bank Act of 1844, which had already been suspended twice, would break down again, a catastrophe which it was believed on all hands would give the death blow to the obnoxious system. The day was always invoked when another deputation of bankers and money dealers might wait on the Government with threats of an universal suspension of payments, if the magic letter were not conceded to put an end to that intolerable system — doubtless the deputation would have called it a cast-iron system — whereby men are prevented from fulfilling engagements into which they have knowingly entered beyond their means. (reprinted in Goschen 1905, pp. 14–15)

So the Bank did not see its restrictive policy as a measure enforced by Peel's Act to prevent it from encountering liquidity problems, but as a kind of stringent measure to force the spread of sound funding methods. The priorities set by the Bank of England directors are very clear from the answer by Governor Morris to Lord Bentinck before the Parliamentary Committee of Inquiry of 1848 (BPP 1847/8, Part 1, evidence Morris and Prescott, qq.3788–99). The question was in reference to Morris' comment on the letter from the government allowing the strict cover regulations in Peel's Act to be suspended temporarily, so enabling the Bank to come a little way towards the policy Wright wanted.

Bentinck: You said in your evidence that you thought it would have been very detrimental if the restriction had been taken off the Bank earlier than the period, at which it was removed in the month of October?

Morris: I stated that in my opinion, it would have been detrimental.

Bentinck: You stated that the Bank was perfectly prepared to maintain the law, but 'that there were other political motives which might influence the Government, such as the stopping of mills and so on'?

Morris: I stated that, as far as the Bank was concerned, it was not requisite that the letter should have been issued, but whether the Government had any political reason of their own, such as the stopping of mills or disturbances in the country, that was a subject for the consideration of H.M. Government, not for the Bank of England.

Bentinck: It would, at all events, have been detrimental to the Bank, because it would have reduced their profit.

Morris: I meant that it would have been detrimental to the interests of the country.

Bentinck: Then you think the stopping of the mills advantageous to the country?

Morris: I am not prepared to say that that which was represented would have taken place, I doubt it very much.

Bentinck: But do you not think the staying of the panic a fortnight earlier would have been the very reverse of detrimental?

Morris: No, because I think it might have checked the importation of precious metals which was then taking place . . . . Gold was coming into the country, and any relaxation making money easier might have been the means of checking the importation of the precious metals, and so far have been detrimental to the interest of the country . . . . The letter being issued earlier might have put off the distress for a short time, but, in my opinion, the result would have been that the interests of the country would have suffered more severely, as it would have delayed the rectifying state of things generally in the country.

The banks and industrialists in the provinces did not see this policy, which was directed to maintaining the convertibility of sterling, as a monetary policy oriented to the medium-term national interest. They were more concerned with the availability of means of payment and credit. The representative of the Chamber of Commerce in Leeds, Cardwell, told the Parliamentary Committee of Inquiry on Bank Acts in 1858, in answer to the question whether the convertibility of the Bank of England notes was 'a matter of no importance, and no consideration' to the inhabitants of Leeds: 'The class of people who are manufacturers, and others, do not enter into these minute questions; they look simply to the mode of getting money to meet their obligations' (BPP 1858, evidence Cardwell, q.5744).

Although the cover regulations in Peel's act were suspended three times — in 1847, 1857 and 1866 — the legislation was not changed. One attempt by Lowe as Chancellor of the Exchequer was rejected as impractical. Lowe wanted to increase the fiduciary issue, if the key rate should rise to at least 12 per cent and the rate for sterling on international financial markets as a whole be satisfactory (Palgrave 1910, pp. 179–81). There had never been a Bank Rate of 12 per cent at that time, nor was there to be in the following decades. A practicable compromise between the 'education aim' as formulated by Overstone and an institutionalized barrier to the collapse of the credit system was not possible.

3.2 The Bank of England and the mid-nineteenth century crises

After Peel's Act the Bank of England was freed of any regulatory responsibility and, initially, it did not act in the provinces any differently from the provincial banks. On the first conflict that arose after 1844, in April 1847, between the growth in the money stock needed for cyclical reasons and a contraction of the circulation to maintain convertibility, the Bank instructed its branch agents to ration credit (BPP 1847/8, Part 1, evidence Morris and Prescott, qq.2864–71, 2987). Except in Leeds and Leicester, the Bank of England discount rate in the provinces remained well below 5 per cent and so clearly below the London level. The only way to intervene in such conditions was to ration credit. The storm of protest which the measure evoked probably surprised the Bank of England. In the autumn of 1847 it therefore acted differently. This time it raised the minimum discount rate for its branches to more than 5 per cent, so that their top rates were actually above the London level. This did not completely prevent the Bank from acting as lender of last resort, but interest rates at such a level were sufficient, apart from emergency cases, to prevent a demand for Bank of England notes in the provinces that would be contrary to the Bank's objectives. Since many provincial banks were still not prepared to charge their customers more than 5 per cent, the old top rate under the Usury Laws, it was not to be expected that they would fund at 5½ per cent to 7½ per cent.[3] Accordingly, the bill holdings by the provincial branches rose by only 13 per cent in the crisis year 1847 from the previous year. In the last crisis year before Peel's Act was passed the rise was 68 per cent (BofE, SDC Reports, C 30/3).

These figures are averages for the year and they do not tell us anything about the way the Bank acted during the weeks of the crises. In fact, very little is known about this. As the example of the Leicester branch shows, the Bank was, however, endeavouring in the autumn of 1847 to avoid giving the impression that it was imposing credit restrictions. At the beginning of November some smaller textile firms asked the branch agent if they could discount bills at the Bank of England, since their own bank, Pares Leicestershire Banking Co., had refused to grant any more credit. The Governor agreed as an emergency measure, but the amount was not to exceed a total of £5,000 (BofE, LBALB Out No. 1,

5 November 1847 and In No. 1, 6 November 1847).

Probably all the branches gave assistance to this extent. Larger rescue operations are known to have been launched during the three crises in 1847, 1857 and 1866 only in Liverpool (BPP 1847/8, Part 1, evidence Morris and Prevost, q.2645) and Newcastle. As explained in Chapter 2, the Bank of England had succeeded by the end of the 1830s in linking almost all the banks in Durham and Northumberland to it by circulation accounts. Unlike agents in many other branches, the agent in Newcastle succeeded in maintaining good relations at least with the two most important regional banks, Lambton & Co., and the Northumberland & Durham District Bank, during 1844. Newcastle had actually become by far the most important rediscounting branch for the Bank of England by the end of the 1840s. The reason why the local banks clung to their contact with the Bank of England was presumably that they depended on the Bank as a local lender of last resort, owing to the nature of their lending business. Most of the Newcastle banks had been founded as 'coal banks', or they served other sectors of heavy industry. They had to lend according to the securities offered. With the great capital intensity of the local industry, most of these were illiquid securities, and especially in times of depression, they were inconvertible. An additional problem was that some of the directors had a personal interest in ensuring that certain firms were given particularly generous credit.

Although mismanagement almost always played a determinant part (McCord 1979, pp. 62–3; Thomas 1934, p. 546), it was rather due to a structural problem in the British banking system after 1844 that these industrial banks had hardly a chance of survival. Covering long-term loans with short-term deposits could only succeed if there was a funding institution that on principle acknowledged that imbalance. The Bank of England was not willing to, nor could it, play such a part, and it was almost inevitable that all the Newcastle banks would break down around the middle of the century. The financial market in the north-east of England was worse affected in the crises in 1847, 1857 and 1866 than those in other parts of the country.

The first bank to fail, in the winter of 1846/7, was the relatively small Newcastle Joint Stock Bank. Its collapse did not cause further problems, because the 'gap' it made was easily closed by the other banks. However, the situation was to be very different with the collapse of the North of England Joint Stock Bank in April 1847. The additional demand from customers of this 'coal bank', whose circulation account limit until recently had been £100,000 (Newcastle Joint Stock Bank for comparison £10,000, see BofE, BBO Bank Note Composition C 79/26) could not so easily be met by the other local banks. In particular, the largest of these, the Northumberland & Durham District Bank, had considerable problems (BofE, NBALB, Out 24 April 1847 and 15 May 1847). After some hesitation the Bank of England Head Office agreed to extend the credit lines for the District Bank from £400,000 to £500,000. Since the discount turnover of the Newcastle Branch did not rise noticeably in 1847, it may be assumed that the net increase was about the same amount that the North of England Joint Stock Bank had previously enjoyed. But despite the intervention of the Bank of England to ease the pressure on the District Bank, public confidence was shaken. The District Bank alone had lost around half a million pounds in deposits since the collapse of the North of England Joint Stock Bank. Since the branch manager of the Bank of England was not in a position to give further support, the manager of the District Bank went to London to speak to the Governor of the Bank in person (BofE, NBALB Out 19 October 1847).

The Newcastle, Shields & Sunderland Union Bank, that could not hope for a similar support action since it was a bank of issue, was the third local bank to go down within a year, despite an intervention by Lambton on 21 October 1847.[4] The run that followed this collapse surprised the Bank of England and the other banks considerably, as the Newcastle, Shields & Sunderland Union Bank had been suspect for a long time and its failure had actually been expected (BofE, NBALB Out 21 October 1847). But clearly this was the last straw. Confidence in the Newcastle banks was now really shaken and the District Bank found itself facing a run the next day as well.

Meanwhile the manager of the District Bank had returned form London without any tangible results. He knew that his bank could hold out against a run for only a few hours, unless he could find funding immediately. The Bank of England branch agent was now faced with the alternative of intervening at once on his own responsibility, or letting the fourth local bank within a year go down, and this time the largest. A few days later he sent the following report to his head office:

> It was a critical moment, there was no time for hesitation. I must either take on myself the entire responsibility of supporting them to an infinite and probably immense extent, or suffer them to stop payment at once, throw the town and neighbourhood for some time into a state of barter, and in all probability the two counties into a state of insurrection. There could be no half-measures, any advance short of the full amount they wanted would be only a useless exhaustion of the Bank's resources. I felt the responsibility was great but I at once determined to support them at any cost, on their depositing good security of any sort, with 50 per cent margin. The run on them was tremendous, the excitement in the town fearful, parties constantly arriving from the neighbourhood by railway jumped into coaches and made them gallop up to the bank, but it was evidently the run of a panic and I had little doubt if the bank could be carried through the greatest proportion of the money drawn would be replaced. I supplied them to an extent which enabled them to meet boldly every demand in notes or gold, as the party wished, they kept open an hour longer than usual and at the close of the day they had drawn from us £136,000. Saturday was market day which brought a number of the country people into the town . . . and before 12 o'clock they had drawn from us £128,0000, at this time it quite subsided, confidence was restored,

> parties who came for money went away without asking for it, others brought their money back . . . by the close of the day they were enabled to pay us back £30,000. (BofE, NBALB Out 26 October 1847).

Naturally the Newcastle branch was not in a position to meet such demand from its own resources. On the very first day of the run the gold holding had shrunk by more than half; nor would the stock of notes have sufficed to meet the demand expected on the following day. The Leeds branch sent enough gold to replenish the Newcastle stock and bring it back to the level at the beginning of the previous day (BofE, NBALB Out 22 October 1847).

The Bank of England was very much more restrictive in regard to the customers affected by the collapse of the Union Bank than it had been in its support of the District Bank. The failure of the Union Bank meant that many companies were unable to pay their wages on time, for the other local banks refused on principle to offer assistance in the first few days after the collapse for any but their own customers. Although the failure to pay wages made the situation dangerously worse,[5] the branch agent was very reserved towards these requests ('not wishing to open a door which might bring all the collieries on our shoulders', BofE, NBALB, Out 22 October 1847).

Although its support was limited mainly to local banks, the Bank of England did pursue a highly responsible policy in 1847 and did act as local lender of last resort, quite in contrast to the prevailing ideology. In view of the fortunate end to the crisis and the Bank's success in preventing the total collapse of the local financial market, it is not surprising that the head office subsequently approved the action of its agent in Newcastle. However, it should not be overlooked that this was an autonomous operation carried out by the North of England branches out of their own resources, that is, without recourse to London. Nor should it be disregarded that the Bank of England was on principle not prepared to support 'industry banks' whose portfolios were necessarily much less liquid than those of London banks. In addition to the criticism, which was fully justified, of the preferential treatment given to some firms (including that of the managing director), the Bank of England also objected on principle to the business policy of the country banks in industrial regions. The District Bank

> is agrounded on that shoal on which all joint stock banks run, viz., by investing deposits on securities which tho' perfectly safe are useless in times like these, and which the District Bank above all others should, from experience, have steered clear (BofE, NBALB Out 15 November 1857).

The Bank of England intervened in Newcastle in the crisis of 1857 as well, though this time the intervention was not spontaneous, it was a planned operation of quite a different kind from the action in 1847. Again the Northumberland & Durham District Bank was at the centre of the trouble. The Bank of England had had to support this bank until well into 1848 and, in doing so, intervened strongly in its affairs. The District Bank had had to reveal overdrafts given to its customers (BofE NBALB Out 14 March 1848) and dismiss one of its directors, who had allowed his private business to become too involved in the business of the bank (BofE, NBALB Out 17 March 1848). Although accommodation was drastically reduced from 1849, the District Bank remained dependent on funding through the Bank of England.

The Bank of England finally ceased giving direct assistance to the District Bank in November 1857, after its London agent had dishonoured its drafts. At the same time the Court of Directors authorized the Deputy Governor to start negotiations with the customers of the District Bank to limit the damage to the local economy. The branch agent, who was greatly in favour of this solution, said:

> I beg to acknowledge . . . the former authorizing me to assist as much as possible the manufacturies and collieries in this neighbourhood in meeting the pays of their workmen . . . . I beg to say that this liberal concession has been of the utmost benefit, as by it all the workmen in this district will this day receive their pay as usual, and thereby a calamity of the most disastrous kind has been averted from this locality . . . . Our counter has been completely besieged by parties wanting assistance to meet their wages . . . not one person having a pay to make . . . has been sent away without getting the required assistance. (BofE, NBALB Out 27 November 1857)

From the account by the branch agent one gains the impression that unlike 1847, when the Bank was not prepared to rediscount for non-banks, this time it mobilized additional resources for the north-east. But this was not, apparently, the case. The data on the lending business by the Newcastle branch shows that the sum, which totalled about £250,000 (see BofE NBALB Out 28 November 1857), was not additional credits which the Bank was pumping into the region. A comparison between the increase in the average bill holdings at the Newcastle branch (see Table 2.9) and the turnover in the discount business, divided into bankers' bills and traders' bills, shows that the increase in demand in 1854–7 was mainly from the local banks. Probably most of this was rediscounting for the District Bank, for the turnover in bankers' bills rose between 1854 and 1857 from £3.6 million to £5.3 million. After the fall of the District Bank it dropped to a total of £275,000 in 1858. Since the traders' bills rose from £1.2 million in 1857 to £1.8 million in Newcastle, contrary to the development at the other branches (BofE, SDC Reports C 35/4), the Newcastle branch does not appear to have experienced much more through the collapse of the District Bank than a shift in its lending business from rediscounting for that bank to discounting bills for some of its customers. Since at the same time its average stock of deposits rose from only £80,000 before the crisis to more than £400,000 after it (see Table 2.8), the branch could probably have coped with the situation alone in 1857 (or with temporary support from one of the neighbouring Bank of England branches).

It is very difficult to make a general assessment of Bank of England policy in the provinces during the financial crises around the middle of the nineteenth century. In view of the interventions in Newcastle during the crisis weeks in 1847 and 1857, which was very courageous under the circumstances and very effective, and the internal comments by the branch agents quoted above (pp. 84 and 86), McCord reaches the following conclusion: 'The action of the Bank had been taken, not on commercial grounds primarily but explicitly to cushion society in the area against the sudden stoppage of funds normally provided by the failed bank' (McCord 1979, p. 64; see also McCord 1980, p. 42). The fact that the Bank incurred only a very slight risk and did not have to pump any of its London resources into the provinces, does not in itself contradict the fact that the Bank was acting as local lender of last resort, contrary to the prevailing ideas and mainly under pressure of a real need.

However, if one remembers that the Newcastle operations were absolute exceptions, and that the Bank otherwise oriented its business policy in the provinces almost exclusively to its own interests, ultimately a more critical view seems appropriate. What choice did the Bank of England have in Newcastle in 1857 and what might have been the consequences?

First, the Bank could have again shored up the District Bank, but this would most probably have meant throwing good money after bad. This was probably the worst of all options from the standpoint of the Bank of England.

Second, the Bank could have declined to rediscount bills for the District Bank and simultaneously rationed the funds available to the Newcastle branch for lending to its customers. The result would have been an immediate suspension of payments by the District Bank and most probably a run on the other banks. In this case a complete breakdown of the local finance market would have been inevitable, even if the Bank were then prepared to intervene as it had in 1847. The Bank would also have come under extreme pressure from the public. It had once before pursued such a course, in April 1847, but had to revoke the credit rationing at its provincial branches after public criticism that it had been empowered to set up its provincial branches in 1826 in order to support the various local finance markets which had suffered from the failure of dozens of country banks. Even worse, the breakdown of the Newcastle finance market would have caused the bankruptcy of many of the District Bank's customers. The Newcastle branch bank's bill portfolio was full of local bills rediscounted for the District Bank, and most probably a large portion of these would have been protested. Bad debts would then have been inevitable, because many of these customers could be expected to pay less than 20s in the pound.

The third option, shoring up the local finance market, would avoid these bad debts, it meant in short that the Bank enabled 'the manufacturies and collieries in this neighbourhood' to pay their debts, both for the workmen's wages and to their creditors, i.e. the Bank of England itself.

3.3 Tenderness for domestic trade and industry?

For many observers, Bank of England policy during the middle third of the nineteenth century was anything but satisfactory. Within forty years, between December 1825 and May 1866, the credit system broke down six times altogether — three times in the pre-Peelite era and three times under Peel's Act. The Bank of England must be held largely responsible for the fact that every downturn from the peak of the cycle during this period entailed a credit crisis. This was partly because the Bank did not yet know how to handle the instruments available to it (particularly during the 1830s), and partly because it did not want to use them (as in the vanguard of the 1847 crisis). In part, the Bank was also powerless in view of the existing legislation. During the following half-century the Bank's policy had very much more positive results. There were no credit crises between 1867 and 1913, although the Bank certainly had the opportunity to bring one about during this period, particularly in November 1890. The outflow of gold was stopped by raising the level of interest rates in good time by a moderate but effective amount. This also facilitated the adjustment process and prevented a breakdown of the payments system that depended on credit. For once the credit system was shaken, the Bank could do no more under Peel's Act than it actually did in the crisis weeks in 1847, 1857 and 1866.

The Bank could pursue such a forward-looking policy even under the restrictions imposed by Peel's Act, and after the crisis of 1866, the calls for it to do so became ever louder. It is evident that from the 1870s the Bank was endeavouring to prevent the collapse of the credit system, and succeeding. Anna Schwartz has therefore given the Bank of England good marks for its central bank policy, for she sees the task for state or quasi-state institutions in the finance sector as largely to prevent 'real financial crises'.[6] By giving 'timely predictable signals to market participants . . . to make available an augmented supply of funds' (Schwartz 1986, p. 21) the Bank fully met its responsibility as a central bank, according to her. It could do this either by measures to maintain its minimum reserves (raising Bank Rate and/or open market policy) or by special measures like setting up a guarantee fund for the London merchant bank Baring Bros. when it was in trouble, and directly acquiring gold from Russia and France in the autumn of 1890.

Apart from that one exception, however, it needed do no more to that end than pursue a policy directed to maintaining its own liquidity. While the Bank also accepted that the market regarded a central bank reserve of at least £10 million as desirable in the 1870s and 1880s (and £20 million before the First World War), and regarded a central bank reserve of £10 million plus as adequate to guarantee the solvency of the Bank of England and so the financial sector as a whole, this mutual illusion prevented a collapse of the credit system after 1866.

Measured by its later experience and by other central banks at this time, the Bank of England was working in literally ideal conditions for a central bank. Whether gold was exported from California, Australia, Russia or South Africa to Germany, France, Italy or elsewhere, it passed through London and often disappeared for a time into the vaults of the Bank of England. The Bank's key rate was not particularly effective in relation to the market rates in London, but if the Bank succeeded in raising the level of interest rates in London, it could draw as much gold from the major world financial centres as it believed was necessary to secure the convertibility of sterling. In many cases it was sufficient simply to raise Bank Rate to induce the Banque de France, the Reichsbank or another central bank to come directly to the support of the Bank of England and prevent either an uncontrolled outflow of gold from these countries to London, or competition over interest rate rises with the Bank of England (see p. 94 below). It was these extremely favourable conditions which gave the Bank of England power of disposition over the gold stocks of the world. Bloomfield therefore concludes that 'the success of the classical gold standard seems to have been attributable . . . primarily to a combination of unusually favourable institutional circumstances rather than adherence to any specific code of rules of central banking behaviour' (Bloomfield 1968, p. 30; see also Sayers 1957b, pp. 13–15; de Cecco 1974, pp. 117–20; de Cecco 1986, pp. 12–16; Drummond 1987, p. 21 and Bopp 1951, p. 244, n. 39).

However, does this conclusion really justify the statement quoted earlier: 'The first consideration of the Bank is the welfare of the trade of the country'? Without wanting to step outside its historical role, could the Bank really not be expected to do more than concern itself with its own solvency? The 'mercantile and banking community' of the City would certainly have given an affirmative answer to this question on the eve of the First World War. A hundred years of the gold standard, about seventy of them under Peel's Act, had made the City of London the 'mart and banker' of the world. The gold standard had become a sterling standard and almost the entire trade of the world was handled through sterling bills drawn on London: 'The multilateral system of payments . . . ensured that every thread of the world's commercial and financial networks passed through London, so that it was between 1870 and 1913 that the City was truly the economic heart of the world' (Crouzet 1982, p. 370). The prosperity of the City was thus largely independent of the prosperity of the 'workshop of the world'. Whether steel from Germany, Belgium, Great Britain or elsewhere was exported to the United States, Argentina or Australia, the payments were almost always handled through London, and the ships, if they were not British ships anyway, were at least insured in London. Thanks to the earnings in the services sector, the chronic trade balance deficit that had persisted since the 1870s was changed to a comfortable surplus (a very brilliant account in Hobsbawm 1980, pp. 143–4). Great Britain had become the most important creditor country in the world.

And the other side of the coin?

> To put it crudely, whilst many British industries were suffering from foreign competition, the City of London was in its heyday, funding and arranging and insuring and shipping — and thus profiting from the growth — in the trade of foreign countries. (Kennedy 1981, p. 49)

Naturally, this is not to say that a policy 'for the welfare of the country' means that the Bank should have actively concerned itself with the problem of the finance of industry, the structural weaknesses or the location problems of British industry, as it started to do in the interwar years (see Heim 1984, pp. 533–50; Sayers 1976, Vol. 1, pp. 314–30). But to concern itself exclusively with the success of the emergent services and *rentier* economy, to create conditions only for that, which permitted it to ensure at least a balance of payments equilibrium, was certainly not enough. There can be no doubt that within the 'rules of the gold standard' as well as under the constraints of Peel's Act a certain consideration for counter-cyclical policy was possible.

The way the Bank of England handled the key rate is a test case. As already explained, an increase in the interest rate level in London not only brought an inflow of gold from abroad, it also attracted gold to London from the domestic circulation (in addition to the deposits at commercial banks). Although interest rates in the provinces were generally very slow to move, this could cause sudden leaps in provincial rates, which were often contrary to the trend needed for the economic recovery. It was assumed even by contemporaries that the Bank of England was increasingly aware of this problem in its discount policy and would attempt to cope with it by refining its policy instruments. Sayers adopts this view when he says:

> In the development of the technique of market control the Bank was obviously looking, on many occasions, simply to its end of keeping the market close to its own rate in order to give some reality to the latter's control of the foreign exchanges. But in doing this it had learned that, to some limited extent, market rates and Bank rate could be looked upon as independent weapons. Once this was realised the Bank could to some extent meet the public demand that it should resort to the method of raising the Bank rate as sparingly as possible . . . . Subsequently out of tenderness for home trade, the Bank endeavoured to avoid raising Bank rate . . . by resorting to these other devices for raising market rates. (Sayers 1936, pp. 68–9)

Sayers sees proof of this in the significant decline in the fluctuations in the Bank Rate from 1902 to 1905. During this period the rate was varied only about two to three times a year. The range of fluctuation was also very narrow, between 2½ per cent and 4 per cent, particularly since a Bank Rate of up to 4 per cent was regarded as harmless even during a depression phase (Sayers 1936, p. 89).[7] As an alternative to a further increase in the Bank Rate beyond 4 per cent, the Bank exerted more influence on the market rates with an active open market policy, so that the differences between the market and Bank rates were clearly less in these years than during the comparable cyclical phases in the mid-1890s and the second half of the 1880s (Palgrave 1903, Table 4, p. 33; Mitchell 1988, Table 15b, p. 683). Intervention on the gold market was also conducted in great style.[8]

After 1907, however, the restraint was over. In that year the Bank raised its key rate to the alarm figure of 7 per cent for the first time since 1873. In the following years it had frequent recourse to its discount policy and the questions arise: why could the Bank not expect the economy to take a Bank Rate of 7 per cent in 1899 but did so in 1907, and why did the Bank want to spare the economy more expensive credit during the depression and recovery phase, from 1902 to 1905, while in the comparable phase of the following cycle (1908 to 1910) it kept its Bank Rate well above 4 per cent for months at times? It also needs to be said that the more frequent variations in Bank Rate from 1907 to 1910 were just as significant as the reduction from 1902 to 1905. Their frequency actually regained the level of the 1880s, when the Bank's open market policy was still in its infancy.

A different motive must therefore be assumed for the differences in the Bank of England's handling of its central bank policy instruments during the first and second business cycle of the twentieth century than 'tenderness for home trade and industry'. The Bank's experience in handling its discount policy during the 1880s and 1890s was that market rates react extremely sluggishly to increases in the Bank Rate. Recourse to open market policy measures, like 'borrowing in the market' or selling Consols or other gilt-edged securities had been necessary to make its key rate bite and achieve the desired effect on exchange rates. In doing this the Bank had discovered that with an effective open market policy moderate increases in the key rate were sufficient to achieve the desired objective.

The Boer War brought the Bank out of the experimental phase and caused it to develop a systematic open market policy. Immediately after the outbreak of the war the British government appeared as a large borrower on the capital market. As banker to the government, the Bank of England now saw its task as keeping the level of interest rates as low as possible. The only meaningful way to do this was to develop its open market policy. The decision was facilitated by the fact that the heavy demand from the government gave the Bank an unusually strong position on the money market (see *Bankers' Magazine*, Vol. 71, January 1901, pp. 83–4). After this success, the Bank used its open market policy during the ensuing depression, particularly since the issue of more Treasury Bills had greatly strengthened its market position from 1902. Instead of, as hitherto, having to meet the government's short-term lending needs largely alone, the Bank of England could now take money out of the market by issuing Treasury Bills, as it felt appropriate (*The Economist* 9 August 1902, pp. 1243–4).

Very probably this policy was also even cheaper than the traditional discount policy. Measures that had a rapid effect quickly stiffened the market and the outflow of gold could be stopped at a relatively early stage. Both borrowing in the market and selling gilt-edged securities had their price, but raising the Bank Rate would first have only widened the gap between key and market rates and consequently have affected interest earnings, owing to the loss of competitiveness in the lending business. In this context Beach quotes the Chairman of the London Joint Stock Bank, who regarded the Bank of England's open market policy as extremely positive for the banks' earnings (Beach 1972, p. 131, note 5). The Bank of England tended to the same view, as *The Economist* had already rightly assumed in 1881.[9] Comparing the depression of 1901 to 1903 with that of 1893 to 1895, discount earnings in each of the weakest years of the depression in the 1890s were £8,200 (1894) in Threadneedle Street and £32,800 (1895) at the branches. The comparable figures in the depression during the following cycle were £39,000 (1901) in Threadneedle Street and £65,000 (1902) at the branches. Related to the best year in the previous boom the figures were 12.2 per cent (1894 over 1890) and 37.9 per cent (1901 over 1900) in Threadneedle Street, and 40 per cent (1895 over 1890) and 64.4 per cent (1902 over 1899) at the branches.

During the depression in the mid-1890s the Bank made the mistake of 'employing' its funds with additional investment in various securities, and in this way further depressing interest rates. In the depression phase of the following cycle it had to pay out around £12,000 in the 1901/2 accounting year and around £1,000 in 1902/3 in interest payments on open market operations. But this expenditure was quite disproportionate to the improvement in the discount earnings during this period and, if the open market policy should become too expensive, the Bank still had the possibility of inducing a direct inflow of gold by raising its buying price for gold coin.[10] Sayers also sees the need to lower costs as the evident motive for the active gold policy that was pursued on occasions. 'In the circumstances of the moment, making higher rates effective would have been an expensive business', he says. Accordingly, it is hard to see why Sayers accepted the profit motive as the reason for the alternative between open market policy and gold market intervention, but not for the alternative discount policy versus open market policy/gold market interventions. Clearly he regarded open market policy as more expensive on principle (see *The Economist* 15 February 1890; Sayers 1957b, p. 10). He could not explain the open market period from 1902 to 1905 otherwise. He expressly stressed that intervention on the gold market was the cheaper solution in view of the need to consider counter-cyclical policy: 'and in many cases the Bank was probably unwilling to embark on a high rate policy while home trade was so slack' (Sayers 1936, p. 95).

Why the Bank returned almost exclusively to the old discount policy after 1907 is something Sayers cannot explain in his interpretation. He only establishes the fact in his *Bank of England Operations* of 1936 (pp. 99–101) and sees it as due to the extraordinary success of discount policy in the crisis of 1907 and later. In his great monograph on the Bank of England of 1976, however, he appears able to remove this fault from his argument. He quotes an internal study in the Bank on the effects of varying the Bank Rate on the provinces (and thus on industry). Remarkably the Bank commissioned this study from its branch agents shortly before it raised the Bank Rate in October 1909 within only two weeks from 3 per cent to 5 per cent — during the same period market rates in London rose from 2.125 per cent to 4.5 per cent.

The study was carried out quite unsystematically by the individual agents, and bankers were questioned rather than borrowers. The statements reported accordingly differed widely. While a banker from Newcastle said that key rate variations (he no doubt meant increases) were good to show customers that interest rates had to be increased, the agent in Bristol saw a direct relation between a high Bank Rate and the increase in the number of bankruptcies. The principal of the branch banks' office also concluded, in his summary of the study, that the major customers of the commercial banks might be in a position to be given special conditions when Bank Rate was high, but 'the cotton business both at Liverpool in the raw material and at Manchester with the mills and spinners, and the wool trade generally and shipbuilding throughout the country is very much affected by the fluctuation of the Bank rate' (BofE, BBO Special Reports No. 534). In the best case the Directors could disregard the study. But to interpret the renaissance of Bank Rate as having proved that an active discount policy would not have negative effects on the domestic economy, as Sayers was a little inclined to do (Sayers 1976, Vol. 1, p. 44) hardly seems possible.

Naturally this is not to deny that the variations in the Bank Rate were generally intended to affect international capital flows. However, it cannot be contested that they also affected the credit supply in the provinces, and a central bank policy that was at least distinguished by consideration for counter-cyclical policy, must have taken that into account. The fact that credit rates were never really low in the provinces on account of the usual minimum deposit rate there of 2.5 per cent is no reason to see the increase in the level, that had been stable for so long if relatively high, as harmless. Only when the Bank Rate in London was high was it the 'effective rate in the provinces, whether it is so in London or not', as stated in *The Economist* of February 1890.[11] So the increase in the key rate by 2 percentage points within only two weeks in the autumn of 1909, when the domestic cycle was just beginning to recover, is simply indifference to counter-cyclical policy. The branch agents' survey did not alter that.

In another context Sayers' reasons for the renaissance in discount policy may, however, be very meaningful. He was certainly right to say that the increases in the key rate from 1907 had a faster and more direct effect than formerly. In the autumn of 1906 the Bank of England had established that it was not the interest differential between London and the other finance centres that was causing a 'free' inflow of gold, but that the Banque de France was buying bills to the value of £2.5 million in London for central bank policy reasons, paying in gold and so providing considerable relief in London. A year later the Bank of England discount rate again 'persuaded' the Banque de France, the Reichsbank and other central banks to come to the aid of the Bank of England's gold holdings, in their own interests (see Foreman-Peck and Michie 1986, pp. 392–3).[12] The US time rate was 13.5 per cent at the beginning of November and it did not drop below 10 per cent for the entire month. A key rate of 7 per cent in London could not therefore stop the outflow of gold to New York. To prevent a further rise in the Bank Rate in London, which would have inevitably disrupted the money markets in France and Germany even more than a rate of 7 per cent was doing already, the Banque de France and the Reichsbank preferred to come directly to the aid of the Bank of England in order not to prevent the uncontrollable outflow of gold on their side by raising key interest rates further. Altogether more than £19 million flowed to London in this way (see Beach 1972, pp. 143–6; Sayers 1936, Ch. 5, pp. 102–15; Hawtrey 1962, pp. 116–18; Clapham 1944, Vol. 2, pp. 391–2; Sayers 1976, Vol. 1, pp. 58–60).

There were a number of other cases in the following years when the Banque de France provided the Bank of England with gold reserves to prevent increases in the key rate in London. In so far, the huge gold reserves of the Banque de France were the '*masse de manoeuvre* of the Bank of England at almost no cost' (de Cecco 1986, p. 19; see also Kindleberger 1978, p. 189; Collins 1988, p. 157). It cannot be proved, but it is quite conceivable, that the Bank of England used the effect of its Bank Rate on the other financial centres to induce the Banque de France to place its gold reserves at the disposal of its central bank policy, not only in exceptional situations, like 1839 and 1890, but relatively regularly. Certainly, this recourse to the French gold holdings was cheaper for the Bank of England than either a corresponding increase in its own reserves or an active open market policy, such as it had pursued in the early years of the twentieth century. This was, of course, precisely the motive: to achieve an effect comparable to the old policy at very much lower cost. That is why the Bank gave up its discount policy in favour of open market/gold market policy from 1898/9, and that is why after 1906/7 it returned to its old policy, but under different conditions. To that extent, the interlude of open market policy had nothing to do with counter-cyclical considerations.[13] If the Bank had been concerned to pursue a monetary policy oriented to the domestic economy, it could not at any time during the quarter century before the First World War have had fewer scruples in raising the key rate strongly than in 1899 and 1900. The economy at that point in the cycle was overheated and a high rate could actually have been beneficial as a signal. This time the Bank did not raise the rate on account of the government's need for credit, but it did in 1907, when there was no such overheating (see also Clapham 1944, Vol. 2, pp. 391–4). So there can be no question of 'tenderness towards home trade and industry' from the Bank of England in the last two decades before the First World War either.

4

The Bank and industry: the example of Birmingham 1880–1905

Our account so far has been limited in the main to general trends in the Bank of England's policy towards the provinces or (industrial) borrowers there. The argument that the Bank was indifferent to counter-cyclical policy put forward in the last chapter has not really been proved yet. Our concern was rather to show that the thesis of 'tenderness towards domestic industry and trade' needed modifying. However, we were only able to show that the application of certain central bank policy instruments was not, or at least was not primarily, due to consideration for the supply of credit in the (industrial) provinces. Only a detailed examination of the Bank's business policy in the provinces would definitely show whether the Governors of the Bank were really, as has been maintained, 'indifferent to counter-cyclical policy'. The Birmingham branch is particularly appropriate for this, since its region was one of the industrial centres and the cradle of the 'new' (capital-intensive) industries in Britain. Moreover, 'Birmingham' to contemporaries was the national counterpart to the 'City', because its bankers and industrialists were traditionally the most outspoken opponents of a monetary policy oriented to the rules of the gold standard.

During the ninety years or so of its existence, up to the First World War, the Birmingham branch went through a very varied history, probably more varied than that of any other Bank of England branch. After its establishment it was one of the most active and profitable of the Bank of England's branches, but this was only of brief duration. From the mid-1830s it was overtaken by a growing number of other branches, and half a century after its establishment it was losing more than any of them. In the lending business it had fallen to seventh place behind the 'small' branches like Hull and Bristol. In the 1890s, finally, it experienced a sudden upswing, but again this was only of short duration. The 'M' curve especially (see Figure 4.2) in the lending business (advances and discounts) in the 1890s seems worth a more careful examination, particularly since this curve differs clearly from the development in the other provincial branches (Figure 4.1).

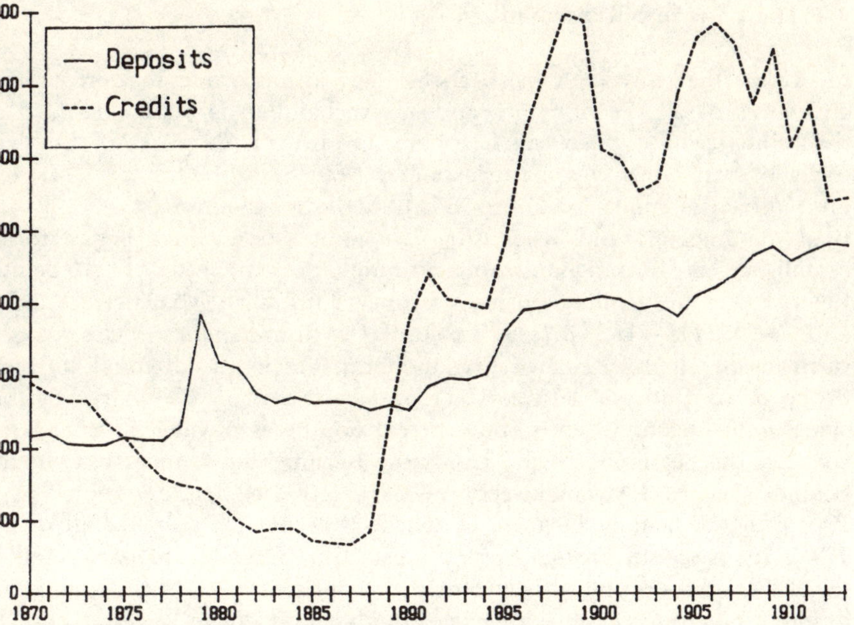

Figure 4.1 Bank of England branches' lending and deposits, 1870–1913 (£000)

Source: see Table 2.19.

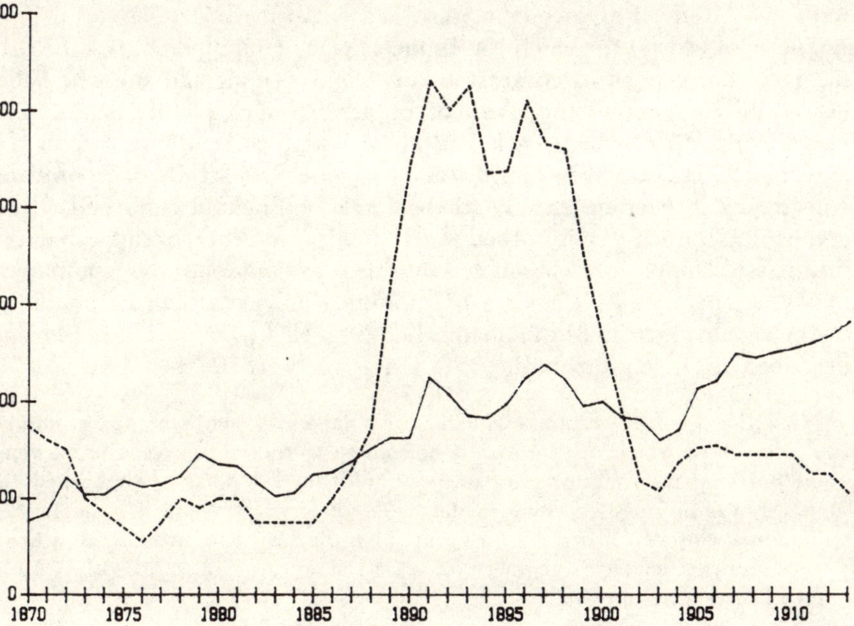

Figure 4.2 Birmingham branch lending and deposits, 1870–1913 (£000)

4.1 The crisis in bill discounting

In 1830 the Birmingham branch had around one-quarter of the customers of all the branches and it was handling around one-third of the total discount business (Clapham 1944, Vol. 2, p. 115). Only as issuer of banknotes was it surpassed by Manchester (see Table 2.3). But after the local banks had responded to the competition started by the Bank of England and when the first joint stock banks began to be established in Birmingham, the Birmingham branch fell back behind Liverpool in the lending business (from 1832), then Manchester (1834) and Newcastle (1839) (see Table 2.4). Birmingham's share of the turnover of all the Bank of England branches in the discount business dropped from 30 per cent in 1831 to 12 per cent in 1840. It kept that share until the mid-1850s, but thereafter it was always under 10 per cent. At the beginning of the 1860s the Birmingham branch was already behind Liverpool, Manchester, Leeds, Newcastle and at times even Bristol in the lending business (Table 2.9). From the second half of the 1860s the discount business was almost entirely limited to banks and in the 1870s traders' bills had largely disappeared from the Birmingham branch's portfolio. Even taking over the business of the Leicester branch, which had been closed in 1872, only brought four new customers with any discount business of note (BofE, BBO Special Reports No. 503a; see also Ziegler 1989b, pp. 19–21). At the end of 1876, of the former 250 active drawing accounts (not including stock accounts) only 111 remained (BofE, BBO Annual Statistical Reports C 79/21).

The high esteem in which the branch agent, Chippindale, was held by the local banks was in contrast to his slight commercial success. When he retired as agent of the Bank of England branch all the banks made him a present, to which each had contributed no less a sum than £30 (Sayers 1957a, p. 155). The esteem was due precisely to Chippindale's consistency in keeping strictly to the Bank of England rules and so not competing directly with the local banks in the normal banking business.[1] Chippindale's branch was also available to the commercial banks at any time as a source of funding,[2] but even then he could not do more business in Birmingham. Looking back, his successor Barham described the situation in the 1860s and early 1870s as follows:

> These [local banks' accounts with the Birmingham branch] were ten in number . . . seven of which never thought of coming to the Bank except to exchange old notes for new ones or sometimes for gold . . . . [It was] an established idea that it was no good to come to the Bank for anything . . . . The banks here are much closer to their London agents than they are at Manchester and Liverpool, and the managers go there for assistance of all sorts (BofE, BBALB Out No. 20, 6 October 1887).

It was in this situation that F.F. Barham took over the branch. Unfortunately we do not know whether the directors had chosen him in order to pursue a different policy in Birmingham, but it is certain that Barham began immediately 'to induce the banks to work with us and to keep accounts with some sort of life in them'. He did succeed in winning new customers or interesting old customers in the services the Bank could offer. Two years after Barham took over the branch the number of active drawing accounts had risen to 161 and to 167 (BofE, BBALB Out No. 18, 30 December 1878; 30 December 1879). However, this did not have any positive repercussions on the deposits maintained at the branch. Barham was not able to induce the banks to hold higher minimum balances if he wanted to do any business with them at all.[3] Instead the Birmingham branch's lending business improved markedly. The stock of bills in its portfolio rose, against the trend at the other branches, from on average £88,000 in 1876 to on average £139,000 in 1877 and £173,000 in 1878 (Table 2.11). The Birmingham branch's share of the discount business transacted by all the branches rose from 5 per cent to 9 per cent (1877) and 12 per cent (1878).

However, the growth potential in the lending business was now exhausted, and thereafter the trend in the discount business at Birmingham was more or less parallel to the general trend. The branch's share was relatively constant up to 1888 at 10 per cent to 15 per cent. Barham soon recognized that an expansion of the lending business was no longer possible in the traditional way, for the bill had largely been replaced by the cheque in the region, and bill discounting by advances on securities or overdrafts.[4] Since the branches were still denied any flexibility in interest rates, they were not competitive against the commercial banks in the provinces as long as the private discount rate did not apply there. For that reason Barham tried to win for himself more scope in interest rates in 1879. The answer from London, however, gave him no hope of vitalizing his discount business:

> This concession is only rarely made even in London and then to those firms who kept their sole accounts with us. It has never yet been extended to the branches, nor do I [the Principal of the Branch Banks' Office is writing here on behalf of the Deputy Governor] imagine there is any probability of its being so. (BofE, BBALB in No. 11, 22 July 1879)

The directors were still not interested in leaving the path they had taken in 1844. That applied to the direction of the provincial branches generally and their relation to the provincial banks in particular. The relation between the Bank of England and the provincial banks had improved slightly in the course of time — particularly in Birmingham — but the Bank of England was not prepared to revise the discount agreements concluded with the provincial banks on such stringent conditions. At the end of the 1870s it might have been opportune for a central bank interested in good relations with the commercial banks to make concessions. The old agreements of 1844, under which former banks of issue had received either a compensatory payment or a discount account at preferential conditions, had proved a disadvantage in the latter case for the commercial banks. From about the mid-1870s the margin between the Bank of England's key rate and the market rates had widened noticeably. The market rates were often under the 'preferential rate' and the commercial banks had to rediscount at the Bank of England at a rate at which they in turn could not invest.

Since 1845 the Bank of England had had a revised circulation account agreement with the Birmingham & Midland Bank, in the 1870s the second largest bank in Birmingham (BofE, CB No. 67, 30 January 1845). When the agreement was due to be prolonged at the end of 1879, the Birmingham & Midland Bank asked for a reduction in the current credit lines from between £36,000 and £40,000 to between £15,000 and £30,000 (BofE. Out No. 18, 17 November 1879; CB No. 102, 20 November 1879). A few months later it then suggested that it could handle its entire funding through the Bank of England, if it could rediscount at market rates at the Birmingham branch (BofE, BBALB Out No. 19, 19 April 1880).[5] But London would not agree:

> The Deputy Governor . . . regrets he is unable to hold out any hope of such concession being granted . . . . Discounting under Bank Rate (except in the Commutation Accounts) has not been extended to the Branches and in London is confined to firms (other than banking and discount houses) who kept their sole account with the Bank. (BofE, BBALB In No. 10, 19 April 1880)

In taking this attitude the Bank of England again missed the chance to take charge of monetary policy as a quasi-government body. Instead it was, in Sayers' words, 'prepared to miss an opportunity of strengthening its direct hold upon the country banks; it drove [them] back to the traditional channel of the London agent' (Sayers 1957a, p. 143).[6] It is extremely unlikely that a more co-operative attitude on the part of the Bank of England could have prevented the Birmingham banks from shifting their head offices to London in the next two decades, but the conversion of the commercial banks in Birmingham onto 'London and provincial banks' also took away from Barham his last theoretical chance of enlivening his lending business by co-operating with local banks and establishing the Bank of England as a 'bankers' bank'.

4.2 The rise of the 'industrial branch', 1880–93

It had been apparent to Barham around 1880 that in view of the slight scope the branch managers enjoyed, a reactivation of his discount business would not be enough to get the Birmingham branch out of the red. To achieve that he would have to adapt to the conditions that governed his competitors, the commercial banks. Since the overdraft which the commercial banks gave were on principle still forbidden for the Bank of England, the only way was to make his terms for advances on securities so attractive that they would be competitive against the overdraft terms of the commercial banks. This was by no means impossible. When rates were low, the Bank of England could always underbid the provincial banks with its interest rates without running the risk of loss, particularly before the introduction of private discounting and private lombard rates in the provinces. The requirements for the quality of the securities were a bigger problem. In the past these had been so restrictive that advances were rarely asked for (see Chapter 2.3.3). Since there were no prospects that this rule would change, Barham had to try to create other scope for himself and he could only do this if the branch banks' office tolerated his side-stepping the rules.

The first time Barham exceeded his competence in granting a loan was in July 1879. However, this was presumably not yet a deliberate attempt to create more scope for himself by establishing a case of precedence. There followed an interesting discussion between the branch banks' office[7] and Barham, in which the different attitudes are very plain. These differences were to play a determinant part in the history of the branch over the next two decades. The discussion is further illustration of the relationship between the Bank of England and the provincial banks.

The Midland Banking Co., a provincial bank of medium size with a paid-up equity of £300,000 and reserves from undistributed profits of £50,000 (before the City of Glasgow Bank crisis) had decided after the crisis to increase its paid-in capital by £200,000. The sum was not, however, to be provided by a call on the capital not yet paid in, but solely by the directors, as a sign of the strength of the bank. One of these directors, an industrialist (presumably in the iron industry) was also a customer at the Birmingham Bank of England branch. To raise his share of £20,000 he had handed in an accommodation bill for £14,000 for discounting and asked for a mortgage loan of £6,000 (the value of the land was given as £30,000). Barham had already transacted the business without consulting London when he informed the branch banks' office (BofE, BBALB Out No. 18, 30 July 1879). He would probably not have been given permission for the deal, for he had broken two rules at once. First, accommodation bills were on principle excluded from discounting and second, the Bank never gave mortgage loans. So the branch banks' office telegraphed as soon as it received the communication, demanding that the deal be stopped at once. When Barham telegraphed back that it was already transacted — although only for £8,500 and not £20,000 — London telegraphed back again that Barham should at least try to get 'freehold land producing rents' as security.[8]

The same day the Deputy Governor again explained the reasons for his disapproval of Barham's independent action and the Bank's principles in regard to securities for advances:

> The Deputy Governor wishes me to say that as the deeds offered in the present instance were those of landed property producing rents he would, if it had proved necessary, have taken the application under consideration though it would not have been in accordance with the Bank's usual practice to do so. If, however, the deeds had been those of works of any description, he considers the local banks who would necessarily be better able to judge the value of such property, would have been the right people to apply to. Advances on such property is not considered 'banking business' in the Bank's acceptance of the term. It was also a matter of consideration with regard to the bill of £14,000 . . . whether such bill was based on a purely mercantile transaction or was not rather of the nature of an accommodation bill . . . to obtain funds from the Bank of England . . . to assist the Midland Banking Co. (BofE, BBALB In No. 11, 31 July 1879)

Of particular importance in this 'lesson' is the distinction drawn by Grenfell, whose wife came from one of the largest land-owning families in England, between pledging agricultural land and pledging factory buildings and plants. Even if it cannot be said that he had a personal interest in the distinction, it is surprising that the decisive factor was not that the creditor might perhaps be in a better legal position over a mortgage loan of this kind but that the Bank would not have to assess the value of an industrial enterprise. However, the main bank of a firm ought to be able to judge the inherent value of such a security as well as Grenfell felt he could judge ground rent.

In this specific case it may be assumed that the director of a commercial bank would not have all his accounts with the Bank of England, and Grenfell's mistrust was justified. But his remarks also applied to the hypothetical case that a customer for whom the Bank of England was the main bank would offer a debenture bond (in the case of a joint stock company) or a title deed on works (in the case of a family firm). Clearly this was application of London business practices to the provinces here. 'Sound banking' still meant trade credit, or in Grenfell's words, 'Bills . . . based on a genuine trade business' (BofE, BBALB In No. 11, 2 August 1879). The City still regarded mortgage loans with great scepticism,[9] but they were usual in the social circles in which the Bank of England directors moved. However, the Bank of England totally refused to finance fixed capital investments. Its ban applied even to advances to be invested in circulating capital, where a return flow within a foreseeable period was possible.[10] Current account lending was forbidden on principle.[11]

Barham did at first accede, but only two weeks later he again went on the offensive by giving a loan of £5,000 to an iron and steel firm in Wolverhampton, and taking as security *inter alia* Lehigh Wilkes Bane Colliery 6 per cent mortgage bonds.[12] The Deputy Governor agreed, although he stressed that 'the securities deposited . . . are not of a class the Bank usually advances upon'. He only insisted on a safety margin of 20 per cent and an interest rate of 3 per cent (one percentage point above

Bank Rate). The term of the loan was not to exceed one month (BofE, BBALB In No. 11, 19 August 1879). The customer was not satisfied with the interest rate and Barham supported his demand to be charged only 2 per cent, since interest rates were on a low level ('Their request seems not unreasonable in itself and their account is one of the class that we ought to see more of' (BofE, BBALB Out 26 September 1879)). However, with the security the borrower could offer he would probably not have obtained so low a rate in any other bank in Birmingham, for as Barham's successor reported later, the interest rates on current account loans in Birmingham were as a rule one percent above Bank Rate, but at least 4 per cent.[13]

In this case Barham had succeeded in compensating the competitive disadvantage he suffered in granting overdrafts by charging a lower interest rate. The provincial banks, with their high deposit rates, could not compete with the interest rates charged by the Bank of England when London rates were low. To expand that side of his business, Barham had to convince the directors that business in gilt-edged securities was not to be had in Birmingham. On the whole he was successful in this even in the 1880s, for clear criteria for the acceptance or rejection of securities by the Deputy Governors are not evident. Securities could be rejected on one occasion and a little later comparable securities, or those of even worse quality, could be accepted.

In January 1884 Barham sent to London an application from an entrepreneur in the non-ferrous metal industry in Birmingham

> who has for some time had an account here and discounts a few hundred pounds of very fair bills. He now wishes the power to discount his promissory notes for not more than £1,000, and hands me as security the title deeds of his works (to the value of about £800) . . . and four policies of the Metropolitan Life Insurance Society [to the value of about £200 for each policy]. (BofE, BBALB Out No. 19, 10 January 1884)

The Deputy Governor agreed (BofE, BBALB In No. 11, 14 January 1884). This is surprising, bearing in mind Grenfell's remarks on this class of security in 1879. But four years had passed and there had been two changes in the supervision of the provincial branches in the meantime. Three years later Barham proposed starting negotiations with another firm which wanted credit of up to £20,000 'on security of title deeds of the works, valued for the Company at £81,000' (BofE, BBALB Out No. 20, 17 March 1887). Although Barham recommended the business, the Deputy Governor refused firmly this time (BofE, BBALB In No. 12, 18 March 1887) — again it was a different Deputy Governor.

The situation was similar for shares that were not yet fully paid up. After the Bank had accepted fully paid-in Muntz Metal Co. shares as security in 1880 (BofE BBALB Out No. 19, 1 July 1880; In No. 11, 2 July 1880),[14] the same customer offered a package of shares in 1882 for another loan, some of which were not fully paid up (BofE, BBALB Out

No. 9, 30 January 1882). Deputy Governor Gilliat said on principle: 'The securities . . . are not of a class the Bank would care to make an advance upon. As a general rule the Bank does not make advances on securities, however good, upon which there is a further liability' (BofE, BBALB In No. 11, 31 January 1882).[15] Three months previously the same Deputy Governor had approved a loan of £2,000 (for three months) to a director of a local steel firm. The security was '400 shares of J. Russel & Sons Ltd. . . . they being £10 shares £6.10 paid'. Not only were the shares not fully paid up, they were not even marketable locally, but Barham saw this as due to the special quality of the shares (BofE, BBALB Out No. 19, 25 April 1881).

In this case, to obtain these credit conditions Barham may have made use of the rotation among the directors and the change that had just taken place in the supervision of the provincial branches. It is striking that he went on to do more when he had the approval for £2,000, raising this to £3,000 on his own initiative and accepting as additional security '100 £25 shares £20 paid of the Great Bridge Steel and Iron Co. Ltd' (BofE, BBALB Out No. 19, 28 April 1881). The Deputy Governor may not have had the firmness to turn the application down, particularly if it had been approved jointly by the agent and the principal of the branch banks' office.[16] He had previously been a member of the Committee for branch banks, but a junior member, and so excluded from the main decisions of the Bank. He had been a member of the real centre of power, the Committee of Treasury, for only a few months. A short time later, when he had assimilated his duties as Deputy Governor, he no longer approved such securities.

They were indeed risky. In order not to be registered as shareholders of the company, with an obligation to pay in on the equity, the provincial banks generally did not have the shares they took as security for loans transferred to their names, they were content with what was known as a 'blank transfer'. This was a document in which initially the name of a recipient was not entered. If the loan was repaid the creditor returned the security and the blank transfer to the borrower. Only if the borrower was not in a position to repay the loan did the creditor enter his name on the transfer document; he was then entitled to have himself registered as owner of the share against presentation of the completed paper and the share certificate. The risk was that only now was the condition created for realizing the security. Should the borrower die or go bankrupt the blank transfer was worthless, for a transfer of the shares could not now take place. They would pass in the first case to the borrower's heirs, who were not obliged to pay the debts of the deceased before the end of a year (see Rae 1903, p. 37). In the second case they formed part of the bankrupt's assets. In his *Dictionary of Political Economy* Palgrave says: 'The holder of a (blank) transfer ought to exercise great care' (Palgrave, *Dictionary* 1901, Vol. 1, 'blank transfer', p. 155). Writing in the 1890s, the *Bankers' Magazine* could not understand why, after some striking verdicts against creditors in the 1880s, banks were still accepting blank transfers at all (*Bankers' Magazine* Vol. 53/1, 1893, pp. 727–8, 913–4; Vol. 55/1, 1895, pp. 553–4). Blank transfers were on principle forbidden at the Bank of England[17] and the provincial banks probably prolonged loans secured in this way only in rare cases.

It was presumably on looking through the securities deposited with the branches that Deputy Governor Collet on taking office four years later noticed this loan. It had apparently been prolonged without difficulty for four years, although in the meantime the first verdict on a blank transfer case (Société Générale de Paris v. Walker) had been decided against the creditor (*Bankers' Magazine* Vol. 53/1, 1893, p. 727). Collet, who knew the provincial branches' business better than almost any other Bank of England director,[18] immediately required Barham to ask for 'repayment before long unless more suitable securities can be found' (BofE, BBALB In No. 12, 31 March 1885). In fact, the loan was repaid a short time later (BofE, BBALB Out No. 20, 30 May 1885). Barham was not to be convinced by such reversals that the rules which applied to the provincial branches might be suitable for the largely anonymous lending business, as that in Birmingham might appear to be in London. He believed that, thanks to his close contacts with a number of leading local industrialists, he could judge far better when a loan really needed securing and when the debtor was security enough in himself. So it was not only the business as such that led him to grant certain customers special conditions, it was the information he got from his constant contact with them (BofE, BBALB Out No. 20, 2 March 1886, 1 May 1886).

Barham's attitude to the London rules is very clear from the following dispute with Deputy Governor Lidderdale, who, like his predecessor Collet, took his supervision of the branches much more seriously than most other Deputy Governors. Again, the case was a blank transfer. This time, however, the problem was not paying in the shares; presumably the customer, the owner of several coal mines, did not want to lose his voting rights in the canal company concerned. Unlike Collet, Lidderdale's reaction to this new breach of the rules for the branches' lending business was rather restrained:

> The Deputy Governor would have preferred that you should have submitted to London [this] application before acceding to it. The Bank has of late endeavoured, as far as possible, to avoid making advances on securities on a blank transfer unless the amount were small . . . . In the present case no length of time is stated . . . and the inference is that [your customer] will want the £10,000 quoted for a considerable period. (BofE, BBALB In No. 12, 19 August 1887)

This response, to disapprove the action but not necessarily the conditions for the loan, brought a reaction from Barham that was evidently on the offensive, and which shows that he saw himself as country banker rather than agent: 'I should certainly not have proposed a blank transfer except when confident that borrowers would be undoubtedly good for the full amount in both means and character' (BofE, BBALB Out No. 20, 20 August 1887).

By 1886/7 Barham had succeeded in taking Birmingham from being the least profitable branch, as it was ten years before, to fourth place behind Liverpool, Manchester and Newcastle, with a loss of 'only' £395. Apart from that one year, the improvement in Birmingham was slight, but while the other branches had to suffer growing losses as the discount business slid into seemingly unstoppable decline, Barham did succeed in preventing at least a further deterioration. It can hardly be doubted that he did so because he was able to balance the decline in the discount business by increasing his lombard lending against securities. In the 1887/8 accounting year, directly before the reform of the rules on the provincial branches' credit business, the lombard business in Birmingham had reached the size of that of all the other provincial branches together.

Unfortunately we know the extent of the lombard business in the Birmingham branch only from 1887, but there is evidence to suggest that these loans to the above-mentioned local firms were still exceptions. Presumably the breakthrough that made the Birmingham branch the 'industrial branch' of the Bank of England came only in 1885/6, after business relations were taken up with the leading local stockbroker, N. Lea & Son. In May 1885 Lea opened an account with the Bank of England to lombard first class securities (BofE, BBALB Out No. 20, 14 May 1885). Deputy Governor Collet at first insisted that really only first class securities should be deposited and that loans must not be prolonged. He also demanded that London should be informed by telegraph of each additional loan (BofE, BBALB in No. 12, 15 May 1885, 13 July 1885, 14 July 1885, 20 July 1885).

Of course Lea did not keep to the securities he initially pledged, shares of the Great Eastern Railway Co., the Southwark & Vauxhall Water Co. and the Buenos Aires New Gas Co. The loan rapidly took on a permanent character, as it was topped up virtually from settlement to settlement, and the additional securities were not always first class. Unlike his predecessors, Collet, however, kept the development under observation and only intervened at the end of August, when it looked like getting out of hand (BofE BBALB In No. 12, 26 August 1885). In the next few weeks Barham took shares of only leading railway companies as security (BofE, BBALB Out No. 20, 14 September 1885, 15 September 1885, 29 September 1885).

The decisive breakthrough came at the end of 1885. Lea's credit had reached £33,000, which alone was equal to one-third of the discount business transacted by the Birmingham branch that year. Moreover, Lea had now transferred all his accounts to the Bank of England and so Collet was presumably prepared to make concessions. He agreed to Barham's suggestion of

> taking from them, in case of need, some of the best local securities regularly quoted at par or at a premium on the Birmingham Stock Exchange. It might happen that their clients, buying local and neglecting London securities, might make it convenient to provide cover entirely in the latter. (BofE, BBALB Out No. 20, 11 March 1886)

It was the spring of 1886 before Lea deposited shares of the Birmingham Small Arms & Metal Co. as security for the first time (BofE, BBALB Out No. 20, 11 March 1886)[19] and over the next few years local securities probably made up only a small part of what he pledged. However, the official recognition of local securities by the Deputy Governor created considerable scope for Barham in the future negotiations with industrialists in the region.

In the same month as Lea, another customer also received a loan against shares of the Birmingham Small Arms & Metal Co., and the Birmingham & Aston Tramway Co. (BofE, BBALB Out No. 20, 2 March 1886). Shortly after business relations began with the Chamberlain Group (see p. 108 below) with a loan to Walter Chamberlain, again against shares of the Birmingham Small Arms & Metal Co. (BofE, BBALB Out No. 20, 11 August 1886). This laid the foundation for the enormous expansion of the lombard business for the Birmingham branch. At the end of 1886 there were sixteen advance accounts in Birmingham (see BofE, BBALB Out No. 26, 8 January 1887, annexed), but the Lea & Sons' account was by far the most important. Even in 1888 it alone comprised half the total lombard business in Birmingham.[20]

Local securities still presumably accounted for only a minority of the securities pledged, but the Governors were observing the development with distrust. At the beginning of 1889 Barham was told: 'The Deputy Governor has been looking over your advance statements and thinks you should not have too much under advance against industrial and local undertakings the price and status of which cannot well be ascertained in London' (BofE, BBALB In No. 13, 16 March 1889). But Barham was not to be dissuaded from the path he had taken. The criticism from the following Deputy Governor was also rather half-hearted. Objections were raised again and again to the high proportion of local securities in the advance statements from Birmingham (BofE, BBALB In No. 13, 9 October 1989, 1 March 1890, 2 January 1891, 12 August 1891) but if Barham proposed a specific transaction London almost always agreed.

The reform of 1888, which gave the branch agents greater independence of the branch banks' office in fixing the conditions for their loans, did not leave any evident traces of the correspondence between the agent and the branch banks' office. However, there must have been a considerable rise in the lending to local firms in 1889, as the rise in the lombard business that year (see Table 2.18) was certainly not due to loans to stockbrokers like Lea & Sons. The main factor was the new independence in fixing the interest rates, since in the following years there were frequent differences of opinion between Birmingham and London on the level.

At the end of the 1880s Barham had also begun to operate as a private businessman outside the Bank. Some of these activities were known to the branch banks' office, but not all of them; some were discovered only when the management of the branch was examined in 1894. The Bank did not, of course, permit its agents to hold subsidiary posts, as a director of joint stock companies or similar positions, and Barham tried to conceal these activities. More or less honorary posts, however, were welcomed in London, particularly if they involved moving in top social circles. Unlike the other agents, however, Barham sought contact with potential customers less as a member of the local financial aristocracy than as a businessman.

The start of the official side of this activity was to have far-reaching consequences. Barham became a member of a committee that was working on a reconstruction scheme for the Patent Shaft and Axle Tree Co. in Wednesbury (BofE, BBALB Out No. 21, 15 July 1889). Very soon the Chairman of the Board of Directors of the Patent Shaft Co., Walker, was asking for a loan of £10,000 from the Bank of England (and obtained it), and was declaring himself ready to move the accounts of his firm from the Birmingham & Midland Bank to the Bank of England. The Governors hesitated to accept securities like shares and preference shares of the Patent Shaft Co. and the Allsopp Brewery, which belonged to Walker's wife's family, for what would evidently be large borrowing requirements (BofE, BBALB Out No. 21, 20 December 1889, In No. 13, 20 December 1889), but finally business relations were established. Only ten years later was the Bank of England fortunately able to loosen these ties again without incurring losses (for details see Ziegler thesis 1988, pp. 395–9).

The second business partner Barham won through his activities outside his work as Bank of England branch agent was the Chamberlain Group. The group consisted of the three brothers Walter, Arthur, and Joseph Chamberlain, together with Edward Nettlefold, Edward Hookham and a few other industrialists, who had a metal and electrical empire in the Midlands. The Chamberlains and their firms had been opening advance accounts with the Bank of England since 1886; one of these firms was the Birmingham Trust. At about the same time as the account was opened, the Director of the Trust, Arthur Chamberlain, invited Barham to act as trustee for the bonds that the investment trust would issue against special (local) securities (BofE, BBALB Out No. 21, 21 July 1890). Although this increase in activities with the local business world on the part of Barham, who was of course identified with the Bank of England in the eyes of the general public, went too far for the Deputy Governor (BofE, BBALB In No. 13, 22 July 1890), business relations do seem to have developed between the Trust and Barham as a private businessman at this time (BofE, CB No. 117, 9 August 1894).

Within a very short time the Trust owed the Bank of England £208,000 (BofE, BBALB In No. 13, 13 August 1891). This was 20 per cent of the total lombard business at the Birmingham branch and around 7.5 per cent of that of all the provincial branches put together. Lidderdale, who had probably been taking a more critical attitude to industrials since the Baring crisis, was certainly not pleased, and in 1891 he demanded that the credit be reduced (BofE, BBALB In No. 13, 12 August 1891, 18 August 1891, 29 August 1891). But Barham resisted on the following grounds:

> All our prospects of doing business depend upon keeping the customers we have who are mixed up with all that is going on in this place. Our loans are much more personal in character than ordinary fortnightly loans to brokers . . . . The Birmingham Trust has a large uncalled capital and strong shareholders in addition to the margin of securities. It is certainly more trustworthy than a firm of brokers on this account because the securities pledged are its own and not the property of its clients . . . . The loan on the Small Arms Co. debentures is soon to be paid off. It has given the Trust but a very little profit . . . . To charge them highly is therefore to render business impossible which is absolutely safe. The endorsement of the Trust makes business possible which we could not do otherwise. (BofE, BBALB Out No. 21, 31 August 1891)

Barham had to be called to London to be told who was ultimately responsible for the credit policy of the provincial branches (BofE, BBALB In No. 13, 3 September 1891). In fact, he did have the loan reduced in the next few weeks, but by November he was already approving an increase (BofE, BBALB Out No. 21, 10 September 1891, 22 October 1891, 9 November 1891). Unfortunately we do not have exact figures but a later list suggests that the loans to the Chamberlain Group between 1892 and 1894 were on average around half a million pounds (BofE, BBALB Out No. 28, 9 December 1901), about half the total lombard business in Birmingham.

It cannot be maintained that the Bank of England directors forced the expansion of the 'industrial branch', but they were informed of the development at every phase. They did nothing to stop the branch agent's attempts to make use of certain competitive advantages over the local banks. They only intervened when the intended business seemed too risky (for instance in the case of shares not fully paid up) or if they felt they were losing control altogether (as in the case of 'industrialists' as security, the value of which only the agent could judge). No efforts to improve relations with the commercial banks after the Baring crisis are evident; on the contrary, the commercial banks watched the new activities of the Bank of England provincial branches with the greatest mistrust. The active credit policy of the Bank of England in Birmingham, and elsewhere, was in direct contrast to the Bank's assurances that it would serve the commercial banks as central bank and ensure the convertibility of sterling with their interest-free reserves. By using these reserves to operate itself as buyer on the money market, the Bank not only reduced the central bank reserves, which were generally regarded as too low, it was actually competing with its depositors in their very own field of business.

Understandably, therefore, complaints from the banks in Birmingham went to the directors immediately after the Bank had extended its private discounting and private lombard rates to the branches. Howard Lloyd said as early as 1890 that the Bank of England Birmingham branch was competing directly with him 'for certain classes of local business'. A short time later Lloyd's branch manager in Smethwick complained of 'the very undue competition of the Bank of England' (Sayers 1957, p. 154). Lloyd thereupon complained directly in London, pointing out that this practice was in direct contrast to the efforts by the Bank to build up larger central bank reserves using the commercial banks' deposits. A talk between Lidderdale and Barham in 1891 did not, apparently, yield any concrete results (Sayers 1976, Vol. 1, p. 21), for a year later Lloyd complained again — presumably without avail this time too (BofE, BBALB Out No. 22, 19 November 1892).

4.3 A London scandal and the reverberations in Birmingham 1893/4

It is difficult to tell when, and on what projects, Barham's private business activities conflicted with his obligations and loyalty to the Bank of England.[21] Certainly accepting a director's post at a brass foundry was a breach of faith to the Bank. He took it to obtain a post as manager there for his son. Naturally the Deputy Governor knew nothing of this connection when Barham opened an advance account for 'his' firm with the Bank of England in 1893 (BofE, BBALB In No. 14., 30 April 1894, private letter from Deputy Governor Sandeman). Unfortunately Barham's connections with another firm are less clear, for which he had also opened an advance account; possibly he was only a private shareholder in this case. Nevertheless, Deputy Governor Powell insisted that the account be closed as soon as he heard of the connection, particularly since the securities deposited were inadequate. Barham resisted the demand as if there were no rules on extraneous activities in the Bank:

> Your inquiry is directed into matters in which you know me to have a personal interest. I am of course bound to give you officially any information for which you may ask but I shall take it kindly if you would tell me straight if at any time you are curious as to my personal connections with anything . . . . There is really nothing to know beyond what is patent, that I have sometimes a few shares in things that are going forward. It is impossible in a place like this to get business at all, at least for a concern like this, without intimate personal relations with those and those alone [with whom] business can be done. I have acted and worked with such men as the Chamberlains, Nettlefolds, etc., because they are the most intelligent and active men in this place, and I have found it possible to meet their wishes and become thoroughly acquainted with

> their enterprises . . . . I should never have got them here and should not keep them if I could not meet their wishes as other banks would. You cannot, I am sure, wish us to fall back in the state we were in a few years ago. I do therefore beg of you to give . . . such encouragement as you can find to those who have some other idea than the old one of keeping out by doing nothing. All incentive comes from the Agents who must suffer everything if they are wrong and have every inducement to avoid responsibility. (BofE, BBALB Out No. 21, 21 November 1891, private letter to Deputy Governor Powell)

Naturally the Deputy Governor could not tolerate such a combination of private business and Bank of England agency, but his answer was restrained[22] and it showed that he trusted Barham to balance the requirements of the local lending market with the Bank's security requirements.

Presumably the full extent of Barham's breach of confidence would never have become known if the scandal over the chief cashier of the Bank had not erupted, making the directors hypersensitive to the private activities of their senior staff and causing them to cut down the scope allowed to their branch agents in fixing credit conditions, at least for a time. Therefore the beginning of the end of the Barham era in Birmingham was not a bankruptcy on the part of one of his customers but a scandal in London, which revealed to the public the weakness of amateur management by the directors and Governors in London and the lack of supervision of the senior staff. A few days after the scandal broke, the branch banks' office wrote to Barham: 'Since the recent events at the Bank, the Governors are more particular than ever as to the character of the securities against which advances are made' (BofE, BBALB In No. 14, 21 November 1893).

The Court of Directors also appointed a Special Committee 'to Examine into the Advances now Standing'. In February 1894 the Committee presented new Regulations 'to Govern Advances to Customers at the Branches'. They stipulated that the securities deposited must be realizable at any time (see Chapter 2.3). Under the new rules the lending business in Birmingham had to be totally reorganized, as Barham had not only accepted securities over the past two years that could only be traded on the stock market in Birmingham, he had also taken shares and bonds of private companies that could only be sold even in Birmingham on the informal market. Not only had he accepted some of these securities from his major customers, like Walter and Arthur Chamberlain or Edward Nettlefold, but also some had come from the companies themselves.

As early as 1892 the Deputy Governor had demanded exact information on such securities (BofE, BBALB In No. 13, 12 February 1892). Barham had described their marketability as:

> It is certain that the securities . . . could not be sold in the open market for the new settlement. But they are all of them sound local concerns which the market could absorb in reasonable time. The persons to whom the advances have been made are identified with the management of the business in question

> and I have regarded the advances as being of the nature of running accounts such as country banks are in the habit of giving to their customers. These advances cannot be put on the same footing as loans on the Stock Exchange from account to account. They enable some parts of the funds of the Bank to be used in the manufactures of the country . . . . This is a manufacturing district with little or no Stock Exchange speculation and the advances are those which the district requires. I can say with confidence that there is no security of the local kind in the list that is not a sound and genuine property creditable to everybody associated with it. Moderate sums could of course be sold at once. (BofE, BBALB Out No. 22, 13 February 1892)

This satisfied the Deputy Governor.

The situation was similar a year later, when Barham wanted to give the Midland Trust, an investment trust and issuing house like the Birmingham Trust, a loan for £8,000. The loan was to be secured mainly by shares and bonds of local firms. The Deputy Governor objected to the quality of the securities: 'The list of securities comprises some that had perhaps be better left out . . . . They are generally speaking of the local industry class . . . you have enough already held as securities for advances at your Branch' (BofE, BBALB In No. 13, 29 March 1893). When Barham then stressed that the securities were after all widely distributed and so the security for the loan did not depend on a single sector (BofE, BBALB Out No. 22, 29 March 1893), the branch banks' office replied that the Deputy Governor certainly did not think it was advisable to grant 'advances made on nothing but "industrials" however "mixed" they may be'. Nevertheless, Barham was able to carry out his business (BofE, BBALB In No. 13, 30 March 1893).

Then in the summer of 1893 Barham opened the account for 'his' brass foundry. In his own words this was 'a small private company, the shares of which would be saleable by private contact' (BofE, BBALB Out, No. 22, 4 September 1893). The company had now transferred its accounts to the Bank of England and the movements on the account enabled its business to be carefully scrutinized. It was particularly attractive business, since it would build up the deposits, which had been falling well behind the growth in the lending business for some time.

When, after some hesitation, Deputy Governor Wigram finally agreed to a loan of up to £700 against £1,000 6 per cent preference shares in the company, Barham again saw a chance to widen his scope.

> I hope the Deputy Governor will not think . . . that as there are no jobbers in industrial shares, at any rate in the market, anything like a parcel can only be disposed of by a special arrangement, of course at a low price, or gradually as real investors come forward. Investors gladly take sound local industrial concerns, but speculative investments taking up numbers of shares rapidly are rare. The amount of local investment demand depends on the condition of the local trade, but I do not doubt that a very moderate revival of local business would enable us to sell all our local investment shares in the course of a few months. I do feel very strongly that our only genuine business here must be

> in local industries, and that moderate distributed loans on shares of this class, the real intrinsic merit of which we know something about is sounder for us . . . than loans to stock brokers on American or Argentine rails of which we know nothing. If the Deputy Governor would permit me to enable very moderate loans on debentures of a few local companies . . . I am sure that we could safely hold or readily sell the debentures and that we could gather a sound and sufficient number of good trading and manufacturing accounts earning us commission and giving us substantial balances. (BofE, BBALB, Out No. 22, 11 September 1893)

The Deputy Governor agreed to that proposal, 'provided that you were well acquainted with the real position and intrinsic merits of each company' (BofE, BBALB In No. 14, 13 September 1893). In the next few weeks Barham thereupon set up accounts for three more private companies at the Bank of England.[23]

All this came to an end, of course, when the May scandal broke in the middle of November 1893, and, without exception, all further requests from Barham were turned down in the next few months.[24] Instead, the Deputy Governor instructed him to have all the bonds of private companies exchanged for better securities (BofE, BBALB In No. 14, 8 January 1894). A short time later, the Committee of Inquiry set up after the May scandal stated that the state of the lending business in Birmingham was highly unsatisfactory:

> The Birmingham advances have given the Committee a considerable amount of trouble. The amount employed is larger than at any other branch, and the business done in advances seems in many cases of doubtful benefit to the Bank. Two local Trust Companies have very considerable advance upon speculative and rather doubtful securities, in many cases advances . . . against securities of a purely local character. (BofE, CB No. 117, 8 March 1894)

Naturally Barham defended his practice in his interview with the directors. They acknowledged the difficulties he faced and had to admit that the quality of securities in the provinces was a major problem, since bill discounting had largely been replaced by current account lending:

> Securities quoted . . . at the London Stock Exchange are not often to be had, and the Agent is therefore anxious to be allowed to take as securities for advance for really good customers Debentures secured by a floating charge on the stock in trade and book debts of the customers business.

If the directors were to force him to keep strictly to the rules, Barham, according to his report, saw no hope of keeping his customers (BofE, CB No. 117, 8 March 1894).

Interestingly, the Committee did not make any recommendation to the Court of Directors on how the lending business in Birmingham should now be handled. A month after new rules had been laid down it might have been expected that the directors would endeavour to ensure that they were really applied. But this did not happen. The Court of Directors themselves put off the issue and only instructed the Committee for

Branch Banks to undertake a special examination of the business in Birmingham. It is certainly not too speculative to assume that the presentation of the accounts for the half-year 1893/4, which enabled a dividend of only 4½ per cent to be paid in April for the six months, the lowest since 1877, was responsible for this restraint. Since 1892 the Birmingham branch had been the most profitable provincial branch after Liverpool. The risk of slipping back to the 1880s, when the provincial branches were making losses of up to £30,000, needed very careful consideration, in view of the fact that they were now earning that amount.

The Committee for Branch Banks presented its report on Birmingham at the beginning of May. It showed that the major part of the current advances, which amounted to about £900,000, were covered by local securities, but the lombard business had not so far incurred any losses and it seemed, as the report concluded, that none were to be expected, since these were almost without exception sound firms. The report also found that it was not always 'satisfactory' to keep strictly to the rules, and it proposed that at least bonds of local firms should be acceptable as security. However, the branch banks' office was to be regularly informed of the creditworthiness of the companies involved (BofE, CB No. 117, 3 May 1894).

The report, presumably written from Barham's information, would probably have enabled him to continue running the branch without any further changes, if the directors' confidence in him had not been badly shaken a few days later. Enquiries by the Committee at the local stockbrokers had produced a very much less favourable picture. In a report 'on local industrial companies' sent from Birmingham the Committee for Branch Banks had examined altogether sixteen firms. They included some of first class standing, like Nettlefolds, the Birmingham Small Arms & Metal Co. and Kynoch, whose shares were also marketable in London. However, most were small firms whose securities would be difficult to sell even in Birmingham. Of the Midland Electric Light & Power Co., for instance, that was part of the Chamberlain Group, the Bank held 2,982 of 5,000 shares (BofE, BBALB Out No. 23, 12 May 1894). A short time later the Committee for Branch Banks said tersely in a memorandum: 'The Committee is seriously alarmed at the large amount lent out at Birmingham Branch on local industrial securities' (BofE, BBALB Out No. 23, 2 June 1894).

However, there was no thought of dismissing Barham. Only his subagent was moved and replaced by another (BofE, CB No. 117, 17 May 1894). Barham's competences were also reduced in that the new subagent conducted the negotiations with the branch's customers on the withdrawal of the non-marketable securities. Another task for subagent Smith was to loosen the strong ties between the Birmingham branch and the Chamberlain Group. With Arthur Chamberlain he agreed that the loans (currently £88,000) should be reduced by 15 per cent a year (BofE, BBALB Out No. 24, 25 June 1894), but there were difficulties with the

Birmingham Trust. Reducing its loans, which accounted for more than two-thirds of the Trust's investment, (Birmingham Trust Co. Ltd., Balance Sheet as per 30 April 1894, in BofE, BBALB Out No. 23), higher interest rate charges and exchanging some of the securities were the main concerns of the directors. The Trust proved co-operative, agreed to a reduction in its loans and exchanged the non-marketable securities for 'bonds of a well-secured character' (BofE, BBALB Out No. 23, 9 June 1894).

When the Bank then announced that in future higher interest rates would still have to be charged on the loans to the Trust, the directors of the Trust felt obliged to ask for offers from the London & Westminster Bank and the National Provincial Bank. Both agreed to take the accounts and not charge over Bank Rate. Smith thereupon proposed that the Bank of England should refrain from raising its interest rates and also continue to charge Bank Rate, if the Trust were prepared to continue reducing its loans (BofE, BBALB Out No. 23, 11 August 1894). Deputy Governor Sandeman, who had also been Chairman of the Committee of Enquiry, agreed, as 'it will no doubt satisfy the Chairman [Arthur Chamberlain] and assist you in retaining the Chamberlain group' (BofE, BBALB In No. 14, 14 August 1894). Clearly the directors were still concerned, despite all their fears regarding the securities, to keep the branch competitive. If all the Chamberlain Group accounts had been withdrawn, the branch would certainly have moved back into the red, and in the current situation that was too high a price to pay.[25]

But Barham's position in the Bank was growing increasingly untenable. After the directors had also complained of the inadequate cover on his own account, he had had to repay some of his loans and take up a loan from the Birmingham Trust. That was a second serious breach of faith, for the staff of the Bank of England were strictly forbidden to ease temporary financial embarrassment by 'dealing with professional money lenders'. Any infringement of this rule would result in instant dismissal (Acres 1931a, Vol. 2, p. 558). Moreover, Barham had exposed the Bank to blackmail by the Birmingham Trust in taking the loan. His debts at this time were about seven and a half times his annual salary, and about 40 per cent was owed to the Birmingham Trust. Repayment was quite out of the question, since he had lost the money in speculative dealing and the securities did not nearly cover the loan (BofE, CB No. 117, 9 August 1894). The Birmingham Trust could now bankrupt him and cause a second, Barham, scandal only a year after the May scandal. Barham's speculative business had been of a purely private nature and of a much lesser order than that of May, but that would hardly have interested the general public. A thorough-going change in the management structure and the division of work between professional managers and amateur directors would have been unavoidable.

That Barham's offer of resignation was not accepted, on Smith's recommendation, shows the importance that was attached to him personally in maintaining local business ties. For the relations he had built up, in the style of a private banker, could not simply be taken over and continued by a new manager sent from London and who had no knowledge at all of the region. Smith felt he could not do without Barham's intimate knowledge of local affairs, and despite his mistakes, he said of him in July 1894: 'I can honestly say, I do not think there is one in the service, who equals him in ability' (BofE, BBALB Out No. 23, 6 July 1894). Instead of dismissing Barham, the Bank appears to have given him a larger credit line, enabling him to repay his debts to the Birmingham Trust. However, in the end Barham's private financial problems got so out of hand that he was no longer capable of working and in the August 1894 he had to be retired (BofE, BBALB Out No. 23, 26 August 1894). He received the normal pension, £800 after final earnings of £1,700 (BofE, BBO Misc. Papers, C 79/30).

4.4 The old policy under new management 1894–7

After he had assumed sole responsibility for the Birmingham branch and as the pressure from London eased, Smith, the new branch agent, endeavoured to conduct the business as Barham had done until the summer of 1893, that is, before he began to take bonds of private companies. In October 1894 he presented a list of all the local companies whose shares and bonds were, in his view, acceptable as securities for advances (BofE, BBALB Out No. 23, 24 October 1894). On principle Smith felt that all the bonds of local manufacturing companies and the shares of ten firms should be acceptable. Only with the bonds of collieries and tramway companies was he selective. Cycle and tube shares were on principle excluded, since the Bank would not accept securities whose prices could fluctuate strongly. This meant that all securities subject to speculative dealing were excluded from the lombard business. The same applied in London, where no gold mine shares, for instance, were accepted.[26] In contrast with London, Smith had to admit of his local securities, 'None of these are saleable in quantity at any time' (BofE, BBALB Out No. 23, 17 October 1894). So the standing, position and business of the borrower were still of crucial importance.

In the next few months Smith began to expand once more the credit lines for his industrial customers. In November 1894, for example, a brewery was given an additional loan 'although I am aware a reduction is looked for in London' (BofE, BBALB Out No. 23, 21 November 1894). Six months later Smith actually increased the credit for the Birmingham Trust again. The Trust had financed the reduction of the credit to £110,000 by June 1895, agreed with the Bank in 1894, with loans taken up from the Commercial Bank of Scotland. This meant that the Bank of England was no longer the sole banker to the Trust. Chamberlain now proposed returning all his accounts to the Bank of

England, if the Bank would meet his entire borrowing requirements. Smith believed this was advantageous because

> there is an inevitable tendency, which I cannot wholly check, to place the most liquid and well known securities with the outsiders leaving us the balance. By taking over all loans we should certainly improve the average quality of the cover. (BofE, BBALB Out No. 24, 26 June 1895)

After obtaining the basic approval of the Deputy Governor (BofE, BBALB In No. 14, 27 June 1895), Smith negotiated the following credit conditions: the Trust could ask for credit up to £200,000. The interest rate would be fixed according to the Bank Rate with a 10 per cent margin (BofE, BBALB Out No. 24, 4 July 1895; In No. 14, 5 July 1895). That restored the *status quo ante*.

About the same time the minimal requirements for the marketability of the securities were side-stepped again. In order to obtain the account of a metal merchant's firm, Smith gave the customer credit up to £10,000 for both his private and his firm's account. As securities he was to receive 'Life policies, Title Deeds and Mortgages on Real Estates. This is of course not what we like, but I think for the moderate sums mentioned above there would be little or no risk' (BofE, BBALB Out No. 24, 1 May 1895).

Although the rules of 1894 on principle forbade blank transfers, they were still accepted. For Smith, as for Barham, the creditworthiness of the customer was what mattered. In this connection the treatment of the Birmingham Small Arms & Metal Co. shares is very interesting. The Committee for Branch Banks had not expressly rejected these shares in 1894, but the quantity of the shares that the Bank kept as security and had transferred to the names of its authorized signatories in accordance with the rules, had troubled the directors. Smith had thereupon persuaded the customers to withdraw one-third of their Birmingham Small Arms & Metal Co. shares over a period of time and either replace them with other securities or reduce their credit accordingly.

In the summer of 1895 he had given a loan against Birmingham Small Arms & Metal Co. shares, again for the first time, but he had not had the shares transferred, he was content with a blank transfer. When the branch banks' office complained, Smith refused to transfer the shares, although the customer would have agreed. The reason for this unusual action was his fear that if the shares were transferred, the directors of the company would quickly get wind of this and, in turn, if they were customers of the Bank of England, present Birmingham Small Arms & Metal Co. shares as security. That would have made the branch as dependent on the development of the company as it had been in 1894. On the other hand, Smith did not want to deny his customer his loan and he felt that a blank transfer was the most elegant solution (BofE, BBALB Out No. 24, 15 June 1895).

In view of this development the Birmingham branch naturally still had considerable shortcomings in the eyes of the chief auditor, whose task it had been since the May scandal to check the books of the head office and branches independent of the chief cashier and principal of the branch banks' office. The new Deputy Governor, Hugh Colin Smith, who himself had approved the blank transfer only a few days before, therefore asked Smith to keep closer to the rules in future (BofE, BBALB In No. 14, 20 June 1895).

When the chief auditor repeated his criticism, especially in regard to the blank transfers, the following year, Smith defended himself:

> No Agent likes unregistered transfers. I have really few here, but I have to employ them sometimes, or lose my business. Had I better lost the business?. . . Advances are really the vital part of this branch . . . The business is sound and such . . . as should be undertaken by the Bank of England . . . . I presume to make profits for the shareholders is the object of the business. I was told so when appointed ten years ago and with this in mind I have worked . . . . Ten years ago there was no advance business to speak of at any Branch and the Branches generally . . . were dying of paralysis . . . . Some of us have seen the whole advance business build up step by step and have been proud to think at any rate we were doing our best, under the most direct official sanctions and encouragements to make the Bank something more than a nonentity in the provinces. The Chief Auditor condemns all this . . . . That it is better business do discount bills, everyone will admit . . . but how are we to discount what do not exist? (BofE, BBALB Out No. 25, 19 March 1896).

He made his views even plainer at the end of 1896, when the Deputy Governor criticized the security for a new loan:

> I quite understand the Bank's feelings as to local companies . . . . I came here with similar prejudices against local stocks. What have we seen? A very marked appreciation in the price of almost everything local. Breweries double and treble the price they were in 1894. Small Arms and Kynoch prices more than double. Nettlefold's, Perry's, Avery's, the Wagon Companies, all far higher. Concerns honestly managed by good local men have done well. (BofE, BBALB Out No. 25, 23 December 1896)

As far as criticism of the management in Birmingham was concerned, the May scandal, the changes in the rules and the departure of Barham, all had made little difference. The Deputy Governor did express doubts at certain securities, or the interest rates, but he rarely turned down a request from the agent. The reason is probably that between 1894 and 1896 the Bank of England was going through its worst crisis as a commercial bank since 1844. Since the beginning of 1894 Bank Rate had been 2 per cent and the market rates on loans by bill brokers and deposit banks in London had actually been under 1 per cent for months. Accordingly, the private discount rate in London dropped below 1 per cent, and under these conditions it was becoming increasingly difficult to place surplus funds in London. The dividend also looked likely to fall through the floor as soon as the hidden reserves were used up. Only the slowly rising demand for credit in the industrial provinces seemed to offer a way out of the dilemma (Table 2.16).

The branch banks' office therefore tolerated discount rates under 1 per cent in the provinces as well, and at that rate the Birmingham branch could probably underbid its competitors. In November 1895, for instance, a leading iron industrialist from Wolverhampton opened a discount account with the Birmingham branch, because Smith would discount traders' bills for him at the 'absurdly low rate of one per cent' (Smith). The agent did this 'to show our friends they need not go to London discount houses when banking with us. The demoralisation of discount rates by 50 millions "Other Deposits" is unspeakable' (BofE, BBALB Out No. 24, 4 November 1895).

The relative steadiness of the lending business at the provincial branches and especially in Birmingham, which, despite the change in management and the temporary tightening of the credit conditions, still accounted for around one-third of the income from the lombard business at around £25,000 — 20 per cent of the total lending business of the provincial branches — was certainly the reason why London very largely gave the new agent in Birmingham a free hand. The management of the Bank accepted that such a policy would be bound to lead to a further deterioration in the relations between the Bank of England and the commercial banks. So, in contrast to what Sayers believed (Sayers 1976, Vol. 1, p. 22), it cannot be said that the Bank of England was more restrained in Birmingham after the reform of the rules in 1894. The Bank was only endeavouring to maintain the appearance of reserve, while it was in fact allowing its agent to compete successfully with the commercial banks.

One example of the double strategy is the treatment of an application from Edward Nettlefold to transfer all his accounts from Lloyds Bank to the Bank of England. In the report by the Committee for Branch Banks the directors had criticized the fact that a number of customers had received credit to the amount of several tens of thousands of pounds, but were not transacting any 'banking business properly so called' through the Bank of England. One of these customers was Edward Nettlefold. In a conversation Smith pointed this out to him and explained that the Bank wanted to establish a better balance. Nettlefold answered that it had been the Bank that was not very interested in his transferring his accounts. When Lloyds Bank took over the Birmingham Joint Stock Bank in 1889, difficulties soon arose between Lloyds Bank and the Chamberlain Group, which had worked with the Birmingham Joint Stock Bank: but 'Lloyds were very indignant at the idea of losing any of the Chamberlain Nettlefold connection'. The Bank of England therefore took the accounts of Arthur Chamberlain only, while the others went to the National Provincial Bank.

However, Nettlefold was prepared to move his accounts to the Bank of England if the Bank now wished. Smith commented to the branch banks' office:

> I am not prepared to enter into what would be an open war with Lloyds, unless I am sure that I should receive the full support of the Deputy Governor and the Committee [for Branch Banks]. We must either be content with the advance business of such customers as divorced from their banking business — or we must descend into the area to compete with our neighbours, as our neighbours compete with each other. On the whole a large sum of money is involved and for us in the provinces important principles. To do pure banking, on the Bank of England lines, in the provinces . . . is almost impossible. (BofE, BBALB Out No. 25, 2 October 1896)

The answer from London makes the effect of two and a half years of Bank Rate at 2 per cent very clear:

> You must say to him that any action of his to this end must be quite spontaneous as the Bank would never ask for the accounts. If however he were to bring it and maintain a good balance upon etc. the Bank would treat him liberally both as regards advances and in other matters in connection with it. You must however impress upon him that the authorities in London will not continue large advances to persons who principally keep no account with them. (BofE, BBALB In No. 15, 5 October 1896)

In the end the efforts of the bank to permit only advance accounts in connection with an active drawing account were successful in that in 1896 and 1897 the stock of deposits in Birmingham rose noticeably, while the lombard business stabilized at a high level. A number of customers must therefore have moved their accounts to the Bank of England.

At the end of 1896 the situation in London eased a little, the phase of low interest rates, when Bank Rate was 2 per cent for two and a half years, was coming to an end, and with demand for credit growing and interest rates rising, the interest earnings of the Bank of England in London began to rise once more. In April 1897 the Bank was able to pay a six-month dividend of 5 per cent for the first time since 1892. In the provinces as well the main cyclical indicators were moving upwards. The best indicator for the industry located in and around Birmingham, the production index for the manufacturing industry, especially metal-working and mechanical engineering, showed a rapid growth for 1896, while the textile industry was stagnating (see Feinstein 1972, Table 51). It must be assumed, therefore, that demand for credit was rising, not only in London but in Birmingham as well. The region's resources were certainly not enough to meet the need for credit at this time, but there is evidence to suggest that the big banks, the National Provincial, Lloyds and the London & Midland Bank, were certainly in a position to meet the requirement for trade credit from the increase in their deposits.[27] Moreover, a growing number of industrial borrowers were coming to the London capital market to issue preference shares and bonds.[28]

The Birmingham branch also shared in the increased demand for loans sparked off by the boom, if not to the same extent as its neighbours. After a low in the half-year 1894/5, following the Barham affair, when the lombard business reached its lowest level since 1889/90 at on average £719,000, the stock rose in the 1896/7 half-year to almost £1 million on average (Table 2.18). Birmingham remained in second place behind Liverpool, but was clearly ahead of Manchester, Leeds, Hull and Newcastle. However, the increase was not achieved through the diversification that had been demanded in 1894; on the contrary, it came from a reduction in the ties to the Chamberlain Group. For 1897 Smith estimated 'that more than half the interest earned on advances comes from what we call the Chamberlain group' (BofE, BBALB Out No. 27, 10 January 1898). The branch banks' office and the Deputy Governor clearly no longer had any objection.

4.5 The end of the industrial branch

In 1897 a new principal took over in the branch banks' office. The directors had clearly not been satisfied with his predecessor, Courtney, who apparently had not been able (or willing) to stop the constant infringements of the rules by the branch agents after the criticism from the chief auditor. The new principal, Edye, was therefore told when taking office 'that a man was wanted who would obtain and maintain control of the Branches' (BofE, Edye Reports G 15/39, 13 December 1904). The principal was, of course, hardly to blame, the real responsibility lay with the Deputy Governors, who since the beginning of the 1890s had mainly limited themselves to warnings to the agents — for good reason.

Although the change at the head of the branch banks' office should have made it easier to implement a new policy towards the provincial branches, the real reason for the restrictive attitude on the part of London to the provincial branches around the turn of the century was quite different. Demand for credit, especially lombard lending in London, had risen rapidly in 1897. Moreover, the Bank had invested considerably in securities in 1896. The scope for the branches was therefore greatly restricted, since their business was the least desirable of these alternatives. If advances were requested against London securities, this was always preferable to a credit secured by 'local industrials'.

After taking office Edye set about putting the branches on the course desired by the chief auditor (BofE Edye Reports G 15/39, January Report 1898), and by January 1898 he could report his first successes:

> Our brokers accounts have developed both in number and volume and both they and the private people show a tendency to load us with securities of industrial companies. I have recently had a list of these made out. It is a very long one, too long, but I am glad of a very varied character (no mines or cycles) and I am able to add that, where the amount is of any magnitude, it is so split up that no individual holding need cause any anxiety at present

. . . . The great point is that no loan should be dependent upon the possible collapse of a particular security, this has not been looked after in the past.

A second problem that had not been effectively tackled in the past were the blank transfers. As a list (which has fortunately survived) of all blank transfers in January 1897 shows, the Birmingham branch was the only provincial branch that had given loans to any extent against blank transfers. Ten out of a total of twenty-two borrowers were customers of the Birmingham branch and twenty-two out of thirty-six blank transfers were deposited there.[29] They included loans to Edward Nettlefold and Walter Chamberlain, who had clearly not wanted to transfer securities because they were directors of the companies. Similar reasons presumably applied in the case of a hop merchant who did not want to have a number of brewery bonds registered.

All non-registered securities now had to be either registered or withdrawn. In addition, Edye had instructed Smith to reduce drastically ten loans totalling £100,000, since they were covered by 'second rate securities'. By 'second rate securities' he obviously meant mainly bonds of private companies that could hardly be sold even on the local informal market. Thanks to the good economic climate these loans were reduced by around 80 per cent to £21,400 by the beginning of 1898. Altogether, as a result of the more restrictive attitude on the part of the branch banks' office, the lombard business of the Birmingham branch declined in the 1897/8 accounting half-year by around £150,000 (15 per cent) against the average for the 1896/7 accounting half-year, unlike the lending business at the provincial branches, which reached its absolute peak in 1898 (Table 2.18). Despite this reversal, the cumulative effect that Smith had feared if other customers repaid loans that had sound cover, did not materialise. The major industrialists remained loyal to the Bank. They did not have any reason to change their bank, for the other banks in Birmingham would presumably not have given them loans of an obviously permanent nature against blank transfers.

The first sign of a restrictive attitude on the part of London to credit business by the Birmingham branch, which was on a sound basis, was the instruction from Deputy Governor Gladstone to Smith to charge 4 per cent for a prolongation of the credits for three gentlemen in the Chamberlain Group when they fell due. This was breaking the informal agreement given by the Bank that only half a percentage point over Bank Rate would be charged, since Bank Rate was then 3 per cent. The Deputy Governor was no longer prepared to give such 'permanent advances against industrials' at less than 4 per cent if the interest rate level should fall further (BofE, BBALB In No. 15, 19 March 1898). Smith thereupon warned Arthur Chamberlain 'in a friendly way that the Bank did not purpose to follow money down when money becomes easy, to the very low rate two years ago' (BofE, BBALB Out No. 25, 22 March 1898).

Unlike the withdrawal of the blank transfers, this was a step that could seriously impair the competitiveness of the Birmingham branch. The branch had been able to underbid its competitors for about three years as its interest rates were tied to the London Bank Rate, but when the general level of interest rates was fairly high, the Bank of England was generally above the level charged by local banks in the provinces. The advantage of tying interest rates at the provincial branches to the London Bank Rate had become a disadvantage by the late 1890s. If the branch was still not losing customers, this was because the agent was charging the private lombard rate to some,[30] or the customers could count on compensation in times when London rates were low. Now this consideration on the part of the branch banks' office was clearly going to end. The interest rate, the only weapon the branch agents had in the provinces, had been blunted, and an expansion of their lending business was no longer possible. The only thing they could hope for was to maintain their position.

The prospects for this were still quite good in 1898, as apart from the increase in the lending rate, the branch banks' office and the Deputy Governor were still interested in maintaining business relations with the Chamberlain Group and other major borrowers. The Birmingham Trust, for example, had been granted a current account credit to handle dividend payments for the Great Central Railway Co. stock at the beginning of 1898. The short-term nature of the loan was ensured by the dividends received for the securities deposited (BofE, BBALB Out No. 27, 1 January 1898). Nine months later, when the Trust converted a gas turbine company belonging to the Chamberlain Group into a joint stock company and needed an additional loan of £12,000 for the purpose (BofE, BBALB Out No. 27, 26 October 1898), the Deputy Governor refused to transfer shares of the company to the Bank, because they were, of course, not yet quoted on the Birmingham Stock Exchange. However, he did agree to give the loan without additional securities and tolerate an appropriately low safety margin for a time (BofE, BBALB In No. 15, 27 October 1898). In this way the Bank succeeded in maintaining lombard lending at its Birmingham branch at the level of £800,000 reached after Edye's 'purge'.

In 1899 the situation in London had, however, changed to such an extent that it was now the director's aim to reverse the continuing deterioration in the relationship between deposits and lending at the provincial branches. To that end, those branches where the ratio between deposits and lending was very disproportionate, or whose lending business was largely based on 'industrials', were asked particularly to cut back their lending. Since both conditions applied to Birmingham, the branch banks' office set about implementing its objective there with particular energy by raising the lending rates. Consideration for the Chamberlain Group was a thing of the past.

After an increase in interest rates on private accounts, which by all appearances resulted in a reduction of these loans but did not affect the business accounts, the first blow at the companies belonging to the Chamberlain Group came at the beginning of 1899. In January Chamberlain & Hookham asked whether the Bank of England would agree to its name appearing as banker on the prospectus for a reconstruction scheme of the company (BofE, BBALB Out No. 27, 3 January 1899). The Deputy Governor agreed, but only on condition that the Birmingham branch did not accept subscriptions (BofE, BBALB In No. 15, 5 January 1899). With that condition Chamberlain decided not to put the Bank's name on the prospectus, since investors might have been put off if the company's principal bank had not accepted any subscriptions (BofE, BBALB Out No. 27, 28 January 1899).

Smith himself was clearly surprised by this tough attitude on the part of the Deputy Governor. As he said in a private note to the principal: 'I do not understand the true inwardness of not receiving the applications . . . . Mr Chamberlain agreed like a lamb to the stipulation' (BofE, BBALB Out No. 27, 28 January 1898, annexed). Chamberlain's approach was certainly not in any way unusual. In 1890 the Bank had accepted payments on the issue of United Chemical Co. debentures for subscription at its Bristol and Newcastle branches (BofE, Secretary's LB G 23 No. 11, 29 October 1890), so it must be assumed in the case of Chamberlain & Hookham that the directors had already decided to dissolve their ties with the Chamberlain Group.

Chamberlain and Smith must have realized what the strategy was at the next stroke: only a month later Smith was instructed by the Special Committee for Advances to Private Customers to raise his interest rate higher still for a whole number of loans, including all the credits to the Chamberlain Group. The Birmingham branch was still the one whose lending business corresponded least to what the directors wanted to see. A memorandum by the branch banks' office (undated, presumably at the beginning of 1899) stated that the Birmingham branch had by far the largest number of all 'permanent advances' (sixty altogether), with seventeen of its credits running since 1896. Probably those to the Chamberlain Group accounted for the lion's share of the seventeen, at least as far as the amounts of the loans were concerned.

It now became clear that the Bank would make its credit conditions increasingly restrictive until so many credits were 'voluntarily' withdrawn in Birmingham that on aggregate they no longer exceeded the deposits. Smith, who until then had taken all the necessary measures to adapt his business in Birmingham to the London rules without demur, now set to work — albeit cautiously at first — to maintain his current practice:

> Indeed I had hoped that I got the Branch into calm water . . . . I do not like to see business pass us which we can so well handle and I think an extra quarter per cent that you have made me charge will prove dear . . . . I find great difficulty in maintaining the branch figures, indeed I hardly succeed. And I do not know how to succeed if I fail to take into consideration side winds

and side issues that cannot be known to you. (BofE, BBALB Out No. 27, 23 February 1899).

However, while the Deputy Governor reacted cautiously and only stressed that the Committee's remarks were of the nature of recommendations, Edye doubted that other banks would be able to offer better conditions than the Bank of England over the longer term. This must greatly have annoyed Smith. His tone grew stronger and he became more combative. First he invited the directors to come to Birmingham and obtain a view of the situation at first hand:

> My experience is this . . . that the great competing banks have hard rules which they should quote to you and me, but they have General Managers with wide dispensing powers, for whom no such rules exist. These General Managers would not hesitate to quote rates . . . to abstract business from us or any of their neighbours. The long period of 2 per cent '94, '95, '96 completely demoralised country rates and naturally the borrowing public will not go back to the old terms, viz, 4 per cent minimum on secured loans and 5 per cent on unsecured overdraft.

He also added a memorandum on the Chamberlain links in which he actually proposed dropping the interest rates for Walter and Herbert Chamberlain (BofE, BBALB Out No. 27, 24 February 1899). A day later he finally reminded London that it was the advances to private customers that had brought the turnaround 'in the branches' earning power' (BofE, BBALB Out No. 27, 25 February 1899).

Nonetheless he did not succeed in changing the attitude in London. The directors did not come to Birmingham; in a difficult situation (see Chapter 2.3.3) they had other worries than to offer provincial borrowers fair credit conditions. At the beginning of May the agents were told quite openly that the concern was no longer to put the lending business on a sounder base, but to reduce the loans, particularly if they were secured by 'industrials' (BofE, BBALB In No. 15, 17 May 1899). Although there were difficulties at first, because customers were not in a position to sell their securities at short term as local capital markets were not strong enough ('Industrials . . . are slow of sale, even in easy times because buyers and sellers have to be brought together — there are no intermediate jobbers and dealers', BofE, BBALB Out No. 27, 17 May 1899), the lending dropped in the course of June from around £830,000 to £672,000 and presumably again in July to about £600,000. In Smith's view the bottom had now been reached, otherwise his lending business would collapse. The Governor showed understanding for his point of view and in November he actually approved a loan to Walter Chamberlain on newly issued preference shares of his Elliot Metal Co. (BofE, BBALB Out No. 27, 6 November 1899; In No. 15, 7 November 1899). But it was clearly too late. Edward Nettlefold and Arthur Chamberlain had gone to Barclay's Bank and obtained credit there to reduce their borrowing from the Bank of England. Their companies had also drastically reduced their Bank of England borrowing: Chamberlain Bros., for instance, from £60,000 in June to £30,000 in November (BofE, BBALB Out No. 27, 6 January 1899). By the end of October the lending business in Birmingham had shrunk to less than half of what it had been in May (BofE, BBALB, Out No. 27, 28 October 1899).

Reducing the credit naturally created the same problems as in 1894/5. In order to obtain the credit from Barclay's to repay the Bank of England, the Chamberlains and Nettlefold had had to withdraw the marketable securities, 'leaving a good sample of industrial securities, but most certainly "sticky"' (BofE, Out No. 28, 5 January 1900). Nettlefold, for instance, had most of his credit in June 1900 covered with the following securities (BofE, BBALB Out No. 28, 5 June 1900):

- Nettlefold ordinary shares ('an industrial stock of the highest class, but a very narrow market');
- Brunner Mond shares ('more saleable, but with considerable fluctuations');
- Cannon Brewery pref. shares ('tho' solid . . . very difficult of sale with a Bank rate much over 4 per cent').

Nettlefold countered complaints from Smith by saying that he was prepared to go back to the conditions before June 1899 (BofE, BBALB Out No. 28, 13 March 1900). However, the response from the Deputy Governor was: 'The Bank does not desire to further curtail loans and will consider any new business.' The lending business was now largely reduced to the Bank's deposits base, but even so the Bank was not prepared 'to lock-up money in industrials'. Therefore the credit rates charged the Chamberlain Bros. were raised further (BofE, BBALB In No. 15, 14 March 1900, 23 March 1900), and the result was a further decline in the lending business. 'Your advance figures have fallen . . . but the reason for the shrinkage is quite appreciated here', commented the Principal of the branch banks' office (BofE, BBALB In No. 15, 6 June 1900).

In looking through the correspondence it is striking that from 1899 no more requests for new loans had come from Birmingham. Apparently Smith was refusing these himself, since 'special considerations' regarding the securities offered were probably not necessary. That loans were being requested is evident from the fact that during the agent's annual holiday the representative of the subagent (the subagent himself was doing military service in South Africa) sent one such application to London (BofE, BBALB Out No. 28, 26 April 1900). Probably he had been instructed to consult the branch banks' office on all questions that went beyond the routine business. The answer from London to the application was brief and to the point:

> The Deputy Governor does not care to make the desired advance against the securities you name [Birmingham City Tramway Pref. Shares, Brown Marshall Pref. and Ord. Shares, Birmingham Small Arms & Metal Pref. and Ord. Shares]. This account is hardly of a nature as to call for special consideration (BofE, BBALB In No. 15, 27 April 1900)

However, now that he had reduced his lending to the level of his deposits, Smith must have given loans to other customers than the Chamberlain Group against industrials, on his own responsibility. In July 1901 Edye was complaining that the securities of 'commercial concerns' were increasing again, and asking Smith to consult the branch banks' office before giving loans (BofE, BBALB In No. 16, 11 July 1901).

We do not need to speculate on the reasons for the restrictive attitude taken by the head office from 1899 to 1901. The Banking Department reserve had fallen from the undesirably high level of £30 million on average for the year in 1895, and £35 million for 1896, to £25 million in 1897 and £22 million in 1898. With the clear rise in the securities' holding from 1896, the growing demand for credit in London with deposits stagnating[31] was jeopardizing the reserve from about 1898. In 1898/9 the Bank had three possible ways of countering this development. First, it could sell the securities that had been bought in 1896. Second, it could raise Bank Rate and so throttle the demand for credit (especially in London). Third, it could also change the practical application of its rules and throttle the lending business in the provinces.

The first option was out of the question, since the prices of gilt-edged securities had been falling steadily since the end of 1896, so that the Bank could sell only at considerable loss.[32] In addition, it had also invested in paper during these years that was not traded on stock exchanges. These bonds (mainly corporation bonds and debentures of Indian railway companies) could not be sold: they formed a 'lock-up' in the portfolio for years. The only possibility was to throttle the lending business in order to reduce pressure on the reserve. The restrictions that the Bank introduced were of a different quality than those introduced after the May scandal. The Bank followed the old tradition of lowering the demand for credit by making credit conditions more restrictive. Governor Weguelin had told the Parliamentary Committee of Inquiry in 1857 that there were changing majorities among the directors over the question of how the reduction of the demand for loans to reduce the pressure on the Banking Department reserve could best be achieved. He himself was in favour of 'restraint which is placed upon the term of bills' (BPP 1857, evidence Weguelin, qq.311, 326–7), while his colleague G.W. Norman felt that an increase in Bank Rate would be the best solution (BPP 1857, evidence Norman, qq.2569–70).

In this case a moderate increase in the interest rate would probably have had little effect in view of the boom, because the commercial banks would only have followed suit if the Bank Rate in London had been increased. Raising Bank Rate could not be considered, since it was feared at the time that the money market would not follow. Later, a further consideration was that the government was concerned to keep interest rates low in view of the situation in South Africa and the threat of war. The solution adopted, of adapting the business practice to the rules, was therefore a simple and a 'clean' one, because it could be carried out without arousing too much attention. The Bank did not even need to announce a change in its credit conditions, since the rules that now really applied had existed *de jure* since 1894. Applying them only to the lombard business in the provinces was a very rational decision from the commercial point of view, bearing in mind that the securities in the provincial lombard business were of inferior quality to those available in the London discount business, while there was presumably only a very slight difference between the yields.

It is interesting now to ask whether, after the end of the tighter situation on the money market caused by the cyclical downswing and the war, and with pressure easing on the reserve, the Bank permitted a renewed expansion of the provincial branches' lending business by relaxing its handling of the rules. Although the principal of the branch banks' office repeatedly requested this, there was no increase in activity comparable to the years 1896 to 1898. The discount business did grow strongly in the first few years after the turn of the century, in the provincial branches as well, but the Birmingham branch did not share in the upswing, for the change did not benefit Birmingham and the Black Country, unlike the textile regions. Moreover, the local banks, unlike those in Lancashire, were almost all directly connected to the London money market (*Bankers' Magazine* Vol. 96/May 1900, p. 886), and they were not dependent on the Bank of England for funding.[33] A revival in Birmingham would only have been possible through the lombard business. However, the lombard business was not reactivated; on the contrary, the trend at the provincial branches continued to move downward until the First World War. Accordingly the lending business in Birmingham also declined. The end of the 'industrial branch' was the end of its peak as well.

5

The development of central bank policy and the English provinces — a reassessment

The history of the Bank of England in the provinces can be roughly divided into three phases. The first, from about 1830, immediately after the founding and establishment of the branches, to the passing of Peel's Act in 1844, was characterized by a strategy behind which a monetary policy objective is clearly recognizable. To limit the extent to which the provincial banks of issue could undermine its monetary policy, which was oriented to the balance of payments, the Bank of England endeavoured to induce the provincial banks to cease issuing banknotes by co-operating closely with them and offering certain concessions, such as preferential interest rate for rediscounting.

The second phase, up to the reform of the management of the Bank in 1888, was characterized by a withdrawal of the Bank of England from the provinces. This can be seen not only in a reduction in the number of branches, but more generally in that the Bank of England lost interest in being 'the provincial banks' bank' and largely refrained from utilizing its means of intervention in the provinces. In commercial bank policy, this second phase can be subdivided into two sections. While the business largely stagnated in the 1850s and 1860s after a break towards the end of the 1840s (apart from cyclical fluctuations), the lending business at many branches broke down after the start of the bill discounting crisis in the 1870s, and the losses suffered by the provincial branches weighed increasingly heavily on the Banking Department's profit and loss account.

The third phase, finally, after 1888, brought an active business policy on the part of the branches, but unlike the 1830s this did not involve a specific monetary policy strategy. On the contrary, and in contrast with the 1830s, a division of labour did not develop between the provincial banks that were doing business with non-bank customers and the 'bankers' bank'; the Bank of England was now competing directly with the commercial banks in the province.

The first period in the history of the Bank of England provincial branches was certainly their most successful. The branches played an important role, both for the Bank of England's commercial banking interests and in the development of its central bank policy. To perform these tasks the Bank was certainly prepared to see its earnings capacity reduced. In view of the passive business policy the Bank had pursued in London under the 'Palmer Rule', the activation of its discount business in the provinces must be seen mainly as a side-effect of the attempt to increase the circulation of Bank of England notes in the provinces. That it was the commercial success of some of the branches which actually made the Palmer policy possible should not disguise the fact that the development of central bank policy in England at this time was far in advance of any other European country.

There were two main reasons for the standstill or decline in the development of a modern central bank policy from the 1840s. The first was the cover rules for the issue of banknotes by the Bank of England Issue Department. Tying the Bank of England issue rigidly to the gold holdings of the Issue Department, while at the same time allowing the Bank freedom in its business policy, that is, especially in controlling the level of the Banking Department reserve (the second reason for the reversal in the development of a modern central bank policy in England) was bound to mean that the Bank of England could scarcely establish itself as 'lender of last resort'. When the fiduciary issue was fixed, a shift between the components of the money stock cash (notes and coin) and book money in favour of the former was more or less impossible. To maintain confidence that the notes could be converted into gold at any time, the convertibility of the book money into cash (notes and coin) must necessarily remain in question. For anything else would have meant that the growth in book money would also have to be tied to the available gold reserves. The appropriate legislation would have been the ultimate logic under the law of 1844, but even the advocates of the legislation will have realized that such a path was not practicable.[1]

The biggest problem raised by the lack of convertibility of book money for the credit system and so for the economy as a whole around the middle of the nineteenth century in England was the extreme vulnerability to crises. If confidence in the convertibility of book money was shaken, as it might be if a major bank or discount house were to collapse, it would be difficult to prevent a panic. According to Batchelor, the authorities — and in the British case this could only be the Bank of England — had the following possibilities to prevent a loss of public confidence in book money should a major financial institution be in danger of insolvency. It could first try various measures to restore public confidence in the bank concerned and prevent the collapse that way. The handling of the Baring crisis in 1890 is a good example of such a strategy (see Pressnell 1968, pp. 167–228; Clapham 1944, Vol. 2, pp. 326–39; Fulford 1953, pp. 209–12). Second, it could let the bank go down and try to prevent the confidence crisis affecting others by giving certain guarantees.[2] The action during the panic in Newcastle after the collapse of the Northumberland & Durham District Bank in 1857, described in detail above, is a good example of this strategy. It may be assumed that the central bank will choose the first method if it believes that the liquidity problem is only temporary and the business is basically sound. If it regards the business as basically unsound, the central bank will choose the second alternative.

Except under extremely favourable conditions, both these methods required the provision of considerable additional finance by the central bank, either through extending credit (for instance by increasing the fiduciary issue) or by recourse to the central bank reserves. Increasing the fiduciary issue was impossible under the legislation after 1844. The cover rules were suspended in 1847, 1857 and 1866, but understandably the government could suspend the law only after the panic had already broken out. The purpose of the rigid cover rules was to secure the convertibility of sterling, and in the opinion of the majority of contemporaries, a fixed fiduciary issue was a precondition for this. The cover rules could only fulfil their purpose if their suspension could not be calculated in advance. Only the central bank reserve remained, therefore, as an instrument.

However, its Banking Department operated as a normal commercial bank and even the advocates of more central bank responsibility for the Bank of England had to admit that it was a privately owned profit-making institution. As such, it could hardly be expected to invest capital without making a profit when times were quiet, only to build up an emergency fund to use if competitor banks found themselves short of liquidity when times were difficult. In short, the scope for the Bank to act as 'lender of last resort' was very slight. Nor should it be forgotten that the bank expressly refused to play the part of lender of last resort from 1844 until at least the 1870s. It endeavoured to 'teach' the market that each discount house and each bank should keep its portfolio liquid enough not to be dependent on such an institution.

A typical example of this mixture of objective necessity and 'education' was the end of the lending to the London bill brokers and discount houses in 1858. The objective necessity was that the Bank was simply not in a position to satisfy adequately the demand for funding from these sources. The 'educational' aspect was that the Bank wanted to induce the discount houses to invest their own liquidity reserves, possibly in government paper.[3] Even in the Baring crisis of 1890 great efforts were made to stress the unusual nature of this rescue operation.[4]

It is therefore hardly surprising that the action by the Bank of England in Newcastle during the two crises in 1847 and 1857 was also seen as unusual. The support given to the Northumberland & Durham District Bank in 1847 was solely on the initiative and responsibility of the branch agent there, and it is very doubtful whether the head office would have approved in advance. The intervention in 1857 did come from the head office, but the demonstrative effect that every bank should organize its portfolio so that it was in a position to remain solvent without recourse to a lender of last resort was assured by the collapse of the Northumberland & Durham District Bank. Moreover, this rescue operation was clearly possible without recourse to the central bank reserves. Finally, the Bank of England enabled most of the acceptors of the bills it had rediscounted itself and which were accordingly in its bill portfolio at the time, to fulfil their obligations.

As a rule, however, the Bank of England behaved in the provinces as in the case of the North & South Wales Bank in 1847. The collapse of this bank was started by a false report in a London paper that in Liverpool, following the Royal Bank of Liverpool and the Liverpool Banking Co., the North & South Wales Bank had also ceased payment. The bank did not survive the run this caused. The Bank of England was asked for assistance but refused on the grounds that 'the securities [on real property] are not of that description upon which they [the Bank] usually made advances' (Crick and Wadsworth 1936, p. 184 quoting a North & South Wales Bank source).[5] It is clear here that even in Liverpool where co-operation between the Bank of England and the provincial banks was generally held to be good (see Chapter 2.2.2), the support that the Bank of England could give in emergencies was very limited. Generally it was held that these limits were tighter in the provinces than in London, as the credit rationing in April 1847 and the reasons given for this by Deputy Governor Prescott show (Chapter 2.3.1).

After the crisis of 1878[6] there were virtually no more bank failures in the English provinces. At first this might be seen as due to the activities of the Bank of England which, as is widely held, became increasingly aware of its central bank policy responsibility after the 1870s. However, a closer examination of the policy pursued by the Bank of England in the provinces will show that particularly in the 1880s, its contact with the provincial banks was reduced to a minimum, and it can hardly be said that there was co-operation between the Bank of England and the commercial banks in the 1890s. The stability of the system was due to structural causes. The crisis of 1878[7] had shown the provincial banks that only the principles of 'sound banking' would ensure their survival. Accordingly it was precisely the non-availability of a lender of last resort that forced them to keep their portfolios liquid. Instead of investing in *de facto* long-term lending to industrial and other provincial borrowers, a number of provincial banks went over to investing a growing share of their resources on either the London money market or the London Stock Exchange (Collins 1989, p.512). The greater involvement of provincial banks in London often led directly to the takeover of or co-operation with a London bank, but this always also involved the adoption of London business practices, one of the most important unwritten rules of which was never to rediscount a bill. The conversion of the provincial banks into branches of a major bank operating from London reduced the demand for a lender of last resort institutionally, so to speak.

It was not only the provincial finance markets and their institutions that formed closer ties with the London finance market and so were theoretically less dependent on the Bank of England as intermediary between London and the provinces. The Bank of England itself showed no interest at all in acting in this capacity, although this would have created a better position for its supervisory and regulatory functions. The reactivation of business at its provincial branches had nothing to do with an improvement in its relations with the commercial banks in the provinces. On the contrary, the more active Bank of England policy in the provinces towards the end of the 1880s was the result of the serious crisis in the discount business, both in London and in the provinces, and the growing losses suffered by the provincial branches.

The Bank reacted to this development, first by making its provincial branches more competitive, and second by trying to resume business with the London discount houses. Somewhat later it also followed the example of the London deposit banks.[8] They saw the answer to the crisis in bill discounting as giving, in addition to call credits to bill brokers,[9] similar credits to stock brokers ('Bowen advances').[10]

Because the London alternatives did not at first prove successful, the Bank relaxed its resistance to the wishes of those branch agents who were ready and in a position to conduct their branches like normal commercial banks. There had probably always been a latent readiness on the part of the agents to intervene more actively in the local finance markets, and the Birmingham branch agent was probably not the only one who infringed the Regulations for the Management of the Branches,[11] for the agents' salaries were related to their performance, if not directly, certainly indirectly. An agent or subagent could increase his earnings if his branch was commercially successful[12] or he could be moved to the next larger branch.[13] What criteria (apart from length of service with the Bank) determined the personal success of the senior staff of a Bank of England provincial branch was stated quite openly inside the Bank: 'It is the object of the business to make profit for the shareholders' (BofE, BBALB Out No. 25, 19 March 1896).

That higher interest income for the provincial branches could not be achieved with London business practices was clear to the directors, and with the earnings situation catastrophic, they were forced to make their branches more competitive. However, they tolerated provincial business practices only as long as there was no alternative to provincial business. The May scandal of November 1893 did cause the directors to pursue a more restrictive policy in the provinces for a time, but this attempt failed at the outset because the Banking Department, which was operating in commercial banking, was going through the worst crisis since it had been set up in 1844.

Never before had there been such difficulties in paying a satisfactory dividend. The problems were due to the decline in interest earnings on the lombard and discount business, which had fallen by £216,000 in the 1894/5 financial year from the previous year. The Bank had not been able to make this up with income achieved in the current financial year, and it had to use its hidden reserves. The shortfall in London (including the London West End and Law Courts branches) was more serious in this context than that in the provinces. While the share of London interest income in the gross earnings of the Banking Department fell from 20 per cent in the 1893/4 financial year to 12 per cent in 1894/5, the provincial branches' interest income proved very much more stable, declining only from 9 per cent to 7 per cent. To achieve that stability the directors had had to accept securities that they would never have accepted without these problems, or, as the Deputy Governor said quite openly in 1900: 'our only reason for not acting more consistently with our views, was a desire not to unduly reduce the profit earning power of the Branches' (BofE, BBALB In No. 15, 6 June 1900).

When the reforms of the London lending business did have the desired success towards the end of the 1890s, the situation changed. There is not the slightest indication that industrial bonds were more risky as security in 1899 than they had been before, or that they did not seem suitable for other reasons now. Only when the Bank's resources no longer sufficed to meet the demand for credit from its old customers in the provinces and its new customers in London, was the lombard lending against securities in the provinces cut back — independent of the consequences that these measures might have for the branches or their customers.[14] The Birmingham branch agent said resignedly in September 1899:

> Trade in our district is going on very active and prosperous and our neighbours are doing well. We alone are stagnant partly because of the policy of restricting of accommodation rendered necessary by the position of the London money market. (BofE, BBALB Out No. 27, 4 September 1899)

In other words, the restriction of the lending business in the provinces began clearly before the outbreak of the war in South Africa or before the issue of the first war loan. So it cannot be said that the Bank had to strengthen its reserves in order to be able to hold the market under control in the interests of a successful government debt issue. This situation only occurred months after the beginning of the restrictions. Naturally the war considerably accelerated the reduction of the credits at the provincial branches, but how little this exceptional situation was really the cause, is also evident in that the directors did not accede to the wishes of the branch banks' office and did not permit an expansion of the lombard business at the provincial branches from 1902 to 1905. However justified the efforts to improve portfolio liquidity may have been for a central bank and however justified the shift in weight in the Bank of England's portfolio in favour of 'advances on floaters' or bill discounting, and away from the provincial lombard securities business, the Bank was always concerned for liquidity when the earnings on liquid investment were high enough to guarantee an adequate dividend.

The improvement in the relationship between the Bank of England and the commercial banks in the last years before the First World War can therefore certainly also be seen against the background that the increases in earnings on bill discounting by the provincial branches were very largely due to the provincial banks rediscounting. The shift in the relation between deposits and bill discounting at least at some provincial banks presumably caused them once more to look further for new sources of funding. So the improvement in relations was advisable for both sides, if only from the commercial point of view. According to an estimate by the branch banks' office in 1906 the rediscounting of five out of the eight most important provincial banks accounted for around one third of the discount business of the provincial branches (BofE, Edye Reports G 15/39, Memo 20 February 1906). The Bank therefore occasionally departed from its strict rejection of 'foreign bills' for these customers.[15]

If, as in the 1890s, it was not possible to ensure an adequate dividend with liquid forms of investment, the Bank of England was forced to seek alternatives and it was ready to take a higher liquidity risk. The principal of the branch banks' office described this policy in 1902 as follows:

> My idea of good management of the Branches would be in normal times, when the Bank rate is low and the employment of money in London difficult, to allow the Branches greater latitude in lending and to get a better return for the Bank's money than obtainable in London. Similarly in abnormal times . . . I would tighten rules judiciously, reduce commitments and have funds centralised — acting on this principle when the [Boer] war began, we began, the Deputy Governor always approving of what we proposed, to reduce advances. (BofE, Edye Reports 1902, G 15/39)

The effect of applying the procyclical 'rules of the game' on the conditions in the English provinces cannot be put more plainly. So there can be no question of 'tenderness towards home trade and industry' on micro level. Cyclical considerations did not occur to the branch agents, who were only interested in the commercial success of their branches, nor the London-oriented Deputy Governors.

The much-invoked 'tenderness' is not evident on macro level either, and the more cautious handling of the Bank Rate after the turn of the century will serve as an indication of the rudimentary cyclical approach. A more exact examination of the Bank of England's key rate, however, will show that the Bank was only concerned to keep the costs of the influence on the London interest level which it felt obliged to exercise as low as possible. During the first cyclical downswing after the turn of the century, open market policy measures were the less costly alternative with a relatively low Bank Rate (that would certainly help the cyclical recovery), while even in the following cyclical downswing a more active Bank Rate policy was the better solution, thanks to the attraction of foreign (especially French) gold reserves. Since these reserves were attracted not through better co-operation with the Banque de France or other central banks, but only by the threat of a high Bank Rate, cyclical policy considerations cannot be said to have applied here either. Even one of the most important contemporary advocates of the gold standard, R.G. Hawtrey, had to admit that a Bank Rate of 5 per cent could have had harmful effects on the cyclical recovery in 1909 (Hawtrey 1962, p. 119).

If in conclusion we can now say that the development of central bank policy in England before the First World War has so far been greatly overestimated, that does not mean that there was no need for regulation. Charles Goodhart stressed again only recently that the evolution of the modern central bank functions, from the pure clearing office through lender of last resort to supervision and a regulatory body for the banking system, was a process inherent in the market. A study of central bank policy in the British provinces clearly confirms that. As the development during the 1830s shows, the market was ready to accept a central body as clearing house and pay a certain price for the stability it brought (in this case giving up licences to issue banknotes). That after the promising start in the 1830s the other steps to the modern central bank named by Goodhart were not taken much earlier than in the other industrializing countries of Europe was due to specific institutional factors that did not apply in that form in other countries. It cannot be maintained that 'the market' resisted a 'lender of last resort'. The next steps to the responsibility of a modern central bank were prevented only by institutional factors, until the banks, especially those in the provinces, were forced to accept the second-best solution of unconditional portfolio liquidity. This would appear to be one of the main reasons for the 'almost pathological concern with liquidity that plagued English banks' which Cameron complains of (Cameron 1982, p. 106).

Goodhart's second argument, that the Bank of England slowly grew into the role of a modern central bank, cannot, however, be confirmed. According to him

> the metamorphosis from [its] involvement in commercial banking, as a competitive, profit-maximizing bank among many, to a non-competitive non-profit-maximizing role . . . marked the true emergence and development of proper Central Banking . . . . Competition between the other commercial banks and the Bank of England . . . [as well as] an uncomprehending, if not antipathetic, legal code in the form of the Bank of England Act of 1844 . . . complicated, overshadowed, and tarnished [the] adoption of a regulatory role. (Goodhart 1988, pp. 9, 104)

However, as one could meaningfully add, the 'natural' (a term Goodhart repeatedly uses in this context) development of central banking was not prevented by these factors. As a result of this study one can see that the interplay of these two factors not only held up the acceptance of a regulatory role by the Bank of England, it actually largely prevented it:

> the micro functions of a Central Bank, in providing a central (and therefore economical) source of reserves and liquidity to other banks and hence both a degree of insurance and regulation, cannot be undertaken effectively, basically because of conflicts of interest, by a commercial competitor. (Goodhart 1988, p. 8; see also Goodhart 1984, p. 224; Sayers 1947, pp. 71, 132)

To that extent Salin's thesis, which Goodhart rejects as 'historically inaccurate', would seem to be confirmed. Salin believes that only direct government intervention can extend a clearing house function (the first step on the way to the modern central bank as custodian of interbank deposits) to the lender of last resort function (see Salin 1984, pp. 16–17; see also Cairncross 1988, p. 47; Pollard 1970, p. 7; Pollard 1989, p. 245–50).[16] The British government did not, however, feel it was incumbent on it to take on that function,[17] and so the commercial goal of securing a dividend, regarded as adequate, constantly conflicted with the commercial banks and thus prevented their voluntary inclusion in a system of supervision and regulation of the banking system by the central bank.

Until the outbreak of the First World War the Bank of England was not a government interventionary body, not even in embryonic form. It was not a reliable lender of last resort. Its task as quasi-state institution did not differ on the eve of the First World War greatly from what it had been during the period of classical competition capitalism in the middle of the nineteenth century. The low development stage of central bank policy in England is most clear from the Bank's policy in the provinces, for here not only did the profit motive play a central role in the directors' decisions, as it did in London, but also the subordination of the provinces to the requirements of the London money and capital markets was evident. That applied as much to the quarter-century before the First World War as to the 1840s.

Notes

Chapter 1

1. This metaphor is probably intended to counter both Keynes' description of the Bank of England as 'conductor of the international orchestra' (Keynes 1930, Vol. 2, p. 307) and McCloskey's and Zecher's 'triangle player' (McCloskey and Zecher 1981, p. 186).

Chapter 2

1. On the Bank of England's negative attitude to demands for an expansion of the circulation of Bank of England notes in the provinces at the beginning of the 1820s, see Acres 1931a, Vol. 2, pp. 415–16, 426. In addition to a certain pressure on the part of the government (see Clapham 1944, Vol. 2, p. 104), the experience of the Bank of Ireland, that had been through a very similar development two years before, was probably of some significance here, see Hall 1949, pp. 127–32; Barrow 1974, pp. 17–22; Munn 1988, p. 74.
2. According to an internal history of the establishment of the provincial branches written for the Bank's 250th anniversary in 1944 (BofE C 79/51), a Bank of England branch in Bristol was expressly welcomed by Stuckey's Bank, one of the first joint stock banks in England. Whether that view was representative of Bristol must remain open. See also BofE, BBO Misc. Papers: History of Branches, C 79/52, undated, c. 1961.
3. This agreement remained in force until 1844, when the Bank of England declared the old conditions for a circulation account invalid and requested fees for transfers. Wrights thereupon transferred their agency to the London private bank Barnett, Hoare & Co. BofE, BBO Birmingham Circulars, C 84/2, 8 April 1845 and BofE, CB No. 67, 26 December 1844.
4. While Wright himself put his banknote circulation at about £50,000 before the agreement with the Bank of England, it may be assumed that for joint stock banks the upper limit for the circulation account was fixed at about 60 per cent of the paid-in equity. See Collins 1972a, p. 154, n.3.
5. The only exception were bills with a term of up to twenty-one days. At a time when the transportation of banknotes was very risky, bills like those issued by the Bank of England itself (see p. 23 below), served exclusively for the transfer of larger sums of money to more distant places. See BPP 1841, evidence James, qq.1444–51.
6. The Birmingham Banking Co. was the very first bank with which the Bank of England concluded a circulation account agreement (BPP 1837/8, App.8, p. 123). It had been created out of two old private banks, Galton & James and Gibbins & Lovell, as successor to Gibbins, Smith & Goode, originally

the largest bank of issue in Birmingham. However, it failed in 1825 (Moss 1981, pp. 541, 549).

7. The private banks Attwood, Spooner & Co., with an authorized note issue of £23,695, Moilliet & Sons with £18,232, and Taylor & Lloyds with £38,816. The amount circulated by the National Provincial Bank of England branch in Birmingham is not known, however, and it may be assumed that the total provincial circulation was around £100,000 (Banking Almanac 1845, List of Private Banks Which Issue Notes, p. 118).
8. Th. Attwood (Attwoods & Spooner), however, stated in 1832 that they were still charging the top rate of 5 per cent. He justified this by saying that the bills he was discounting were of worse quality than those the Bank of England was discounting at 4 per cent in Birmingham: see BPP 1831/2, evidence Attwood, qq.5582, 5589.
9. The Bank was not able to reduce the scope for lending by the contract banks on its own but it could sell the bills deposited as security on the London money market and so 'withdraw a certain portion of the circulation' (BPP 1837/8, evidence Curtis, q.125). As these bills were not discounted at the Bank and so did not bear its endorsement, this practice was not against its rule of not rediscounting on principle.
10. The second Bank of England branch in Yorkshire, Hull, also had only one agreement on an open account at this time, with the private bank Harrison, Watson & Pease, and an agreement with T. & R. Raikes (East Riding Bank), on a circulation account.
11. Hudson says elsewhere: 'There is also evidence that Yorkshire, unlike Lancashire, was notorious from the later 18th century for the proliferation of bank notes' (Hudson 1981, p. 380; see also Crick and Wadsworth 1936, p. 210).
12. With skilful questioning Grote made the interview of the country banker I.C. Wright before the Commons Committee on Banks of Issue in 1841 a kind of crown witness hearing against the private banks of issue which Wright's own bank had been a few years before. See also the speech by the Chancellor, Wood, during the parliamentary debate on Peel's Act in 1844, Hansard Vol. 74, 20 May 1844.
13. Originally presumably a distance of fifteen miles from the location of the Bank of England branch applied (BofE, BBO Circulars, C 79/5, 28 December 1833). The Regulations for the Branch Banks as revised in 1843 state that all banks were excluded 'who issue their own notes which are payable in towns where Branches are established' (ibid., 11 October 1843).
14. Remarkably this hostility on the part of the Bank of England to the provincial banks of issue was later described as 'absurd' by Governor Hodgson himself. See BPP 1875, evidence Hodgson and Palmer, qq.7872–3, evidence Seebohm q.4700.
15. Jones' statement does not match that by the Chairman of the Manchester & Liverpool District Bank, Cooke, in 1875. Cooke said that he only ceased issuing notes in 1844, after his experience of the 1839 crisis (BPP 1875, evidence Cooke, qq.6570–1, 6710–11). However, this is not in line with the report by the Commons Committee on Joint Stock Banks of 1837/8, which lists all the contract banks in its statistics. According to this report, a circulation account agreement with the District Bank branch in Liverpool had been in force since November 1833 and with the District Bank branch in Manchester since November 1834 (BPP 1837/8, App. 8, p. 123). Cooke seems to have overlooked this.

16. Data on the deposits at the provincial branches is available only from 1853, but since the development of deposits was always clearly upwards in all the later crisis years (1858, 1866, 1879 and 1891), this can also be assumed with some certainty for 1839.
17. Clapham refers to a letter from D. Salomons (London & Westminster Bank) written in 1848, urging the Bank of England to join the London Bankers' Clearing House. Salomons argues *inter alia* that 'all Newcastle [clears] at the Bank of England Newcastle branch'. Bankers' clearing houses were set up as independent institutions in the 1870s only in some provincial cities. Newcastle was the second after Manchester to have its own clearing house. According to the *Bankers' Magazine* (Vol. 33, October 1873, p. 974), its establishment was very largely due to the initiative of the Bank of England branch agent Goddard.
18. Thomas says of the causes:

    > presumably because the local banks in these areas were very firmly entrenched, and because the farming classes were averse to change and were not disposed to take their business away from private banks which had served them well for generations (Thomas 1934, p. 87)

    In later years this may, however, have changed. Comparing current banknote circulation and authorized issues by provincial banks the *Bankers' Magazine* reached a different conclusion (Vol. 34, November 1874, p. 885). It showed that the circulation of provincial banknotes in industrial regions was very close to its upper limit, while the banks of issue in agricultural regions were having difficulties in utilizing their quotas.
19. The exact figure for the fourth quarter of 1836 is £1,089,000. The notes from the National Provincial Bank of England are not even included. As this bank operated a number of branches in these counties a figure of £1.25 million hardly seems an exaggeration.
20. The National Provincial had tried every means to keep its licence. A special amendment to the legislation was introduced by Gladstone in 1865 in the hope of enabling the bank to keep its licence although it had a new branch in London, but the legislation to abolish the 65-mile zone came to nothing because the provincial banks themselves saw in it a deterioration of their current position. The National Provincial had proposed a banknote tax of 2½ per cent and a general limit on all issue licences to twenty-five years, to persuade the government to reform through the tax system and the Bank of England to make this palatable with the time limit (BPP 1875, evidence Seebohm, qq.4790–7).
21. At the beginning of 1845 the Court of Directors decided to charge one-quarter per cent under the published interest rate for the branch in question when rediscounting for 'non-issuing banks' (see BofE, CB No. 67, 2 January 1845). This would still have meant 3¾ per cent for Wrights in Leicester at this time.
22. *Bankers' Magazine* (Vol. 34, December 1874, p. 949) summarized this at the end of 1874 as follows:

    > The vitality of these issues has been greater than was expected at the time of passing the Bank Act of 1844. The Act created a privilege and erected it into a monopoly. The framers of this legislation hardly estimated the value of the concession being made, and the stimulus it would give to measures for its preservation.

23. For such customers the branch agents could either charge one-half per cent

above the London Bank Rate or one-quarter per cent below the rate charged to other customers at the branch (Roberts 1958a, pp. 240–1).

24. 'Drafts of a manufacturer on a London warehouse of the first standing should not be discounted at the minimum rate', according to instructions from the Deputy Governor to the agent in Leicester (BofE, LBALB In No. 1, 11 December 1845).
25. The first four local clearing houses worked very closely with the local Bank of England branches. In Birmingham, Manchester and Liverpool the branch agents or subagents were actually the chairmen of the clearing house committees, on which the representatives of all the banks involved served (*Bankers' Magazine*, Vol. 47, July 1887, pp. 587–94).
26. Roberts (1958a, p. 244) rightly sees the decline in the discount business at the Swansea branch as very important in the decision by the directors to close the branch. It should not be overlooked that other branches had a far smaller discount business and could not be closed on account of their note circulation or for other reasons (see above in the case of the Portsmouth branch). Swansea was not far from Bristol, where the branch could supply the South Wales region and the Naval Yards in Pembroke with banknotes with only a slightly higher expenditure.
27. In addition, the National Provincial Bank of England was circulating its notes in the town, so that a circulation of provincial banknotes of more than £200,000 may be assumed in Leicester alone. The circulation of Bank of England notes was only £127,000 in 1844 and around £200,000 a decade later.
28. In 1884 *Bankers' Magazine* (Vol. 44, March 1884, p. 238) reported constant complaints 'for a long time past of the scarcity of bills in Lombard Street'. See also the results of a Directors' Committee in the London & Westminster Bank in the 1880s on the causes of the difficulties the Bank was experiencing in keeping constant the total of bills discounted there (Gregory 1936, pp. 270–1).
29. Naturally the only banks that are suitable for a comparison with the Bank of England are those which, like the London & Westminster Bank or the Liverpool Union Bank, did not take over other banks and also exercised restraint in opening new branches. (On the Liverpool Union Bank see Nishimura 1971, Table 19, p. 97 and on the London & Westminster Gregory 1936, pp. 305–6.) In the balance sheet of the London & Westminster Bank 'Loans and Discounts' are unfortunately shown only together. But since here too the relation between 'Loans' and 'Discounts' will certainly have shifted in favour of the latter, as it can be shown to have done at the London & County Bank for instance, the decline was probably of the same order.
30. It is not quite clear when this rule was lifted, for what mattered was not when it was crossed off the official Regulations Concerning the Management of Branches but from when the agents were able to ignore it with London's tacit consent. In the case of Birmingham it is pretty certain that much of the lombard lending against securities was not in keeping with the rule even before 1888.
31. In the branches where the lombard business was in any case insignificant by the mid-1890s (Plymouth, Portsmouth, Bristol, Hull and Leeds) and in Liverpool and the London Law Courts branch there was nothing to object to. In Newcastle one credit, in Manchester two and at the London Western branch

four were objected. Altogether £19,000 was regarded as sufficient risk provision (BofE, CB No. 116, 8 March 1894). For comparison, £250,000 was set aside as risk provision for Threadneedle Street alone in January (BofE, CB No. 116, 14 January 1894).

32. Both indicators reached their peak in 1900 (at current prices) and 1899 (constant prices): see Feinstein 1972, Tables 3 and 5, 47 and 48. This data matches the observations of contemporaries. *The Economist*, for example, dates the turn of the cycle in the last quarter of 1899, but it certainly does not see the development in 1900 as recessive. See the supplements 'Commercial History and Review of . . .' 1899 and 1900, *The Economist*, 1900 and 1901.
33. For the provinces the lombard lending against securities cannot be separated from the bill lombard loans. The latter were not, however, of any great importance there, and the distortion of the figures is probably very slight.

Chapter 3

1. The decision could also be interpreted as opposition by the Currency School to the influence of the Banking School, the leading representative of which, Tooke, was a director of the Bank from 1843 to 1857. The Currency School also had two of its leading representatives in the Court, Norman and Hubbard. On the basic theoretical positions of the two sides, see Fetter 1965, Ch. 6, pp. 165–97, White 1984, pp. 35, 153 and Crockett and White 1978, pp. 208–17.
2. The provincial bank I. & I.C. Wright in Nottingham, for instance, was not prepared to charge its customers more than the top rate of 5 per cent under the old Usury Laws. See BPP 1847/8, Part 3, evidence I.C. Wright, q.2920.
3. According to official statistics this was the discount rate applied on 5 October 1847 by the provincial branches of the Bank of England. See BPP 1947/8, Part 2, App. 15, p. 184.
4. The Union Bank resumed operations a few years later, but it finally collapsed in the crisis of 1857. See Thomas 1934, p. 444, App.M, p. 660.
5. In private correspondence McCord judges the situation in Newcastle as follows:

   > The banking crisis of 1847–8 in North East England, associated with the collapse of several local banks . . . coincided with other temporary strains. I include especially the last great phase of Chartism which for a time seemed to present a serious challenge to the established order.

6. > A financial crisis is fuelled by fears that means of payment will be unobtainable at any price . . . . It is precipitated by actions of the public that suddenly squeeze the reserves of the banking system. In a futile attempt to restore reserves, the banks may call loans, refuse to roll over existing loans, or resort to selling assets . . . . A real financial crisis occurs only when institutions do not exist, when authorities are unschooled in the practices that preclude such development, and when the private sector has reason to doubt the dependability of preventive arrangements. (Schwartz 1984, pp. 11–12)

7. In the view of the Bank of England branch agent in Birmingham a Bank Rate of up to 3.5 per cent would not have affected local lending rates, while in the view of the agent in Newcastle a Bank Rate of 4.5 per cent would not have affected them there. See BofE, BBO Special Report No. 534.
8. Sayers sees the gold market intervention in the boom year 1899 as an

attempt 'to spare the trade and business of the country the burden of a seven per cent rate' (1936, p. 91), and that in the depression year 1904 as 'the Bank was probably unwilling to embark on a high rate policy while home trade was so slack' (1936, p. 95).

9. 'It would be judicious for the Bank and probably profitable too, to take money off the market by borrowing on their Government Securities' (*The Economist* 8 October 1881, p. 1241).
10. Interest expenditure in the half-year 1903/4 was actually higher, at £30,000, than discount interest earnings in Threadneedle Street during the same period (£29,000). For one and a half years the Bank therefore refrained from 'borrowing on stock' (BofE, Stock Estimates (ADM 19), Profit and Loss Accounts) and shifted entirely into raising the gold price (see gold prices in the weekly statements by the *Statist* in October and December 1903 and March, June and July 1904). On the Bank's gold policy, see Sayers 1936, p. 82 and 1976, Vol. 1, pp. 47–53.
11. Beach says: 'A high Bank rate was therefore regarded as an affliction by the industry dependent upon the local banks' (Beach 1972, p. 160).
12. The dilemma for the Reichsbank in such a situation was the relatively slight influence it could exert on international gold flows. In this it was at a considerable disadvantage against the Bank of England. The Reichsbank therefore had to put its key rate much higher than the current key rates in London and Paris. However, if it became known that the Reichsbank was putting its key rate so high only to attract gold, confidence in the Mark would be shaken and balances withdrawn from Germany. Moreover, in view of the gold reserves that were everywhere felt to be too small (with the possible exception of France), the central banks were competing directly with each other. Interest rate rises in Germany provoked interest rate rises elsewhere, and this weakened the desired effect. The Reichsbank had to take particular account of the Bank of England here, for according to Mosbacher it had little means of effectively countering an increase in Bank Rate in London. The Reichsbank therefore avoided forcing the Bank of England to adopt compensatory measures. The gold market intervention (also known as 'external discount policy' in contemporary German terminology) was therefore of different and clearly greater significance for the Reichsbank than for the Bank of England: see Mosbacher 1976, p. 33.
13. Without going into this in more detail, Bloomfield also comes to a rather pessimistic conclusion regarding the counter-cyclical motivation of the Bank of England's open market policy (Bloomfield 1959, p. 46).

Chapter 4

1. In 1869 a customer of the Birmingham branch of the Bank of England moved to Lloyds Banking Co. because of the 'inconvenience of their [the Bank of England's] restrictions' (quoted from Sayers 1957, p. 154).
2. However, up to 1866 that did not apply to Lloyds Banking Co., which had an issue licence and so was not permitted to rediscount.
3. Ten years later Barham was in heated controversy over this with Deputy Governor Lidderdale, who long before the Baring crisis wanted to force the commercial banks to keep larger reserves with the Bank of England. See the personal letters from Lidderdale to Barham in BofE, BBALB In No. 12, 10 October 1887, 27 October 1887, 9 November 1887, 11 November 1887

and 15 December 1887. After Lidderdale took the negotiations with the banks in Birmingham in hand himself (BofE, BBALB In No. 12, 21 December 1887), the average stock of deposits did rise by around 20 per cent.

4. This was revealed by a survey in the city of Birmingham in the mid-1880s (BofE, BBALB Out No. 20, 9 November 1886).
5. Barham did not mention that an offer on his part (in February) had preceded this application from the Birmingham & Midland Bank (in April). The Midland Bank in turn used the February enquiry to achieve better terms from its London agent, the Union Bank of London. See Holmes and Green 1986, pp. 81–2.
6. Sayers is referring here to a case in 1846, when the Bank of England excluded the private bank Taylor & Lloyds (later Lloyds Banking Co.) from rediscounting at its Birmingham branch, in annoyance that the private bank would not renounce its issue licence. Thereafter Taylor & Lloyds rediscounted exclusively at its London sister bank, Hanbury, Taylor, Lloyd & Co.
7. The Deputy Governor of the Bank was always responsible for the policy towards the branches. Since the supervision of the provincial branches changed every two years as the Governors rotated, there could be considerable frictional losses. Some of the Deputy Governors were more interested in effective supervision of the provincial branches while others left the branch agents more scope. The following quotation from Henry R. Grenfell, Deputy Governor from 1879 to 1881, could, however, have come from any of his successors. It is very characteristic of the approach of the London directors generally.
8. The telegrams from London have not survived, but the contents can be surmised from the answers. The texts of the answering telegrams are to be found in BofE, BBALB Out No. 18, 31 July 1879.
9. Bank of England director Hankey put this very plainly in a reader's letter to *The Times* in January 1879, a few weeks after the City of Glasgow Bank crisis:

   > A merchant may with perfect propriety grant his acceptance against the consignment of goods or against a variety of engagements, the risk of which he is supposed to be able to calculate, and for which kind of business he is entitled to charge a remunerative commission. Not so with a banker . . . . Above all it is indispensable for a good banking security that the acceptor intends to pay his acceptance at the date of maturity and not to contemplate a renewal of the bill . . . . The bill cannot be made to depend on any external circumstances, such as the sale of goods or a counter engagement of any other person. This I hold to be the main difference between a bill of exchange and a mortgage. (*The Times*, 18 January 1879)

10. Hilferding makes a distinction between two kinds of lending to industry:

    > Monetary capital may be required for conversion to circulating or fixed capital. The difference is important, on account of the different ways the funds flow back. Monetary capital, advanced to buy circulating capital, will flow back in the same way, that is, its value is fully reproduced after the turnover period and reconverted to monetary form. The situation is different with advances that are to be converted into fixed capital. Here the funds only gradually flow back over a long series of turnover periods and the money is tied up throughout that time. The difference in the reflow therefore determines the different degrees in which the bank's money is locked up. (Hilferding 1910, p. 113)

11. Both types of capital lending mentioned above can appear in a bank's balance sheet as overdrafts. Only a bank that is very well informed about

its customers' affairs can be really sure that repayment may be expected over the medium term thanks to the reflow. Very frequently reflows were needed again immediately to enable the production to be continued to the order already achieved — or the undertake rationalization investment that was needed. In such a situation a bank was hardly in a position to enforce repayment.

> Money advanced on overdrawn account without security to an agreed-on limit is not usually subject to such prompt repayment. The debtor on this form of advance has therefore a longer time for getting into trouble, if his affairs should tend into that direction. (George Rae 1903, p. 34)

Rae almost felt that it was a moral obligation to restrain industrialists from using current account credits over extended periods. He describes in detail the fate of an industrialist who had been granted generous credit initially by the branch manager Littleworth (Rae 1903, pp. 47–9). In regard to portfolio liquidity capital lending of the second type could therefore be very advantageous, for joint stock companies could issue bonds which were actually quite a liquid form of investment if they were marketable.

12. This was not a local security, but it was not the class of security the Bank would have chosen to invest in. The Lehigh & Wilkes Bane bonds had been issued in 1874 by Bonar Thompson in London. They were also guaranteed by an American railway company, which is why they are listed by Adler as 'American Railway Security' (Adler 1970, App. 1, p. 208). That was the first time the Bank accepted securities for advances in which it did not invest itself.
13. 'The provincial banker while allowing two and a half per cent on deposits must buttress with a minimum charge on overdraft' (BofE, BBO Special Reports No. 534). This report dates from 1909, but it is very unlikely that the interest rates were lower thirty years before, when almost all the banks in Birmingham were still dependent on the resources in the region that bore interest at 2½ per cent. The fact that some customers were powerful enough to put pressure on the banks and achieve a slight undercutting of the minimum rate on occasions did not alter that.
14. The Muntz Metal Co., incorporated in the middle of the nineteenth century, was not a company of only local standing. Even in the first half of the nineteenth century it was one of the leading non-ferrous metal processing firms in England and one of the largest industrial enterprises. Its shares were also already being traded in London in the 1880s. For details on the history of Muntz' brass alloys, see Timmins 1866, pp. 313–16; see also Allen 1929, pp. 34–5.
15. In explanation here we can quote a prize-winning essay 'On Bankers' Securities' by the branch manager of a commercial bank, in *The Bankers' Magazine* (Vol. 46, 1886, p. 958):

> As registration gives a complete title, it also involves all the liabilities attaching to a shareholder, and it would be folly for a banker to register any shares in his own name before becoming acquainted with all the liabilities they carry. Shares not fully paid up should never be registered in the banker's name, for by doing so he would render himself liable for all the unpaid portions of the shares . . ., and in the event of any company becoming insolvent his supposed security might be converted into a heavy loss.

16. The tone of the memorandum leaves no doubt that good relations existed between the principal, Courtney, and Barham. The memoranda from Courtney's successor, Edye, who was regarded as wanting to see an active business

policy in the provinces (Sayers 1976, Vol. 1, p. 21, n. 1) were much cooler.

17. The official Birmingham Circular of the branch banks' office states:

> The Deputy Governor [Collet] directs me to draw your special attention to . . . the grounds upon which the Bank must decline to accept blank transfers as security for advances: Under the last Bankruptcy Act, the Receiver or Trustee to every estate becomes possessed *ipso facto* of all the property of the Bankrupt . . . . The effect of this is to render all blank transfers of stock absolutely valueless as security, under the circumstances which would make it necessary to put them in force (BofE, BBO Birmingham Circulars, C 84/1, 26 June 1885).

18. Collet had been an employee of the Bank of Liverpool from 1840 to 1848, before becoming a partner in the merchant bank Brown Shipley in Liverpool in 1851, after spending some time in the United States. He remained for another thirteen years in Liverpool, before founding the London branch of Brown Shipley in 1864. Two years later he was elected a director of the Bank of England.
19. Shares and bonds of the Birmingham Small Arms & Metal Co. were certainly 'first class' local securities at this time. The company, founded in 1861 with the support of the War Office, had, however, suffered a sales crisis since the late 1870s, and only a few years before it had moved into bicycle production as a sideline. This was still not very successful in the 1880s, and in 1885 the firm temporarily ceased to produce bicycles since its capacities were fully utilized owing to the tension between Britain and Russia in Afghanistan (see Allen 1929, p. 219; and Davenport-Hines 1984, p. 48). Its shares were still totally unknown in London in the 1880s, neither traded on the London Stock Exchange nor even circulating outside the official market (BofE, BBALB In No. 12, 6 October 1888).
20. According to a list dating from summer 1888, Lea's credits had reached a total of about £120,000 (BofE, BBALB Out No. 20, annexed).
21. Up to 1839 employees of the Bank were allowed to engage in secondary activities without restriction and even without the approval of the Bank. When bankruptcies of Bank of England staff began to mushroom, the Court of Directors in 1836 ordered that any employee who became bankrupt would face instant dismissal. Finally in 1839 it forbade employees on principle 'to carry on any trade, profession or business, either directly or indirectly, either as principal or agent' (quoted from Acres 1931a, Vol. 2, p. 487).
22. That you have personally connected yourself with several of our customers in various ventures in order to benefit the Bank indirectly, and that you think the Bank for its own sake ought therefore to support these ventures, though it would probably not do so on their own merits . . . I must say that seems to me a dangerous position for both you and the Bank. For the Bank because it would be departing from its usual prudent course of advancing against high class and easily realizable securities only (BofE, BBALB In No. 13, 22 November 1891).
23. An electrical firm in the Chamberlain Group (security £10,000 bonds, BofE, BBALB Out No. 22, 20 October 1893); a mechanical engineering firm (security £3,000 bonds, op. cit., 7 November 1893); and a brewery (security £5,000 op. cit., 24 October 1893).
24. See BofE, BBALB Out No. 22, 6 December 1893, 12 December 1893, No. 23, 1 January 1894, 2 March 1894; BBALB In No. 14, 7 December 1893, 13 December 1893, 2 January 1893, 2 January 1893, 3 March 1893.
25. At this time the directors could no doubt foresee that the August results would be catastrophic, for a day after the Deputy Governor had indicated that Smith should accommodate the Chamberlains, the Bank sold bonds for

the value of £340,000 to mobilize hidden reserves and at least maintain the autumn dividend at 4 per cent (BofE, General Ledgers ADM 7).

26. See the interview between the US Monetary Commission and the Bank of England Governor in 1909 in BofE, CB No. 132, Appendix. An extract is given in T.E. Gregory 1964, Vol. 2, p. 311.
27. At the end of 1898, at the peak of the cycle in other words, Smith reported to London:

> Very much to my regret new business does not come our way. Our big neighbours growing bigger daily, hinge their finances much more on London money market methods than formerly and are not in the least afraid of large amounts. Consequently people are less constrained, down here, to seek our assistance. And our rate debars us from a share in the staple business of the Midlands (BofE, BBALB Out No. 27, 17 November 1898).

28. A calculation of the new issues of securities by joint stock companies by Tilly using data from the *Investor's Monthly Manual* (R. Tilly 1986, Table 8, p. 228) shows a rise in new issues of preference shares of £0.85 million in 1895 to £7.1 million in 1896 and £12.3 million in 1897, and of bonds from £5.8 million in 1895 to £18.8 million in 1896 and £20.6 million in 1897. Although cumulative effects from issues to redeem fixed-term bonds were not taken into account, the trend is evident. The situation was different for ordinary shares. Here too Tilly's figures show a clear increase in demand. However, the issue of ordinary shares certainly did not mean that these would reach the public. Generally, especially on conversions, the previous owners took the shares in order not to lose control of the company. The investment needs were financed by issuing preference shares and bonds, but the firm had to be converted into a joint stock company for such securities to be issued.
29. The longest list of blank transfers at all the branches was at the Western Branch in London, where fifteen more customers had deposited blank transfers. The Western branch blank transfers differ, however, from those in Birmingham in that they were not 'industrials' but securities that were much more marketable (British and overseas railway paper, colonial and foreign government stock).
30. 'When the bank rate exceeds 3.5 per cent the class of securities and chances of competition by my very eager neighbours rule the rate that I charge' (BofE, BBALB Out No. 27, 17 November 1898).
31. The stock of deposits at the Bank was about £50 million on average for 1895, 1897 and 1898, and £60 million in 1896.
32. In fact the Bank in these years sold securities that could be sold without loss. That was the case with foreign government stock (Danish 4 per cent bonds, Turkish 4 per cent bonds and Russian 3.5 per cent bonds) and ordinary shares of railway companies (Midland Rail ord. stock and deferred ord. stock, and London & North Western Rail ord. stock, BofE, General Ledgers ADM 7).
33. A parallel development occurred for the local clearing houses. During the peak of the boom in 1899 the Birmingham clearing house had fallen back to fourth place behind Liverpool, Manchester and Newcastle in turnover. The reason was given by *The Economist* as: 'It is now banked chiefly by companies having a London clearing' (*The Economist*, 17 February 1900, Commercial History and Review of 1899).

Chapter 5

1. The reason for not including commercial bank deposits was a naive definition of money stock by the Currency School (see Fetter 1965, pp. 171, 187–92; Collins 1978, pp. 381, 387) but even if their representatives had thought out their theory consistently they would hardly have been able to implement it over the longer term. For Peel's Act could only remain in force for seventy years because the necessary tying of the 'money stock' to the gold reserves of the central bank was undermined by the development of cheques as means of payment and so did not constitute a barrier to the growth in the money stock (in the modern definition).
2. The other possibilities given by Batchelor, to let the bank go down first and then help it back on its feet again, or systematically to suppress the level of information on the difficulties being suffered until the bank could help itself (Batchelor 1986, p. 69) are more of a theoretical nature and it is hard to imagine a situation where they could be applied.
3. See BofE, CB No. 80, 4 February 1858; National Discount Co. Ltd., Board of Directors Minute Book, Vol. 1, 19 March 1858, Guildhall Library Ms. 18, 131; Clapham 1944, Vol. 2, pp. 240–1; see also a more critical account of the 'Rule of 1858' in King 1936, p. 284.
4. See the speech by Governor Lidderdale at the annual general meeting in April 1891, in *The Bankers' Magazine*, Vol. 51/1891, pp. 704–6; *Economic Journal* Vol. 1/1891, p. 195; Crump 1891, p. 394.
5. It should be remembered that banks of issue like the North & South Wales Bank were on principle not allowed to rediscount at the Bank of England.
6. This crisis was generally seen as due mainly to the collapse of the City of Glasgow Bank. However, Collins has recently shown that since this crisis had little impact on London, its effects on the provinces in England have been underestimated (Collins 1989, pp. 504–27).
7. According to Landes this process started after the crisis of 1866 (Landes 1960, p. 113), while Collins attaches greater importance to the crisis of 1878 (Collins 1989, p. 526; see also Jeffreys 1938, pp. 18, 119; Kennedy 1976, p. 160; Kennedy 1987, pp. 120–34).
8. Sir Felix Schuster, Governor of the Union of London & Smiths Bank, a competitor who was critical of the Bank of England but in general rather well disposed, commented later on this step to the US National Monetary Commission. First, the Bank of England had permitted the commercial banks 'to grow round them and get very strong and powerful, and, having perceived that, they rather tried to retrace their steps and get a little of that business themselves' (National Monetary Commission interviews, p. 49).
9. 'Money at call' loans were not given by the Bank of England, but after 1890 it did resume direct lending to bill brokers and discount houses, after breaking this off itself in 1858. Although turnover in the discount business rose again noticeably when the discount houses etc. were again permitted to rediscount in Threadneedle Street, the reform had not yet had a really positive effect on gross discount earnings, owing to the short terms of the loans and the depression of the mid-1890s.
10. 'Advances on floaters' or 'Bowen advances' (after the chief cashier, Bowen, who succeeded May in 1893 and did all he could to build up this part of the business in the depression during the 1890s) were short-term loans to stock jobbers to finance their transactions. The only security offered for the

loans were 'floaters', that is, British government bonds, Indian stock, railway bonds and so on. From May 1895 the chief cashier's office issued its own 'stock exchange rate, communicated by the broker of the Bank to the stock jobbers with whom the Bank was doing business' (Sayers 1976, Vol. 1, p. 20). At about the same time the advances on floaters were shown separately from the other loans in the Bank's statistics, and this enables a very reliable assessment of their quantitative significance in the Bank's total lending. In 1895 they accounted for about 10 per cent of the lombard business in Threadneedle Street (without 'quarterly advances'). Only when the Bank also accepted terms of just three days for the loans, as it did from December 1897 (instead of a week as formerly) did the turnover rise, by around 300 per cent within a very short time. Gross interest earnings in the 1898/9 financial year amounted to £13,000, or about 10 per cent of the gross earnings on lending (discount and lombard) in Threadneedle Street. After the turn of the century advances on floaters accounted for 30 per cent of turnover.

11. The agent in Leicester, Wright, also side stepped the rules in the 1860s: first, that under which no overdrafts were to be given, by discounting bills of exchange which had not yet arrived at the branch. Second, he discounted bills of firms that did not have a regular discount account with the Bank of England, by crediting the amount to the drawing account of one of the partners in the firm. This was also contrary to the rules. In doing so, he used the rule for an exceptional case, under which could be discounted only bills of customers who only had their sole account with the Bank of England. This criterion did not apply to the firm, but it did to the partner (BofE, LBALB In No. 2, 1 April 1867, 2 July 1869, 6 July 1869, Out No. 8, 2 April 1867, 5 July 1869; Ziegler 1989b, p. 16).
12. It is hardly surprising that Barham's salary was raised from £1,500 to £1,700 in 1889. If the commercial success of the branch had continued it would have been promoted to a 'first class branch' like Manchester or Liverpool (BofE, BBALB Out No. 29, 5 April 1902) and the agent could have expected to earn up to £2,000 a year. On the salaries of agents and subagents, see BofE, BBO Misc. Papers C 79/30.
13. The agents at the branches in Liverpool and Manchester earned between £1,500 and £2,000 a year; those in Leeds, Newcastle and Birmingham between £1,500 and £1,800; those in Bristol, Hull and Leicester between £750 and £1,000; and those in branches that were suffering considerable losses, Portsmouth and Plymouth, only up to £800. That put them below the level of the subagents in Liverpool and Manchester, who could earn up to £1,000. See BofE, BBO Misc. Papers C 79/30.
14. It does not matter in this context whether the former borrowers at the Birmingham branch really found it difficult to raise the credit they needed from other banks, the decisive fact is that the Bank did not care what the effects of its credit restrictions were. However, it should be mentioned that the Birmingham Trust obviously had difficulties in raising the necessary funds. To repay a loan of £50,000 from the Bank of England, Chamberlain tried to obtain the appropriate credit from the London & Midland Bank, but since the bank wanted him to transfer all the Trust's accounts to the Midland Bank before it would give a loan of such a size, the deal does not appear to have been done (Midland Bank Archive, Holden Diaries 22 May 1901, Midland Minute Books, Vol. 20, 31 May 1901).
15. The branch banks' office gives examples from Newcastle, Manchester and

Leeds (BofE, BBO Special Reports No. 607b).

16. Defined as follows:

> It is absolutely fundamental to the Bank's position as a central bank that it should always be prepared to lend to the market when called upon. It must never refuse to help the market. It can charge whatever rate it thinks fit, but it must lend. (Sayers 1947, p. 90)

Salin's argument is historically 'inaccurate' only in so far as he maintains that the development of modern central bank policy was not inherent in the market. As we have seen, the market accepted a central bank, but the Bank did not voluntarily become a non-competitive non-profit-maximizing institution.

17. Cairncross summarizes the relation between the Bank of England and the government as follows in a recent article:

> It was not until Norman's Governorship [i.e. after the First World War] that . . . [the Bank's] evolution into a central bank was complete. For much of its earlier history the Bank was not conscious of any responsibility for control over the monetary system nor did the government think in these terms . . . . There were very few occasions on which the government and the Bank were at cross purposes . . . . In any event the government was not equipped to cross swords with the Bank of England: there were at most only two or three people in government service who were thoroughly familiar with monetary problems and it was only in a crisis or in matters of debt management that contact between the two bodies extended much beyond exchanges between Chancellor and Governor. (Cairncross 1988, pp. 45–6).

Bibliography

Acres, W.M., 1930a: Closed Branches of the Bank of England: Exeter, *Old Lady of Threadneedle Street* Vol. 6, pp. 80–1

———, 1930b: Closed Branches of the Bank of England: Gloucester, *Old Lady of Threadneedle Street* Vol. 6, pp. 152–4

———, 1931a: *The Bank of England From Within*, 2 Vols, Oxford University Press

———, 1931b: Closed Branches of the Bank of England: Swansea, *Old Lady of Threadneedle Street* Vol. 7, pp. 168–70

———, 1931c: Closed Branches of the Bank of England: Norwich, *Old Lady of Threadneedle Street* Vol. 7, pp. 91–2

———, 1931d: Closed Branches of the Bank of England: Leicester, *Old Lady of Threadneedle Street* Vol. 7, pp. 250–1

———, 1932: Closed Branches of the Bank of England: Portsmouth, *Old Lady of Threadneedle Street* Vol. 8, pp. 84–5

Adler, D. *1970: British Investment in American Railways, 1834–1898*, University Press of Virginia, Charlottesville

Allen, G.C., 1929: *The Industrial Development of Birmingham and the Black Country*, 1860–1927, Allen & Unwin, London

Anderson, B.L. and Cottrell, P.L., 1975: Another Victorian capital market: a study of banking and bank investors on Merseyside, *Economic History Review* Vol. 28, pp. 598–615

Andreades, A., 1966: *History of the Bank of England, 1640 to 1903*, fourth edition, Cass, London

Ashton, T.S., 1953: Bills of exchange and private banks in Lancashire, in: Sayers 1953, pp. 37–49

Baber, C. and Williams, L.J., 1986: *Modern South Wales: Essays in economic history*, University of Wales Press, Cardiff

Bagehot, W., 1873: *Lombard Street: The description of the money market*, King, London

Barrow, G.L., 1974: *The Emergence of the Irish Banking System*, Gill & Macmillan, Dublin

Batchelor, R.A., 1986: The avoidance of catastrophe: two nineteenth century banking crises, in Capie and Wood 1986, pp. 41–76

Beach, W.E., 1972: *British International Gold Movements and Banking Policy, 1881–1913*, Greenwood, Westport/Conn.

Bloomfield, A.J., 1959: *Monetary Policy Under the International Gold Standard, 1880–1914*, Federal Reserve Bank of New York

———, 1968: Rules of the game of international adjustment?, in: Whittlesey and Wilson 1968, pp. 27–46

Boot, H.M., 1984: *The Commercial Crisis of 1847*, Hull University Press

Bopp, K., 1951: Bank of France policy, *American Journal of Economics and Sociology* Vol. 11, pp. 229–44

Bordo, M. and Schwartz A., 1984: *A Retrospective View of the Classical Gold Standard*, Chicago University Press

Cairncross, A., 1988: The Bank of England: relationship with the government, the civil service and Parliament, in: Toniolo 1988, pp. 39–72

Cameron, R., 1982: Banking and industrialization in Britain in the nineteenth century, in: Slaven and Aldcroft 1982, pp. 102–11

Capie, F. and Rodrick-Bali, G., 1982: Concentration in British banking, 1870–1920, *Business History* Vol. 24, pp. 280–92

Capie, F. and Wood, G., 1986: *Financial Crises and the World Banking System*, Macmillan, London

Cecco, M. de, 1974: *Money and Empire: The international gold standard, 1890–1914*, Blackwell, London

———, 1986: *Currency, Coinage and the Gold Standard*, EUI Working Paper No. 86/229, Florence

Checkland, S., 1954: The Lancashire bill system and its Liverpool protagonists, 1810–1827, *Economica* Vol. 21, pp. 129–42

———, 1957: The mind of the City, 1870–1914, *Oxford Economic Papers* Vol. 9, pp. 261–78

———, 1975: *Scottish Banking: A history*, Collins, Glasgow

Clapham, J., 1930, *An Economic History of Modern Britain*, 3 Vols, Second Edition, Cambridge University Press

———, 1941: The private business of the Bank of England, 1744–1800, *Economic History Review* Vol. 11, pp. 77–89

———, 1944: *The Bank of England*, 2 Vols, Cambridge University Press

Collins, M., 1972a: The Bank of England at Liverpool, 1827–1844, *Business History* Vol. 16, pp. 144–59

———, 1972b: The Langton Papers: banking and Bank of England policy in the 1830s, *Economica* Vol. 39, pp. 47–59

———, 1978: Monetary policy and the supply of trade credit, 1830–1844, *Economica* Vol. 45, pp. 379–89

———, 1984: Business of banking: English bank balance sheets, 1840–1880, *Business History* Vol. 26, pp. 43–58

———, 1988: *Money and Banking in the United Kingdom: A history*, Croom Helm, London

———, 1989: The banking crisis of 1878, *Economic History Review* Vol. 42, pp. 504–27

———, and Hudson, P., 1979: Provincial bank lending: Yorkshire and Lancashire, 1826–1860, *Bulletin of Economic Research* Vol. 31, pp. 69–79

Cottrell, P.L., 1980: *Industrial Finance, 1830–1914*, Methuen, London

Crick, W.F. and Wadsworth, J.E., 1936: *A Hundred Years of Joint Stock Banking*, Hodder & Stoughton, London

Crockett, A. and White, W., 1978: The lessons of early 1800s controversy between the British banking and currency school for judging the adequacy of the world's foreign exchange reserves, *Revue Internationale d'Histoire de la Banque* Vol. 16, pp. 208–18

Crouzet, F., 1982: *The Victorian Economy*, Methuen, London

Crump, A., 1891: The Baring financial crisis, *Economic Journal* Vol. 1, pp. 388–94

Davenport-Hines, R.P.T., 1984: *Dudley Docker: The life and times of a trade warrior*, Cambridge University Press

Dornbusch, R and Frenkel, J.A., 1984: The gold standard and the Bank of England in the crisis of 1847, in: Bordo and Schwartz, 1984, pp. 233–73 (including comment by J.R.T. Hughes)

Drummond, I., 1987: *The Gold Standard and the International Monetary System, 1900–1939*, Macmillan, London

Dutton, J., 1984: The Bank of England and the rules of the game under the international gold standard: new evidence, in: Bordo and Schwartz, 1984, pp. 173–99 (including comment by D.E. Moggridge)

Feinstein, C., 1972: *National Income, Expenditure and Output of the United Kingdom, 1855–1965*, Cambridge University Press

Fetter, F., 1965: *Development of British Monetary Orthodoxy*, Harvard University Press, Cambridge, Mass.

Foreman-Peck, J. and Michie, R., 1986: The performance of the nineteenth century international gold standard, in: Fischer, W., McInnis, R.M. and Schneider, J. (eds), *The Emergence of a World Economy, 1500–1914*, Steiner, Wiesbaden, pp. 383–411

Fulford, R., 1953: *Glyn's 1753–1953*, Macmillan, London

Giuseppi, J., 1966: *The Bank of England*, Evans, London

Goodhart, C.A.E., 1972: *The Business of Banking, 1891–1914*, Weidenfeld & Nicolson, London

———, 1984: Comment, in: Pippenger 1984

———, 1988: *The Evolution of Central Banks*, MIT Press, Cambridge, Mass.

Goschen, G., 1905: *Essays and Addresses on Economic Questions (1865–1893)*, Arnold, London

Gregory, T.E., 1936: *The Westminster Bank Through a Century*, 2 Vols, Oxford University Press

———, 1964: *Select Statutes, Documents and Reports Relating to British Banking, 1832–1928*, 2 Vols, Cass, London

Hall, F.G., 1949: *The Bank of Ireland, 1783–1946*, Figgis & Co, Dublin

Hawtrey, R., 1962: *A Century of Bank Rate*, Second Edition, Cass, London

Heim, C., 1984: Limits to intervention in depressed areas, *Economic History Review* Vol. 37, pp. 533–50

Hilferding, R., 1910: *Das Finanzkapital*, Brand, Vienna

Hobsbawm, E., 1980: *Industrie und Empire*, 2 Vols, Ninth Edition, Suhrkamp, Frankfurt/Main

Holland, R.M., 1910: *The London Bankers' Clearing House*, Government Printing Office, Washington

Holmes, A.R. and Green, E., 1986: *Midland: 150 Years of banking business*, Batsford, London

Horsefield, J.K., 1949: The opinion of Horsley Palmer, *Economica* Vol. 16, pp. 143–58

Hudson, P., 1981: The role of banks in the finance of the West Riding wool textile industry, c. 1780–1850, *Business History Review* Vol. 60, pp. 379–402

———, 1986: *The Genesis of Industrial Capital: A study of the West Riding wool textile industry, c. 1750–1850*, Cambridge University Press

Jeffreys, J.B., 1938: *Business Organisation in Britain, 1856–1914*, PhD, University of London

Jones, L., 1983: Public pursuit of private profit? liberal businessmen and municipal policies in Birmingham, 1865–1900, *Business History* Vol. 25, pp. 240–57

Jones, S., 1978a: The cotton industry and joint stock banking in Manchester, 1825–1850, *Business History Review* Vol. 20, pp. 165–83

———, 1978b: The Manchester cotton magnates' move into banking, *Textile History* Vol. 9, pp. 91–111

———, 1985: The Bank of England in Manchester, 1826–1850, *Bankhistorisches Archiv* Vol. 11, pp. 28–47

Kennedy, P.M., 1981: Strategy versus finance in twentieth century Great Britain, *International History Review* Vol. 3, pp. 44–61

Kennedy, W.P., 1976: Institutional response to economic growth: capital markets in Britain to 1914, in: L. Hannah (ed.), *Management Strategy and Business Development*, Macmillan, London, pp. 153–83

———, 1987: *Industrial Structure, Capital Markets and the Origins of British Economic Decline*, Cambridge University Press

Keynes, J.M., 1930: *A Treatise on Money*, 2 Vols, Macmillan, London

Kindleberger, Ch., 1978: *Manias, Panics and Crashes: A history of financial crises*, Macmillan, London

——— and Laffargue, J.P., 1982: *Financial Crises: Theory, history and policy*, Cambridge University Press

King, W.T.C., 1936: *History of the London Discount Market*, Routledge & Sons, London

Landes, D., 1960: The structure of enterprise in the nineteenth century: the case of Britain and Germany, in: 11. *Congrès International des Sciences Historiques, Rapports V: Histoire Contemporaire*, Göteborg, pp. 107–28

Levy-Leboyer, M., 1982: Central banking and foreign trade: the Anglo-American cycle in the 1830's, in: Kindleberger and Laffargue 1982, pp. 66–116 (including comment by P. Temin)

Mathias, P., 1973: Capital, credit and enterprise in the Industrial Revolution, *Journal of European Economic History* Vol. 2, pp. 121–43

McCloskey, D.N. and Zecher, J.R., 1981: How the gold standard worked, 1880–1913, in: D.N. McCloskey, *Enterprise and Trade in Victorian Britain*, Allen & Unwin

McCord, N., 1979: *North East England: An economic and social history*, Batsford, London

———, 1980: North East England: some points of regional interest, in: S. Pollard (Hg.), *Region und Industrialisierung*, Vandenhoeck & Ruprecht, Göttingen, pp. 33–51

Mitchell, B.R., 1988: *British Historical Statistics*, Cambridge University Press

Morgan, E.V., 1943: *The Theory and Practice of Central Banking*, Cambridge University Press

Mosbacher, W., 1976: Reichsbank und Bank von England im Goldstandard vor 1914, *Bankhistorisches Archiv* Vol. 1, pp. 20–51

Moss, D., 1981: The Bank of England and the country banks: Birmingham 1827–1833, *Economic History Review* Vol. 34, pp. 540–53

———, 1982: The private banks of Birmingham, 1800–1927, *Business History* Vol. 24, pp. 79–94

Munn, Ch. W., 1981: *The Scottish Provincial Banking Companies, 1747–1864*, J. Donald, Edinburgh

———, 1988: The emergence of joint stock banking in the British Isles: a comparative approach, *Business History* Vol. 30, pp. 69–83

Nevin, E. and Davis, E.W., 1970: *The London Clearing Banks*, Elek, London

Nishimura, S., 1971: *The Decline of Inland Bills of Exchange in the London Money Market, 1855–1913*, Cambridge University Press

Ollerenshaw, Ph., 1988: The development of banking in the Bristol region, 1750–1914, in: Ch. Harvey and J. Press (eds), *Studies in the Business History of Bristol*, Academic Press, Bristol, pp. 55–82

Palgrave, R.H.I., 1901: *Dictionary of Political Economy*, Macmillan London

———, 1903: *Bank Rate and the Money Market*, 1844–1900, Murray, London

———, 1910: *History of the Separation of the Departments of the Bank of England*, Government Printing Office, Washington

Pippenger, J., 1984: Bank of England Operations, 1893–1913, in: Bordo and Schwartz, 1984, pp. 203–32 (including comment by C.A.E. Goodhart)

Pollard, S., 1970: *The Gold Standard and Unemployment Policies Between the Wars*, Methuen, London

———, 1989: *Britain's Prime and Britain's Decline: The British economy 1870–1914*, Arnold, London

Powell, E.T., 1915: *The Evolution of the Money Market, 1385–1915*, Financial News, London

Pressnell, L.S., 1953: Public Moneys and the Development of English Banking, *Economic History Review* Vol. 5, pp. 378–97

———, 1956: *Country Banking in the Industrial Revolution*, Clarendon, Oxford

———, 1968: Gold reserves, banking reserves, and the Baring crisis of 1890, in: Whittlesey and Wilson, 1968, pp. 167–228.

Rae, G., 1850: (Th. Bullion), *The Internal Management of a Country Bank*, Groombridge & Sons, London

———, 1903: *The Country Banker*, Fifth Edition, Murrey, London

Roberts, R.O., 1958a: Bank of England branch discounting, 1826–1859, *Economica* Vol. 25, pp. 231–45

———, 1958b: The Brecon Old Bank of Wilkins & Co., 1778–1890, *Business History* Vol. 1, pp. 35–51

———, 1986: Banks and economic development of modern South Wales before 1914, in: Baber and Williams 1986, pp. 65–80

Ryton, J., 1984: *Banks and Bank Notes of Exeter, 1769–1906*, Exeter

Salin, P., 1984: *Currency Competition and Monetary Union* (General Introduction), Martinus Nijhoff, The Hague

Sayers, R.S., 1936: *Bank of England Operations, 1890–1914*, King, London

———, 1947: *Modern Banking*, Second Edition, Oxford University Press

———, 1953: *Papers in English Monetary History*, Oxford University Press

———, 1957a: *Lloyds Bank in the History of English Banking*, Oxford University Press

———, 1957b: *Central Banking After Bagehot*, Oxford University Press

———, 1976: *The Bank of England, 1891–1944*, 3 Vols, Cambridge University Press

Schwartz, 1986: Real and pseudo financial crises, in: Capie and Wood 1986, pp. 11–40 (including comment by A.H. Meltzer and D.E. Moggridge)

Slaven, A. and Aldcroft, D.H., 1982: *Business, Banking and Urban History: Essays in honour of S.G. Checkland*, J. Donald, Edinburgh

Sykes, J., 1926: *The Amalgamation Movement in English Banking*, 1825–1924, King, London

Thomas, S.E., 1934: *The Rise of Joint Stock Banking*, Vol. 1, Pitman, London

Tilly, R.H., 1986: Financing industrial enterprise in Great Britain and Germany in the nineteenth century: testing ground for Marxist and Schumpeterian theories?, in: Drukker and Wagener, *Economic Law of Motion of Modern Society*, Cambridge University Press 1985

Timmins, S., 1866: *The resources, products, and industrial history of Birmingham and the Midland hardware district*, Hardwicke, London

Toniolo, G., 1988: *Central Banks' Independence in Historical Perspective*, de Gruyter, Berlin

White, L.H., 1984: *Free Banking in Britain: Theory, experience, and debate, 1800–1845*, Cambridge University Press

Withers, H., 1909: *The Meaning of Money*, Smith, Elder & Co, London

Whittlesey, C.R. and Wilson, J.S.G., 1968: *Essays in Money and Banking, in honour of R.S. Sayers*, Oxford University Press

Ziegler, D., 1988: *Das Korsett der 'Alten Dame'. Die Geschäftspolitik der Bank of England, 1860–1913*, PhD, EUI Florence 1988

———, 1989a: Central banking in the English provinces in the second quarter of the nineteenth century, *Business History*, Vol. 31, pp. 33–47

———, 1989b: *The Bank of England in the Provinces: The case of the Leicester branch closing, 1872*, EUI Working Paper, Florence

Sources

1. Archives:

Bank of England (BofE)

Archive

Court of Directors Minutes (Court Books -CB), G 4
Committee of Treasury Minutes (CTM), G 8
Edye Reports, G 15/39
Secretary's Letter Books, G 23

General Ledgers and General Ledger Supplements, ADM 7
Stock Estimates, ADM 19

Discount Office Ledgers and Accounts, C 22 to C 23 and C 25
Special Discount Committee (SDC) Papers, C 30 and C 35

Branch Banks Office (BBO) Accounts and Papers, C 79

Record Office

Birmingham Branch Agents' Letter Books (BBALB)
Leicester Branch Agents' Letter Books (LBALB)
Newcastle Branch Agents' Letter Books (NBALB)

Midland Bank Archive:

Holden Diaries
Midland Minute Books Vol. 20

2. *Published Sources:*

British Parliamentary Papers (BPP):
Secret Committee on the Bank of England Charter, BPP 1831/2, Vol. 6
Secret Committee on Joint Stock Banks, BPP 1836, Vol. 9
Secret Committee on Joint Stock Banks, BPP 1837, Vol. 14
Secret Committee on Joint Stock Banks, BPP 1838, Vol. 7
Select Committee on Banks of Issue, BPP 1840, Vol. 4
Select Committee on Banks of Issue, BPP 1841, Vol. 5
Secret Committee on Commercial Distress, BPP 1847/48, Vol. 8, Parts 1–3
Select Committee on Bank Acts, BPP 1857, Vol. 10
Select Committee on Bank Acts, BPP 1857/8, Vol. 5
Select Committee on Banks of Issue, BPP 1875, Vol. 9

Hansard
The Times
The Economist
Statist
Journal of the Institute of Bankers
Banking Almanac 1845 and 1912
Bankers' Magazine

Index of People and Places

Acres, W.M. 8
Allsopp Brewery 108
Argentina 89
Attwood, Th. 139
Attwood & Spooner 14, 139
Australia 89

Bagehot, W. 75
Bank of Ireland 138
Bank of Liverpool 24, 35, 40, 146
Bank of Manchester 24, 25
Banque de France 89, 94, 135
Barclay, Bevan & Tritton 38
Barclays Bank 38, 125, 126
Barham, F.F. (BofE Birmingham branch agent) 98–118, 143–145, 149
Baring Bros. 88
Barnes & Co. 35
Barnett, Hoare, Hanbury & Lloyd 38, 138, 144
Batchelor, R.A. 130
Beach, W.E. 92
Belgium 26, 89
Bentinck, George (Lord) 80, 81
Biddulph Bros. & Co. 40
Bilston 14
Birmingham, *see* BofE branches
Birmingham & Aston Tramway Co. 107
Birmingham & Midland Bank 18, 35, 38, 100, 108, 144
Birmingham Banking Co. 15, 138
Birmingham City Tramway Co. 126
Birmingham Joint Stock Bank 119
Birmingham Trust Co. 108, 109, 112, 113, 115–117, 123, 149
Birmingham Small Arms & Metal Co. 107, 109, 114, 117, 126, 146
Black Country 14, 128
Bloomfield, A.J. 89
Bonar, Thomson & Co. 145
Bosanquet, Salt, Whatman, Harman, Salt & Bosanquet 38
Bradford 21
Brecon 15, 24
Bridgnorth 14
Bristol, *see* BofE branches
Brown, Shipley & Co. 146
Brunner, Mond & Co. 126
Buenos Ayres New Gas Co. 106

Cameron, R. 79, 136
Cannon Brewery 126
Capital & Counties Bank 37
Cardiff 6, 16
Carlisle 11
Carmarthen 40
Cassels, W.G. (Northern & Central Bank of England) 25
Central Bank of London 38
Chamberlain, A. 108, 111, 114, 115, 119, 122, 124, 125, 149
Chamberlain, H. 125
Chamberlain, J. 108
Chamberlain, W. 107, 108, 111, 122, 125
Chamberlain & Hookham 124
Chatham 8
Chippindale (BofE Birmingham branch agent) 98
City of Glasgow Bank 65, 101, 148
Clapham, J. 6, 75
Clarke, Mitchell & Philips 9, 49
Cole, A.C. (BofE Governor) 2, 76
Collet, M.W. (BofE Governor) 105, 106
Collins, M. 75, 176
Commercial Bank of England 25
Commercial Bank of Scotland 116
Cooke, Th. (Manchester & Liverpool District Bank) 139
County of Gloucester Banking Co. 34
Courtney (Principal BofE branch banks office) 121, 145
Coventry 14
Cumberland 11

Darlington District Joint Stock Banking Co. 28
Derby 9
Dudley 14
Durham 28, 83
Dyer, J.C. (Bank of Manchester) 24, 25

East India Co. 20
Edye, E. (Principal BofE branch banks office) 121–127
Elliot Metal Co. 125
Exeter, *see* BofE branches

France 26, 88, 89, 94, 143
Fuller, Banbury & Nix 38

Galton & James 138
Germany 89, 94, 143
Gibbins & Lovell 138
Gibbins, Smith & Goode 138
Gilliat, J.S. (BofE Governor) 103
Gladstone, S.S. (BofE Governor) 122
Gladstone, W.E. 140
Gloucester, *see* BofE branches
Gloucestershire 29, 30
Gloucestershire Banking Co. 12, 29–32, 34, 35, 41
Goodhart, Ch. 136, 137
Goschen, G.J. 80
Gosling & Sharpe 38
Great Bridge Steel & Iron Co. 104
Great Central Railway Co. 123
Great Eastern Railway Co. 106
Grenfell, H.R. (BofE Governor) 102, 144
Grote, G. 139

Halifax 21
Hampshire & North Wilts Banking Co. 37
Hampshire Banking Co. 37
Hankey, Th. (BofE Governor) 144
Harrison, Watson & Pease 139
Hawtrey, R.G. 135
Head, J.M. & Co. 11
Hodgson, A. (Bank of Liverpool) 40
Hodgson, K.D. (BofE Governor) 139
Hookham, E. 108
Hubbart, J.G. (BofE Governor) 142
Huddersfield 6, 7, 21
Huddersfield Banking Co. 7, 8
Hudson, P. 21
Hull, *see* BofE branches

Imperial Bank 25
Italy 89

Jones, Loyd & Co. 24

Kent, Surrey & Sussex Bank 10
Kidderminster 14
Kynoch Co. 114

Lambton & Co, 29, 83, 84
Lancashire 13, 19,21, 24, 27, 28, 30, 128, 139
Lea, N. & Son 106, 107, 146
Leamington 14
Leeds, *see* BofE branches
Lehigh Wilkes Bane 102, 145
Leicester, *see* BofE branches
Leicestershire Banking Co. 49
Levy-Leboyer, M. 78
Lidderdale, W. (BofE Governor) 105, 109, 110, 143, 148
Lincolnshire 30
Liverpool, *see* BofE branches
Liverpool (Second Earl of) 5, 31
Liverpool Banking Co. 132
Liverpool Borough Bank 35
Liverpool Commercial Banking Co. 35
Liverpool Union Bank 35, 141
Lloyd, H. (Lloyds Bank) 110
Lloyd, S. (Lloyds Banking Co.) 24
Lloyds Bank(ing Co.) 35, 38, 110, 119, 120, 143, 144
London & County Banking Co. 10, 38, 141
London & Midland Bank 38, 120, 149
London & Westminster Bank 10, 38, 115, 140, 141
London Joint Stock Bank 10, 92
Loyd Jones (London bankers) 38
Lowe, R. 82

Manchester, *see* BofE branches
Manchester & Liverpool District Banking Co. 25, 26, 34, 139
Manchester & Salford Bank 25, 26, 38
Mansfield 49
May, F. (BofE chief cashier) 67, 148
Melksham 37
Merthyr 6, 15
Metropolitan Life Insurance Soc. 103
Midland Banking Co. 101, 102
Midland Electric Light & Power Co. 114
Midlands 27, 28, 30, 108, 147
Midland Trust Co. 112, 113
Moilliet & Sons 139
Morris, J. (BofE Governor) 40, 80, 81
Muntz, P.H. 40
Muntz Metal Co. 103, 145

National Discount Co. 148
National Provincial Bank of England 25, 33, 36, 115, 119, 120, 139–141
Nettlefold, E. 108, 111, 119, 122, 125, 126
Newcastle-under-Lyme 13
Newcastle-upon-Tyne, *see* BofE branches
Newcastle Commercial Joint Stock Banking Co. 28
Newcastle Joint Stock Banking Co. 28, 83
Newcastle, Shields & Sunderland Union Bank 28, 84, 85, 142
Newport 6
Nishimura, S. 51, 54
Norman, G.W. (BofE Governor) 127, 142
North & South Wales Bank 132, 148
Northern & Central Bank of England 25
Northumberland 28, 83
Northumberland & Durham District Bank 28, 83–87, 130, 131
North of England Union Joint Stock Bank 28, 83, 84
North Wilts Banking Co. 37
Norwich, *see* BofE branches
Nottingham 9, 40, 49, 80

Overend, Gurney & Co. 50

Overstone (Lord) 79, 82

Paget & Co. 49
Palgrave, R.H.I. 75, 104
Palmer, E.H. (BofE Governor) 33
Palmer, J.H. (BofE Governor) 5, 6, 20, 77
Pares Leicestershire Banking Co. 42, 49, 82
Parr's Bank 38
Patent Shaft & Axle Tree Co. 108
Peel, R. 32, 33, 36
Pembroke 8, 141
Plymouth, *see* BofE branches
Portsmouth, *see* BofE branches
Powell, D. (BofE Governor) 110, 111
Prescott, H.J. (BofE Governor) 41, 132
Pressnell, L.S. 8

Raikes, T. & R. 139
Reichsbank 89, 94, 143
Robinson & Bradhurst 49
Royal Bank of Liverpool 132
Russel & Sons Ltd. 104
Russia 88, 89, 146

Salin, P. 137
Salomons, D. (London & Westminster Bank) 140
Sandeman, A.G. (BofE Governor) 110, 115
Sayers, R.S. 2, 75, 76, 90, 92–94, 100, 119
Schuster, F. (Union of London & Smiths Bank) 148
Schwartz, A. 88
Seebohm, F. (Sharples & Co., private banker) 30
Shaftesbury 34
Sheffield 21
Sheffield Union Banking Co. 20
Smethwick 110
Smith (BofE Birmingham branch agent) 114–127
Smith, H.C. (BofE Governor) 118
Société Générale de Paris 105
Somerset 30
South Africa 89, 126, 127
Southampton 37
South Lancashire Bank 25
(South) Wales 20, 27, 141
Southwark & Vauxhall Water Co. 106
Storey & Thomas 34
Stourbridge 14
Stuckey's Banking Co. 138
Sunderland 28
Sunderland Joint Stock Banking Co. 28
Swansea, *see* BofE branches

Taylor & Lloyd 139, 144
Tooke, Th. 142
Towgood & Co. 16
Turner, Th.C. (BofE Leicester branch agent) 42

Union Bank of London (Union of London & Smiths Bank) 10, 144, 148
Union Bank of Manchester 25, 26
United Chemical Co. 124
USA 89

Walker, T.E. (Patent Shaft & Axle Tree Co.) 108
Walsall 14
Warrington 38
Warwick 14
Warwickshire 30
Wednesbury 108
Weguelin, T.M. (BofE Governor) 127
West Bromwich 14
West Riding 20, 21
Wigram, C. (BofE Dep. Governor) 112
Wilkins & Co. 15, 24
Williams, Deacon, Thornton & Co. 38
Withers, H. 75
Wolverhampton 14, 102, 119
Wood, Ch. 139
Wright, I. & I.C. 9, 11, 12, 23, 32, 34, 35, 40, 49, 79, 80, 138–140, 142
Wright, J.J. (BofE Leicester branch agent) 149

York 21
Yorkshire 20, 21, 27, 139
Yorkshire Banking Co. 20
Yorkshire District Bank 20, 21

Subject Index

Bank Charter Act 1844 1–3, 20, 26, 31–39, 41, 47, 49, 66, 76–82, 88–90, 129, 130, 136, 140, 148
  suspension of 80, 81, 131
Bank of England
  Banking department 1, 3, 31, 41, 55, 59, 72, 73, 78, 127, 129–133
  'borrowing in the market' 91, 92, 143
  'borrowing on stock', *see* 'borrowing in the market'
  'Bowen advances' 133, 148, 149
  branch banks office 3, 39, 46, 47, 70, 73, 93, 99, 101, 104, 107, 108, 111–114, 117–119, 121–128, 134, 143, 146
  branches, provincial
    Birmingham 3, 6–9, 11–19, 22, 24, 28, 29, 39, 40, 44, 48–50, 53, 54, 57–70, 73, 74, 96–128, 133–135, 141–143, 147, 149
    Bristol 7, 14, 17, 18, 30, 31, 40, 44, 47, 48, 51, 53, 57–60, 63–69, 93, 96, 98, 121, 124, 138, 141, 149
    Exeter 7–9, 17, 18, 28
    Gloucester 6, 7, 12, 14, 15, 17, 18, 28–31, 40, 41, 44, 48, 50
    Hull 7, 8, 14, 17, 18, 28, 40, 47–51, 53–60, 63–66, 68, 69, 139, 141, 149
    Leeds 6–8, 14, 17–22, 44–48, 51–55, 57–65, 68, 69, 74, 82, 85, 98, 141, 149
    Leicester 3, 9, 14, 17, 18, 30, 40, 42, 44–51, 82, 98, 140, 141, 149
    Liverpool 6, 7, 13, 14, 17–20, 22–24, 28, 30, 35, 39, 40, 44, 48, 51, 53--60, 62–65, 68, 69, 71, 74, 98, 106, 121, 141, 149
    Manchester 6, 7, 14, 17–19, 22–26, 28–30, 40–44, 48, 51, 53–60, 63–65, 68, 69, 71, 74, 98, 106, 121, 141, 149
    Newcastle 7, 8, 11, 14, 17, 18, 27–29, 44–48, 51, 53–55, 57–60, 62–5, 68–71, 74, 83–87, 93, 98, 106, 121, 124, 130, 131, 140–142, 149
    Norwich 7–9, 14, 17, 18, 27, 40
    Plymouth 8, 9, 14, 17, 18, 40, 48, 50, 57–60, 141, 149
    Portsmouth 8, 9, 14, 17, 18, 27, 40, 41, 48, 50, 57–60, 141, 149
    Swansea 6, 7, 14–18, 20, 40, 48, 50, 51, 141
  chief cashiers office 67, 149
  'circulation accounts' 11–14, 16, 18–21, 23, 24, 26, 28, 33–35, 38, 40, 43, 44, 49, 83, 100, 138, 139
  Committee for Branch Banks 6, 9, 67, 70, 71, 104, 113, 114, 117, 119, 120
  Committee of Treasury 75, 104
  Court of Directors 36, 42, 67, 70, 73, 75, 86, 111, 113, 140, 146
  discount office 55
  head office 3, 15, 25, 26, 29, 39, 45, 46, 54, 65, 67, 70, 73, 83–85, 92, 118, 127, 131, 141
  Issue Department 1, 31, 41, 72, 73, 130
  key rate, *see* Rate (of discount)
  Law Courts Branch 133, 141
  private rate of discount 55, 62, 70, 99, 101, 110, 118
  'quarterly advances' 22, 26, 46, 47
  Rate (of discount) 2, 26, 35, 39, 40, 43, 54, 62, 70, 74, 76, 82, 88–95, 100, 103, 115–118, 120–123, 126, 127, 135, 141, 142
  Threadneedle Street, *see* head office
  Western Branch 133, 141, 147
banks of issue, provincial 2, 4, 5, 10, 11, 13, 21–25, 28–34, 37, 42, 79, 84, 99, 129, 139, 140, 148
Baring crisis 2, 66, 75, 109, 130, 131, 143
bill brokers 1, 11, 42, 47, 118, 131, 133
Birmingham Bankers' Clearing House 48, 141, 147
Birmingham Stock Exchange 107, 111, 123
'blank transfers' 104–106, 117, 118, 122, 123, 145–147
Boer War 73, 91, 128, 134, 135
Bristol Bankers' Clearing House 48

Chamberlain group 107–110, 114, 115, 119, 121–127, 146
Chartism 142
colonial bonds 67
Consols 91

corporation bonds 67, 127
crises
of 1825/26 4
of 1839 78, 139
of 1847 39, 40, 82, 83, 85, 87, 88, 131, 142
of 1857 42, 44, 83, 85, 87, 88, 131, 142
of 1866 37, 45, 50, 83, 88, 148
of 1878 101, 132, 144, 148
of 1890, *see* Baring crisis
of 1907 66, 94

discount houses 1, 42, 73, 100, 119, 130, 131, 133

East India bonds 12, 46
Exeter Flying Post 7

gold exchange standard 5
gold market (policy) 91–94, 142, 143
gold standard 2, 3, 75, 78, 89, 96, 135

'Industrials' (local industrial securities) 73, 107–114, 121–123, 125–127, 134, 147
industry, British 2, 3, 76, 90–93, 95, 96, 135, 143

Leeds Chamber of Commerce 81
Leeds Bankers' Clearing House 48
Leicester Bankers' Clearing House 48
'lender of last resort' 1, 2, 42, 78, 82, 83, 85, 87, 130–132, 136, 137
Liverpool Bankers' Clearing House 48, 141, 147
local authorities 42
London Bankers' Clearing House 51, 140
London money market 2, 12, 13, 23, 25, 26, 34, 40, 42, 43, 46, 50, 73, 91, 127, 128, 132, 134, 137, 139, 147
London Stock Exchange 46, 67, 72–74, 113, 132, 146

Manchester Banker's Clearing House 48, 141, 147
'May scandal' 70, 111, 113, 115, 118, 127, 133

Napoleonic Wars 1, 77
Naval Yards 8, 141
Newcastle Bankers' Clearing House 48, 140, 147
Newcastle Chamber of Commerce 7

open market (policy) 88, 91–94, 135, 143

'Palmer Rule' 76–78, 129, 130
'Peel's Act', *see* Bank Charter Act

railway companies, British 42, 106, 147
railway companies, Indian 127
railway companies, US 145

savings banks 62
Sheffield Bankers' Clearing House 48
stock brokers 66, 67, 73, 106–109, 113, 133
'surplus fuunds' 1, 118

Treasurer for the Navy 8
Treasury Bills 91, 92

Usury Laws 15, 82, 142